P9-CFD-952

Lyndon B. Johnson

Lyndon B. Johnson. © Getty Images

John L. Bullion

Lyndon B. Johnson
and the Transformation of American Politics

THE LIBRARY OF AMERICAN BIOGRAPHY

Edited by Mark C. Carnes

New York   Boston   San Francisco
London   Toronto   Sydney   Tokyo   Singapore   Madrid
Mexico City   Munich   Paris   Cape Town   Hong Kong   Montreal

Executive Editor: Michael Boezi
Development Editor: Vanessa Gennarelli
Executive Marketing Manager: Sue Westmoreland
Production Manager: Denise Phillip
Project Coordination, Text Design, and Electronic Page Makeup:
  GGS Book Services
Cover Design Manager: John Callahan
Cover Photo: Getty Images, Inc.
Photo Researcher: Rona Tuccillo
Senior Manufacturing Buyer: Alfred C. Dorsey
Printer and Binder: R.R. Donnelley & Sons/Harrisonburg
Cover Printer: Phoenix Color Corporation

Library of Congress Cataloging-in-Publication Data

Bullion, John L., 1944-
  Lyndon B. Johnson and the transformation of American politics / John
L. Bullion.
      p. cm. (Library of American Biography)
  Includes bibliographical references and index.
  ISBN-13: 978-0-321-38325-9
  ISBN-10: 0-321-38325-7
  1. Johnson, Lyndon B. (Lyndon Baines), 1908–1973.   2. United States—
Politics and government—1963–1969.   I. Title.

E847.B85 2007
973.923092—dc22
[B]   2007027001

Copyright © 2008 by Pearson Education, Inc.

All rights reserved. No part of this publication may be reproduced,
stored in a retrieval system, or transmitted, in any form or by any means,
electronic, mechanical, photocopying, recording, or otherwise, without
the prior written permission of the publisher. Printed in the United States.

Please visit us at www.ablongman.com.

ISBN-13: 978-0-321-38325-9
ISBN-10:   0-321-38325-7

    5 6 7 8 9 10—DOH—10

To the memory of my father

Some there are who have left a name behind them
to be commemorated in story.
There are others who are unremembered;
they are dead, and it is as though they had never existed,
as though they had never been born
or left children to succeed them.
Not so our forefathers; they were men of loyalty,
Whose good deeds have never been forgotten.
Their prosperity is handed on to their descendants,
And their inheritance to future generations.
Their bodies are buried in peace,
but their name lives forever.

Ecclesiasticus 44: 8-11, 14

Contents

Editor's Preface

Lincoln during the Civil War, Franklin D. Roosevelt during the Great Depression and World War II, and Lyndon Baines Johnson from 1963 to 1968—these three men presided over the American nation during its darkest hours. The crises confronted by Lincoln and FDR require little elaboration, but were the challenges of Johnson presidency evenly roughly comparable to two cataclysmic wars and the near-collapse of the American economy?

This book answers this question in the affirmative. And largely this is because Lyndon Baines Johnson, perhaps the most powerful politician in American history, had decided to stamp his will upon the nation. Biographer John Bullion explains that from an early age Johnson believed it his Christian duty to help the less fortunate. When he succeeded John Fitzgerald Kennedy following the young president's assassination in November, 1963, LBJ resolved to complete FDR's social revolution. The United States, he vowed, would wipe out poverty, achieve racial justice, and otherwise consecrate the nation to building a "Great Society" for all.

Johnson's legislative successes were both consequence and cause of the social ferment of those turbulent years. His appeals for a "Great Society" underscored the blighted condition of urban ghettoes; and his modest federal initiatives provoked demands for more. Civil rights protests entered a new and more combative phase as Black Power trumped the integrationist message of Martin Luther King, Jr., and as race riots engulfed the nation's inner cities.

LBJ might have coped with these social convulsions; but then came war in Vietnam, a challenge beyond his religious sensibilities or his substantial political aptitude. The war tugged at the social fabric of the nation; by 1968, when LBJ's term of office ended, it had been ripped into shreds.

Biographer John Bullion explores the paradox of a supremely forceful president who encounters an obdurate reality beyond his control. That LBJ transformed the nation—and the world—is indisputable; yet Bullion also depicts a man at war with himself, divided by his responsibilities as a Christian and the impious demands of politics, and by deep-seated psychological demons and self-doubts and an often irrepressible lust for power.

Bullion's complex reading of LBJ dates from his own childhood. In 1965, Bullion's father, Johnson's tax attorney, took his 21-year-old son on a two-day hunting trip with LBJ. On the first day, using a rifle supplied by the President, young Bullion bagged two yearling bucks. LBJ praised his shooting and whispered an order to the Secret Service agent, who went to town and came back with a new hunting rifle, which LBJ presented to Bullion as a gift. But the next day, Bullion missed every shot. LBJ chewed him out. "I'm starting to think I wasted my money. You can't hit anything," he muttered. The gun, Bullion later learned, hadn't been sighted in. Bullion also learned something about a man whose mood could swing from extravagant kindness to blistering fury in an instant.

Bullion's style is suited to his subject. His writing is beguilingly personal, yet at times it is also direct and blunt. LBJ would doubtless have winced at many of Bullion's conclusions, but the brash Texas politician would likely have appreciated the generosity of Bullion's citations, the forcefulness of his prose, and the clarity of his judgments.

MARK C. CARNES
Ann Whitney Olin Professor of History
Barnard College, Columbia University

Author's Preface

I am grateful to Michael Boezi, who invited me to contribute a study of Lyndon Johnson to the Library of American Biography. His was an act of considerable editorial daring: my research specialty is British imperial politics during the eighteenth century, and my only publication dealing with the era of Johnson was a memoir of my family's adventures with LBJ. I hope I have justified his confidence.

I owe a great deal to several people associated with Longman: Michael's able assistant Vanessa Gennarelli; Laurie Panu, who introduced me to him; and the anonymous readers of drafts of the book.

This book is based upon printed sources, with one exception. The Scripps Library at the Miller Center for Public Affairs at the University of Virginia has made over 1,150 interview transcripts from the LBJ Presidential Library available online. I am grateful to the Scripps Library for making these invaluable documents so easily available.

My colleagues Robert M. Collins, Carol Anderson, and Lee Wilkins gave generously and patiently of their time and expertise. Lynn Wolf Gentzler greatly facilitated my search for materials on Johnson. As I have throughout the twenty-plus years we have worked together, I leaned heavily on the good humor, editorial skill, wise counsel, and abiding friendship of Nancy Taube.

During the last five years, I have taught several courses on Lyndon Johnson. My students have made these courses a source of wonderful fun and much inspiration. I would like to thank two in particular: John Kyle Day, for sharing with me his insights into Southern congressional politics during the 1950s; and Tiffany Semm, for enriching my knowledge of Robert Kennedy and for commenting trenchantly on several versions of many chapters.

My principal expert on Lyndon and Texas is my wife Laura. Her frequent applications of common sense and shrewd advice, leavened as always by love and understanding, enriched the book and its author beyond telling. I cannot imagine writing a book without Laura by my side.

As I worked on this biography, I frequently told colleagues, friends, and family that the main difference between this work and *In the Boat with LBJ* was that I'd left the Bullions out of this one. Now I realize that is true only in the literal sense. My approach to Lyndon Johnson has been deeply and subtly influenced by my late father, J. Waddy Bullion, a man whom Lyndon described as "the best." I often disagreed with Dad's assessment of his friend, but I certainly agree with LBJ's judgment of him. For that reason, this book is dedicated to his memory.

JOHN L. BULLION
University of Missouri

Introduction

Whenever criticism stung Lyndon Johnson, he always felt he could fall back on one truth about himself: "I do understand power, whatever else may be said about me." Then he would elaborate. "I know where to look for it, and how to use it." To him, this was neither exaggeration nor boast. It was a fact of his life. It explained his victories in politics and his greatest achievements as congressman, senator, and president.

Quarreling with this self-assessment is difficult. Getting, keeping, expanding, and using power obsessed Johnson throughout his career. Still, as a guide to understanding his life this flat statement is misleading because it is incomplete. How LBJ defined power is left out. Comprehending his definition is central to grasping how he transformed American politics.

Power was not an abstract concept to Lyndon Johnson; it was inseparable from its human agents. Throughout his early career, he sought out and cultivated men and women who would mentor him. As a high school student he figured out that the way out of his tiny isolated hometown in the Texas Hill Country and on to success in the world beyond it depended on connecting with people who could open doors for him—to stop "working just with my hands . . . and make it with my brain"—and then could guide him through the pathways of power. This pattern continued once he arrived in Washington. Some of these men—such as Alvin Wirtz, the premier lawyer–lobbyist in Austin, and Sam Rayburn, the influential congressman from Bonham, Texas, who rose to be Speaker of the House—came to love and respect him. Others—including Herman and

George Brown, founders of the huge Texas construction company Brown & Root; Franklin Roosevelt, the master of politics and the presidency during his time; Richard Russell, the dominant figure in the Senate during the 1940s and early 1950s—were impressed by him, sponsored his ascent, and formed creative and effective alliances with him.

Contemporaries who tried to explain Lyndon's rise in Washington sometimes dismissed him as "a professional son." Although this sneer simplified some complex relationships, it still singled out an important aspect of his political personality. Johnson could read influential older men as swiftly, thoroughly, and penetratingly as master scholars read books. He listened closely to what was said and unsaid, watched body language with total attention, anticipated the direction of people's thoughts, and improved upon their insights with his fast, sharp intelligence. That men who pulled the levers of power in the federal government were impressed by him was not surprising.

These traits did more than help him to make important friends. They enabled him to read the minds of his political opponents. Lyndon was a formidable opponent in campaigns because he had a sure instinct for his rivals' weaknesses and for the crucial, determinative issues of an election. He struck, and struck hard, at the jugular vein. In his first congressional race, he saw the importance of the voters isolated on ranches and farms "at the forks of the creek." He also sensed the deep affection for FDR in the Texas 10th District. In the 1941 Senate contest, he brilliantly appropriated the tactics of a celebrity politician. In the 1948 special election to fill a vacant Senate seat, he exploited the movement of Texans from the country to the city and portrayed himself—complete with the modern marvel of the Johnson City Windmill, the helicopter he used to travel between towns—as the spokesman for the New Texas. Finally, in his presidential campaign he painted Barry Goldwater as a dangerous extremist and made that extremism the defining issue of the election. His keen mind and ruthless drive dominated opponents, and they made him a master of election politics.

This keenness and ruthlessness also allowed him to see how to get things done in the federal bureaucracy and on Capitol Hill. The tactics he employed there often stood in stark contrast to his modus operandi in other areas. Grasping the differences requires a knowledge of how Johnson behaved in campaigns and toward those closest to him.

In elections Lyndon was a ferocious adversary. To his loyal wife, Lady Bird, he was frequently insensitive to the point of callous brutality. As one of her friends once remarked, he could treat her worse than he would a domestic servant. The demands he made on his staff were both legendary and notorious. Horace Busby, who worked with him for two decades, observed that in Washington, "where his reputation as a driving taskmaster overshadowed his role as a considerable achiever, introduction as a new member of Lyndon Johnson's staff evoked, invariably, spontaneous and embarrassing expressions of genuine sympathy from outsiders." For whatever reason, Johnson had decided that to achieve his great ambitions he had to be willing to savage family and staff, using many of his darker characteristics: his hot temper, his overbearing physical presence, his sharp tongue, his unerring assessment of others' hopes and fears, and his cruel willingness to scornfully fling all these in their faces to whip them and himself on.

Bird, Busby, and the others came to recognize that LBJ also could call on another side of his personality when being a legislator. As staffer Joe Phipps noted in some amazement, "Lyndon Johnson had the capacity to split himself in two." "Not," Phipps hastened to add, "the way a classic schizophrenic might." He was adept at "creating for himself a Joseph's coat that would reflect the varieties of [a] tender, loving soul" and presenting this image as "the *real* Lyndon Johnson." In this presentation he portrayed himself as at heart the reverse of "the cold, conniving, flint-eyed, posturing, mail-coated son of a bitch" many people believed he was.

At legislation, he applied his gift for reading men and women to finding common ground on important bills and issues. What could they accept as compromises? How far would they be willing to go? What needed to be done to pass a law? Contemporaries who were wary of his prowess called him a man without principles, someone more concerned with adding more laws—whether they were useful or not—as notches on his legislative pistol than with resolving issues and driving the bad guys out of town. Those more favorably inclined referred to him as a pragmatic legislator who understood what was possible and saw the value of small steps and half loaves. Both perspectives make complicated processes and stratagems a little too straightforward, but each points to the same fact: Lyndon Johnson was always determined to find some way, by fair means or foul, to do something—he was, as he frequently described himself, a "doer"— and he did: as congressman to modernize his district, as majority leader of the Senate to enact a pioneering civil rights law, and as a president who presided over efforts to create the Great Society.

LBJ's successes did not deceive him into believing that power could be wielded effectively by individuals alone. To the contrary: many of the national and international problems confronting his country were too complicated and too vast to be addressed effectively by gifted men and women acting by themselves. This insight reveals another aspect of his understanding of the nature of power: power did not have an exclusively human face; it was institutional as well. Federal agencies, Congress, and the executive branch were repositories of the force necessary to preserve and strengthen what was good and to reform and improve what was deficient or harmful. What's more, Johnson was convinced these institutions needed more force and greater potency. Only when they were strengthened by statutory laws and executive action could they deal with the domestic challenges and the foreign dangers confronting the United States.

LBJ began his political career during the Great Depression. It was obvious to him then that only the federal government could ameliorate the impact of the economic crisis on millions of Americans and provide the stimulus for recovery and the restoration of prosperity. The 1930s were also darkened by a fundamental threat to the nation's security from Nazi Germany, Fascist Italy, and Imperial Japan. It was obvious to Johnson that geography would not keep America safe, despite the protestations of the isolationists about the width of the Atlantic and Pacific Oceans. Safety depended on beefing up the country's military forces and productive capacity and recognizing that war was inevitable.

After the Second World War, the United States faced an even more powerful enemy: the Soviet Union (USSR). The Cold War required more military preparedness, including terrible advances in nuclear weapons, to stave off aggression from more enemies, Communist nations in Eastern Europe, Asia, and the Caribbean. To sustain U.S. strength, Johnson knew an expanding domestic economy was essential. To compete for the hearts and minds of nations poised between the United States and its allies and the Russians and theirs, it was equally necessary to move away from racism and segregation at home and toward equality of opportunity and civil rights. Put in terms more immediately relevant to a senator from Texas, this meant that the South had to be rescued from economic stagnation and Jim Crow laws and customs. To accomplish these national tasks, the national government had to be given the power to play a dominant role.

Robert Dallek, the author of several books on LBJ, summarized Johnson's views perfectly. "Johnson had a huge investment," wrote

Dallek, "in the idea that government was not the problem, it was the solution." That belief rose out of his analysis of the crises of his times. The faith he invested in that idea was confirmed by his success in strengthening the power of the federal government to solve problems and by applying that power to the issues of his day.

What separated Lyndon Johnson from other pursuers of power was his understanding of how a fascination with it could lead to an overestimation of it. Psychologically, power was a seductive temptation, alluring the unwary with visions of being able to accomplish anything and everything. LBJ resisted this temptation better than many. He did not make the mistake of believing either individuals or institutions could do as they pleased. When his vice president advised him in January 1965 that his landslide victory over Goldwater allowed him to act as he wished, he recoiled immediately. As far as he was concerned, such a statement proved that Hubert Humphrey's naïveté bordered on the dangerous. Not long afterward, he marginalized his vice president by cutting him out of substantive policy discussions of foreign and domestic issues. To Johnson, his power and that of the presidency were limited by an array of circumstances.

Foremost among these circumstances was the power of the USSR to destroy the United States and the world. The first step to preserving peace was not wishing for it and assuming other nations did likewise; rather, it was maintaining a creditable deterrence against a nuclear attack. That required the creation and preservation of credibility. LBJ was certain the United States had to be perceived as strong, as determined to resist aggression, as a staunch, loyal ally, and as willing to respond to any attack, be it conventional or nuclear. Losing credibility was provocative. It would encourage acts of aggression and would dangerously destabilize the nuclear balance of power. Failed attempts at appeasing the Nazis convinced Johnson's generation of leaders of the fatality of appearing and acting weak; the Cold War heightened the necessity of the perception and reality of strength.

Having power did not include the liberty of treating potent enemies as LBJ pleased. He could not ignore such threats. Nor could he delude himself into following his heart and thinking that foreign relations should take a distant second place to domestic reform. Power and preference did not allow leaders to do anything that might remotely threaten American credibility. Lyndon Johnson always saw these considerations as restraints on him and his country. Being strong and firm while easing tensions between the great powers of the world were his primary responsibilities as president. He kept these limitations on his actions constantly in mind. Nowhere did they bind him more closely than in the case of Vietnam.

Lyndon's freedom of action was also restricted when it came to domestic matters. Any effort at reform inevitably crossed swords with groups having vested interests in the status quo. Obvious examples were white Southerners, who had installed and maintained a system of racial segregation that was unjust and unconstitutional. It was not sufficient merely to pass laws against Jim Crow. Johnson had to find ways to persuade whites to comply, however grudgingly, with the legislation. Avoiding bitter, enduring, and perhaps violent opposition to the law was a delicate task of persuasion and negotiation. Justice, Johnson was sure, would not be achieved by judicial or legislative fiat. Those tactics had their limits. Going beyond those boundaries depended on more subtle and sympathetic methods.

Weakening the power of segregation in the South was a specific example of a more pervasive and general problem all over the country. Lyndon struggled throughout his career with a persistent suspicion of the federal government and a historically sanctified tradition of the virtues of local and private control. When he was a boy, the residents of his town vociferously objected to the state of Texas improving the highway into town. This was not because of money: improvements were funded by Austin. The opposition was inspired by a fear that the state would undermine the town's freedom to govern itself. Folks were finally mollified (some said bought off) by the hiring of townspeople for the road crews and, more important, by the appointing of locals as the surveyors to plot the direction and siting of the highway. This sort of episode became familiar to Johnson. He had to balance the desire for federal funds and benefits against persistent concerns about federal control over citizens' lives. Ideally, what the people wanted was money with no strings attached and no higher taxes. Dealing with this strong desire always constricted Lyndon's plans for providing the federal government with the means for solving the nation's problems.

How Lyndon Johnson accumulated and expanded power under these conditions is a major subject of this book. So is the story of how he became in the process a potent agent in the transformation of American politics. Some of the changes he planned, worked toward, and achieved. Other changes he fought to avoid, worked to prevent, and deplored when they became realities.

Precisely how and why this mix of good and bad happened remained somewhat obscure to him. That it occurred embittered him, making his years of retirement frustrating and depressing. When he looked for explanations, he often found them to be the result of personal and political hatred directed at him. He was not completely wrong: certainly there were those who hated him. But animus only scratches the surface of explaining the causes of his mixed legacies, which must be sought in two places. First is an understanding of the interaction between Lyndon Johnson's visions of domestic reform and his perceptions of foreign dangers. Second is an appreciation of the interplay between the power he amassed and the limitations under which he used it.

A Steam Engine in Pants: 1908 to 1937

They were all so poor, Lyndon Johnson said about his childhood, that they did not have a name for it. Hard times were any times. Not having electricity, running water, paved streets, all-weather highways, and railroad service were facts of life. By the standards of Central Texas towns in the early twentieth century, his hometown of Johnson City was isolated and impoverished, but this does not necessarily mean he was born into poverty on August 27, 1908.

It is important to grasp that being poor was more apparent to grown-up LBJ than it was to young Lyndon. LBJ lived high, wide, and handsome in Washington; Lyndon knew only his town, and no one there had a great deal. As a schoolmate recalled, if a family had a house, food, clothing, and (by the 1920s) a Model T Ford, it was middle class. The Johnsons had all this. They bought the first bathtub in Johnson City and one of the first cars. By their neighbors' standards, they were not poor.

In fact, they were prominent citizens. In the Texas Hill Country, bloodlines counted for a great deal, and Sam Ealy Johnson was the descendant of two founding families, the Johnsons and the Buntons. His ancestors were prominent cattle ranchers who branched out into land speculation and village development; one of them, James Polk Johnson, surveyed plots for a new town in 1879, then named the settlement Johnson City after himself. Sam, a gregarious man, ran successfully for the state legislature and served with distinction. At a time when lobbyists in Austin routinely bought representatives with bucks, booze, and blondes, he stayed unhitched. He also resisted the political temptations of nativism. Sam strongly defended his German-American constituents against accusations of disloyalty during World War I. In a time when the Ku Klux Klan waxed powerful, he firmly opposed those "kukluxsonsofbitches." Perhaps most important to the voters, he served their interests effectively. Thanks to Sam, the state paved the highway into Johnson City.

Rebekah Baines Johnson had a distinguished lineage, too. In a community respectful of education, that her grandfather had been president of Baylor, a Baptist college in Waco, counted heavily. She had a college degree, and it mattered that she used her learning to give elocution lessons to the town's young women.

To be sure, Sam did not prosper while Lyndon matured. He failed as a stock farmer, as a speculator in cotton futures, and in a variety of real estate deals. His son blamed his heavy debts on too much whiskey; in fact, bad luck played the major role. That he lost more than he won and was in debt distinguished him from very few in Johnson City, nor did his blueprint for his children's success.

The Johnsons wanted their kids to get college educations; to them, the way out of penny-pinching drudgery and toward success was education. This belief did not set them apart. The town was oriented toward academic achievement, and parents' expectations were reinforced by some extraordinary teachers. Students responded by studying hard and moving on and up. "I think everybody there was ambitious," remembered a schoolmate of Lyndon, "because we didn't have much there. . . . You had to figure if you were going to do anything you had to do it somewhere else."

They did. When Lyndon graduated from high school in 1924, every senior but one went on to college. At that time, very few young people graduated from high school, and only a handful of those who earned diplomas enrolled in colleges. The alumni of Johnson City High did not just enroll in college, either; they were very successful. Graduates from 1919 to 1924 became lawyers, teachers, ministers, corporate executives, five university professors, and one president of the United States.

Later, that president observed Johnson City illustrated these truths: "What the average folks want is very simple: peace, a roof over their heads, food on their tables, milk for their babies, a good job at good wages, a doctor when they need him, an education for their kids, a little something to live on when they're old, and a nice funeral when they die." Make their goals realities, and this would be a Great Society. And they would deserve that society, for to LBJ these simple goals proved "people are good."

But what young Lyndon wanted was not simple, and his plan for achieving his desires defied the prescriptions of Johnson City's good people. He was skeptical of the power of education. This was due in part to the fact that the rote learning of the early grades came easily to him: Lyndon skipped enough grades to graduate high school at the early age of fifteen. It was also the product of his learning style. He learned from conversation. He listened closely. So keen were these skills, he could anticipate another's thoughts before they were spoken, and what he discovered in these encounters stuck; his memory was very exact. This method of comprehending the world made him regard formal academics with near contempt. In school he was an average student. Other than assignments, a friend noticed, he never read a book. To his peers and their parents, this marked him as unambitious.

To that failing they added his notoriety for shirking chores. His father railed at his "lazy streak" and doubted he would ever amount to anything. His grandmother predicted he would "wind up in the penitentiary." Lyndon did not plan on jail, but he did not intend to wind up at college either. He was the one in his graduating class who did not go.

He had concluded that college was not the way out. Talking Texas politics with his father and others led him to believe success depended on finding powerful men who could mentor him, then convincing them to help him rise. So he ran off to California, hoping to become a lawyer under the tutelage of a cousin, Tom Martin.

Tom promised more than he could deliver, however. Lyndon came back to Johnson City as poor as he left, with only this bit of self-knowledge: when inspired, he was capable of prodigious work. The person famous for being a workaholic first appeared in San Bernardino, running a legal practice while Martin spent his time drinking and womanizing. He soon learned another lesson: the only job he could get at home was day laborer on a highway crew. This wore him out and led nowhere. Desperate to work with "my brains and not my hands," convinced by failure to find another route to brain work, he told his parents he would do as they wished and go to Southwest Texas State Teachers College in San Marcos.

At college Lyndon continued to be an average student. Outside the classroom, though, he was very successful. The California fiasco had not converted him to making it on his own, but it had taught him that he must choose better mentors. President Cecil "Prexy" Evans gave Johnson important campus jobs, with ever-increasing responsibilities. By the time Lyndon left in 1930, he had persuaded Evans to let him control student employment and manage his appointments. Classmates and faculty had to ingratiate themselves with Lyndon to get the college president's attention. Lyndon also organized a series of successful campaigns in student politics, overthrowing the domination of a social fraternity, the Black Stars, and succeeding in breaking athletic teams' monopoly of student activities funds. By graduation, he was the best-known student at San Marcos. Evans predicted great things for his protégé, praising in particular his "energy, careful thought, and determination."

However, the enduring experience of Lyndon's college years did not occur on campus. Like many students at Southwest Texas, Lyndon had to take a year's leave and teach school to earn enough money to finish his education. In 1928, the superintendent of schools in Cotulla, a small South Texas town, was desperate to find a principal for what the local Anglos called "the Mexican school." Johnson agreed to take the job for $125 a month.

Poverty was very visible in Cotulla. Latinos there literally lived on the wrong side of the tracks, kept in economic peonage by powerful ranchers, farmers, and merchants, their language, religion, and culture the objects of contempt. Their school had no playground equipment; kids played in the dirt. It had no lunch period; families could not afford the meal. It had no meaningful instruction; the five Anglo women who taught came late, left early, and demanded nothing. When Lyndon met his students, he realized that youth did not keep them from feeling "the pain of injustice": "They never seemed to know why people disliked them, but they knew it was so." He became "determined to give them what they needed to make it in the world, to help them finish their education. Then the rest would take care of itself."

The twenty-year-old had grasped insights he acted on for the rest of his life. He saw clearly that Latinos were not inherently or naturally dumb and lazy. What others scorned as racial inferiority, he diagnosed as the by-products of poverty, and he knew the solution for laziness, the very accusation his father had hurled at him: it was hard work. The way to end poverty—indeed, the only way—was education. The way to end sloth was to require and demand academic performance. The school and its students and teachers had to improve.

What triggered those insights was Lyndon's nature. Learning by listening was his style. Using that technique in Johnson City had made him very perceptive about people everywhere. Conversation there was constrained by small town mores, and people frequently communicated with body language and pointed silences what they would not or could not say. Understanding such mannerisms was crucial to comprehending people. As Lyndon later told aides, what was unspoken was the most important thing. Thus he could intuit accurately how his students felt. That enabled him to imagine himself as someone else and empathize with him or her.

Why Johnson acted on that empathy was owing to nurture. He was always very reticent about his version of Christianity. This caused many to assume he was unmoved by religion. Typical of these reactions was a classmate's observation that church and courthouse provided the only entertainment in Johnson City and that he and Lyndon were fonder of the courthouse. Be that as it may, we should not overlook the subtle and profound influence worship had on him. His family went to the Christian Church, a denomination that split from the fundamentalist Church of Christ. The Christian Church allowed musical instruments during services and practiced a more inclusive Christianity. By example and precept, it stressed the duties of the strong to the weak. That morality stuck in Lyndon's mind and heart. As a boy, recalled his sister, he "loved to play church and . . . had to be the preacher." What he preached he applied the rest of his life. As president, he observed to a friend, "We know the Lord doesn't say we're superior. The Lord tells us to help those others [less fortunate than ourselves]. . . . We've got to help them, educate them, train them, and prepare them."

Nature and nurture enabled Johnson's imagination and reason to interact fruitfully. He could imagine others' lives, and that imagination inspired his reasoned analysis of what and why they suffered. Then his power to imaginatively envision a better future informed his plans to solve their problems. His sense of a Christian's duty impelled him to try to help by making these plans reality.

This process can be seen in Cotulla, where he persuaded the school board to buy playground equipment. He started extracurricular activities, financing them with his own money. He outlawed speaking Spanish at school so his students would become fluent in the language of power. He browbeat the teaching staff into really teaching their subjects and insisting the students do the work. He compelled the completion of homework, allowing no one to go home until assignments were finished. And he fought despair: Lyndon understood the crippling effects of the culture of poverty for minorities well before mainstream educators did. Everyday began with this litany: any baby could become a teacher, a lawyer, a doctor, even president of the United States.

Before the year was out, Lyndon had earned the respect of the school board and the thanks of the Latino students and parents of Cotulla.

After he graduated from Southwest Texas, Johnson taught for a few weeks at Pearsall in South Texas and then for a year at Sam Houston High School in Houston. "He was," Luther Jones noted, "a very unusual teacher," prowling the room, restlessly pressing the students, "very enthusiastic, very demanding." He poured energy into the debate teams, vowing they would win state championships. The team of Jones and Gene Latimer made it to the finals and lost in a 3–2 decision. Johnson took the defeat hard and snuck away to vomit. That was nearly his last act as an instructor. Luther Jones believed that Johnson "probably would have been a great teacher, or could have been" had he continued. Instead, he entered the political world of Washington, bringing his debate team with him.

Johnson got there via Texas politics and the discovery of another mentor. In 1930, during Lyndon's last college semester, Welly Hopkins ran for state senator of a district that included Johnson City. Impressed when he met Johnson, he made him his campaign manager for the Hill Country. Hopkins won the area by a landslide and the election by a comfortable majority. Afterward, he stayed in close contact with this wunderkind. When Richard Kleberg, the wealthy owner of the immense King Ranch in South Texas, won a special election to Congress in late 1931, Welly persuaded him to interview Sam Johnson's "wonderful boy" for his administrative assistant (then called a "secretary"). As Hopkins commented, Lyndon was a natural politician: "ability, personality, intelligence, a wonderful memory . . . ; he knew how to approach people." Moreover, "he had a tremendous drive, not only in accomplishing things but in demonstrating to people that he knew how to do things." Johnson justified Hopkins's recommendation during the interview, and Kleberg appointed him as the congressional secretary for Texas's 14th District. Lyndon resigned his teaching job and left for Washington.

Mostly uninterested in politics, involved in playing golf and partying, Dick Kleberg turned over his office to his young secretary. Lyndon responded to the opportunity magnificently. Seven days a week, eighteen hours a day, he drove himself and Jones and Latimer mercilessly, answering mail and intervening with federal agencies for voters made desperate by the Depression. He displayed his precocity in other ways, too. He became Speaker of the Little Congress, a staffers' social club, and converted it into a sounding board for pending legislation. Most impressive of all, he devised a scheme for keeping post office patronage in the hands of Texas's congressional delegation and out of the grasp of Vice President John "Cactus Jack" Nance Garner. Stung by defeat, Cactus Jack angrily asked his old friends, "Who the hell is this boy Lyndon Johnson? Where the hell did Kleberg get a boy with savvy like that?"

Lyndon was savvy enough to realize that Claudia Alta Taylor, the daughter of the richest man in Karnack, Texas, and a journalism and education graduate from the University of Texas, should be his wife. He met her in Austin in 1934 on his way back from the 14th District to Washington and immediately learned her nickname: "Lady Bird." Twenty-four hours later he proposed; less than three months later they "committed matrimony." As Luther Jones observed, in those days Lyndon "had no trouble making decisions . . . ; he either did it, or he didn't, very rapidly." Lady Bird was barely more deliberate. Clearly, she was strongly drawn to him, both by budding love and the shrewd calculation that the surest way for a Texas woman in the 1930s to realize vast ambitions was to marry the right man.

It was the most consequential decision of their lives. Bird epitomized loyalty. She not only loved Lyndon fiercely; she made helping him succeed the passion of her life. How unchallenged his place in her heart was may be gauged by a comment she made after the Johnsons had two daughters. Wives who were mothers had to choose who came first: their husbands or their children. Lyndon was her choice. He relied on her love and commitment and came to depend on her keen mind and efficient management. Jones put it well: she was his "balancing wheel"; "she matched him with calmness, matched his impatience."

Among Bird's most important contributions was one of her first. Her graciousness helped cement his friendship with Sam Rayburn, the most powerful Texas congressman of the time.

In the Texas legislature, Rayburn had known and respected Sam Johnson as a colleague who fought for the people rather than for the railroads and other corporate interests. He recognized in Sam's son a kindred appreciation for the early efforts of Franklin Roosevelt's New Deal, which was intended to enable the federal government to ameliorate the impact of the Depression on Americans. The two shared a feeling that those serving in Washington could and must help out in the immediate crisis and take steps to restore economic productivity. Already a leader of House Democrats, on track to be Speaker of the House if the party kept a majority, master of the legislative process and warmly welcome in FDR's White House, Mr. Sam's clout could make the difference for a young man. The trick was to attract his attention and earn his affection. That Lyndon succeeded in becoming a surrogate son of the bachelor Rayburn owed a great deal to the charms of his bride and Mr. Sam's deep love for her.

Lyndon soon had to call for Rayburn's help. Alarmed by the prevailing opinion that Johnson was the real 14th District representative, Kleberg's wife began to fear that the secretary planned to mount a challenge. It was pure paranoia; Lyndon knew he would have no chance running against Kleberg in King Ranch country. Mrs. Kleberg was beyond reason, however, and wanted him fired. With his job in jeopardy, Johnson was ready to accept a lucrative offer from General Electric to be a lobbyist. This would end any hope of ever winning an election in Texas. He did not want that, but he had no choice.

Sam Rayburn saved the day. He convinced the White House to name Johnson the director of the National Youth Administration (NYA) for Texas. It was the perfect job for Lyndon. Created by executive order in 1935, the NYA was charged with finding jobs for young people between the ages of sixteen and twenty-five so they could stay in high school and college and training them for future employment. Those plans mirrored his goals in Cotulla on a Texas-size scale. The directorship would also give him useful political contacts all over the state. Recognizing how the position meshed with his ideals and ambitions, Johnson had applied quickly for it. He had been rejected as quickly: too young, too inexperienced, unfamiliar with managing public works, the employee of a reactionary congressman who despised the New Deal. Rayburn's intervention overcame these objections. Lyndon became the youngest NYA state director in the nation.

Lyndon and Bird left for Austin in the late summer of 1935. They planned to return. "When I come back to Washington," he swore, "I'm coming back as a congressman."

Luther Jones, who joined the Texas NYA staff, insisted that Lyndon did not doubt he could succeed as director. "I think he was conceited enough, assured enough to feel he could do anything that fate put in front of him, so long as it was within his physical and mental abilities." Marveling at "the Chief's" complete confidence, Luther identified it as "really his long suit, and it was totally contagious."

Certainly his staff caught it. They and "the Chief" worked the usual seven-day weeks and eighteen-hour days. Lyndon was, some-one said, "a steam engine in pants." He found jobs for 15,000 young Texans within the first few weeks and made enough of an effort to help African-Americans that he won praise for being "so conscious of and sympathetic with the needs of all people" from Mary McLeod Bethune, the NYA's Director of Negro Affairs. By early 1937, Aubrey Williams, the NYA's national director, regarded him as the best state director.

So Lyndon now was poised to run for federal office. He did not figure out when, where, or how. He just waited for destiny. He was not a long-range planner, according to Jones. He was "a doer." Johnson "did today's job, and then first thing you knew he would have choices. All during the time I knew him he was always getting opportunities to do other things that would advance him."

On February 22, 1937, James P. Buchanan, congressman for Texas's 10th District, died. "That [is] my district," Lyndon realized. It was comprised of several Central Texas counties, including Blanco (Johnson City) and Travis (Austin). "This," he knew, "[is] my chance." He cancelled appointments in Houston and drove toward Austin and destiny.

What drove Lyndon? Without question, he wanted power. Scholars who point to that craving are not mistaken. Doubtless, too, he wanted to use power not only for himself but also for others. Johnson really did think federal intervention in the nation's economy was essential. He knew he was "a doer" who could bring Washington's ideas and money to the 10th District. Those scholars who point to his practical idealism are correct.

Still, as LBJ was prone to say, "if you are going to understand a man, you have to know all of him—not just the part he lets you see." Ambition and power, altruism and power—these were plain to all. Beneath them, one of his more perceptive staffers saw something else. Horace Busby mused that his "was less a drive to succeed than a drive not to fail." And nothing impelled him more than "his fear he might have inherited a tendency to be 'lazy.'"

The steam engine in pants never forgot his father's accusation, and the memory of coming back poor from California filled him with determination never to repeat that journey.

2

The Best Congressman That Ever Was: 1937 to 1941

W hen Lady Bird learned that her husband wanted to run for Congress, she asked Alvin Wirtz, a prominent Austin attorney and lobbyist, what the odds were. Wirtz told her "that Lyndon was a long shot because he was the least well known of any of the people who were going to run, but that he thought Lyndon had a chance." Reassured, Bird asked how much it would cost. Told $10,000 for starters, she immediately raised the money from her father. One of the reasons he had a chance was his wife.

Another supporter was Alvin Wirtz. He had been impressed with Johnson—energetic, intelligent, extraordinarily skilled at finding his way through the corridors of power—and how he got things done in Washington. Respect soon deepened into paternal love. Wirtz regarded Lyndon as the son he had never had. When Lyndon had become NYA director, the powerful former state senator had served as chair of his advisory board. Had "Senator"—Wirtz's nickname—not endorsed his candidacy, Lyndon would not have run.

Wirtz raised thousands of dollars for the campaign from the oil and gas companies he represented. The exact sum remains unknown because Senator preferred cash and did not document violations of Texas law by giving receipts or keeping books. Surely Lyndon spent between $75,000 and $100,000, a huge sum for that time. Just as crucial as the money was Wirtz's strategizing. He came up with the issue that dramatized and defined the campaign. Johnson would run as the most fervent New Deal candidate, proving his claim by backing Franklin Roosevelt's doomed attempt to enlarge the Supreme Court. *Franklin D and Lyndon B!* became the campaign's slogan.

Still, Senator's big bucks and FDR's long coattails did not guarantee victory. They made winning possible—not inevitable or even likely. That was up to the candidate.

The stage was set ideally for Lyndon. Buchanan's replacement would be chosen in a special election. Had this been a regular Democratic primary, Lyndon would have been required to get 50 percent of the total vote or face a runoff. In a special election, whoever finished atop the first and only ballot won. There were other advantages, too. Special elections attracted a large field of candidates, thereby dividing the vote among many, and voter turnout was typically much lower than in regular primaries. A relative unknown had a far better chance of getting just enough support to carry the day. Those odds were improved when the long shot campaigned seven days a week, twenty hours a day, and had the knack of listening carefully, connecting with individuals, and earning one vote at a time. Lyndon Johnson stood an excellent chance.

From February 28 to April 8, 1937, in sleet and sun, from predawn to midnight-dark, Lyndon worked. He shed forty pounds and resisted the agony of an infected appendix. Ed Clark, a veteran Texas politician, said, "I never saw anyone campaign as hard as that. I never thought it was possible to work that hard."

On April 10, 29,948 residents voted, significantly fewer than the 41,000 ballots cast in the 1936 primary. Lyndon got 8,820 votes, 27.6 percent of the total, and 3,000 ahead of his nearest competitor. His fervent support of FDR enabled him to carry Austin. Sheer energy won rural votes. One staffer noted, "He won that election in the byways." A cousin chimed in that it was not the towns but "the people from the forks of the creeks" who elected him. "Lyndon got his people to vote . . . it was a masterpiece of campaigning," observed Emmett Shelton, the brother of an opponent. Then Shelton summed up the why of victory: "He just absolutely outcampaigned us."

The new congressman soon met with the president. When FDR finished a fishing vacation in the Gulf of Mexico, he summoned Johnson to Galveston, then took him along to Fort Worth. The two hit it off immediately. Roosevelt regarded Lyndon as the sort of "uninhibited young pro" he would have been had he not gone to Harvard. "Uninhibited" to Roosevelt meant Johnson was not intimidated either by conservative Texas Democrats coalescing around Vice President Garner in opposition to the New Deal or by isolationist sentiment among Texas voters. He would respond to favors from the White House by supporting what the president wanted: more New Deal legislation and increased military preparedness against Nazi Germany and Imperial Japan.

Back in the Oval Office, FDR instructed Secretary of the Interior Harold Ickes and Public Works Administration (PWA) Director Harry Hopkins to give the new congressman all the help they could on federal projects for the 10th District. In return, he expected Johnson would vote with the administration in the House.

Lyndon kept his part of the bargain. The only votes he cast against the administration were in opposition to FDR's decision to cut some benefits. That endeared him to New Dealers and did not trouble Roosevelt. Johnson even supported a 1938 bill to reorganize the executive branch, a measure described by its 100 Democratic opponents as "tyranny." On preparedness he always voted aye, despite isolationist pressure back home. Thomas Corcoran, FDR's right-hand man, dubbed Lyndon "the best New Dealer in Texas."

That conferred tangible rewards. Sooner than many representatives, Lyndon understood how the federal bureaucracy could change lives and enrich districts. As one acute New Dealer observed, Johnson grasped that the executive branch was now more important than Congress. His awareness of how this changed a congressman's role swiftly followed. Emmett Shelton ran the Travis County relief agency, so he knew local and state programs were more omnipresent and extensive than federal ones even in the mid-1930s. Old-line congressmen like "Old Buck" Buchanan assumed that was the way things always would be and did not use their power to help constituents get federal grants and loans. As Shelton noted, Old Buck appointed postmasters and did little else. Between 1937 and 1941 that changed in the 10th District. Lyndon brought in over $70 million in federal funds, a stupendous amount for that time. It enriched Alvin Wirtz by funding the Marshall Ford Dam project he was interested in; it brought over twenty grants for housing, relief, electric power, and flood control to Austin; it brought electricity to the Hill Country; it brought Lyndon newborn namesakes from grateful parents. Corcoran's expert judgment sums up his record: Lyndon Johnson was "the best congressman for a district that ever was."

Johnson had no intention of remaining merely the best congressman for 1 district out of 435. His accomplishments whetted his appetite for power in national politics and for election to the Senate.

Once more he looked for a powerful man who could give him a boost. The choice was easy. To ascend, Johnson had to stay hitched to FDR, so he played a crucial role in derailing Garner's run for the presidency by helping arrange the erosion of Cactus Jack's support in Texas. Then, during the fall of 1940, he took over raising and allocating funds for Democrats' House campaigns throughout the nation. To the surprise of politicians and pundits who predicted a Republican sweep in congressional elections, the rejuvenated and replenished Democrats kept their majority. A grateful president designated him the administration's man in the Lone Star State. Lyndon now announced all the federal projects granted to Texas, and his approval was necessary for requests to have a chance for funding.

Johnson reached for this position for familiar reasons: he was ambitious, he wanted power, and FDR was the obvious way of serving both causes. Still, overlooking another factor would leave this picture unfinished. Although Lyndon said little about foreign affairs during this period, his retrospective comments reveal he closely studied Hitler's rise to power. He believed it portended war for Europe and grave peril for the United States. Johnson did not support Roosevelt's efforts to improve our defense because it was politic; in fact, substantial numbers of his constituents were strongly isolationist and regarded rearmament with alarm. He believed FDR was right.

Around the same time, Lyndon became fascinated by Winston Churchill. He admired him as the embodiment and inspiration of British resistance to Nazism, and he believed Churchill had been right to label the appeasement of Germany at Munich in 1938 as an unmitigated disaster. To Lyndon the moral of Munich was obvious: yielding to aggressors, whether from weakness or will, brought on more aggression and ultimately a more dangerous conflict. Throughout his life he never doubted the truth of this. When he was president, this precept guided his thinking. In 1940, it taught him that America had to be strong and had to be led by Churchill's equivalent—at the time that man was Franklin Roosevelt.

Lyndon desperately wanted to play a significant role in this crisis. As usual, he was willing to wait for events to decide what that might be. "With all those war clouds hanging over Europe," he recalled, "I felt that someone with all my training and preparedness was bound to be an important figure."

For a time, Johnson thought he would play an important role in the Senate. On April 8, 1941, Senator Morris Sheppard suddenly died. The scenario of 1937 repeated itself: a winner-take-all special election, this time on June 28 with several candidates competing in the sort of contest that enticed significantly fewer voters to the polls because there were no local issues or candidates on the ballot. Once more, the import of organization and energy would be magnified. Again, the impact of raising money speedily and spending it efficiently would be tremendous.

Lyndon had no money worries. Getting the Marshall Ford Dam paid for and piling millions of dollars worth of other federal projects on top of it had won him the complete support of Herman and George Brown, co-owners of the immensely profitable and rapidly expanding construction firm Brown & Root. The brothers were among the first examples of what became commonplace in Texas business circles: fiscally conservative, bitterly opposed to taxes, socially bigoted, ferociously anti-union, and dead set against federal programs, except when they enriched business. In this the Browns and fellow businessmen took their cues from Southern Democrats in Congress. As historian Randall Woods trenchantly notes, as long as New Deal programs could be manipulated to subsidize and strengthen the powers-that-be, businessmen could see benefits to Roosevelt's programs. When the president used law and administrative rulings to construct more liberal coalitions and threaten the local elites, especially on race, most Southern Democrats became ferocious opponents.

Insofar as the Browns were concerned, the fact that Lyndon was a strong New Dealer meant less to them than that he delivered the contracts and strengthened the Texas economy. The Browns praised Lyndon for being "practical." To quote George Brown: "Basically Lyndon was more conservative, more practical than people understand. You get right down to the nut-cutting, he was practical." Sure, he was for minorities and labor and the little man. "But by God . . . he was as practical as anyone." A key part of that practicality was Johnson's quick comprehension of what military preparedness could mean economically, as well as the speed with which he funneled large parts of this money to the Browns and into the Texas economy.

The oil and gas industry in Texas shared the Browns' appreciation of Lyndon's practicality. They slopped virtually unlimited sums into his trough. National labor unions and liberal New Dealers contributed generously, too, as the White House put out the word to help the best New Dealer in Texas. Favors and dollars from the U.S. Treasury made for strange bedfellows; a man who could turn on Washington's cash spigot was prized by people across the whole spectrum of politics. Lyndon counted on his ability to keep everybody happy by bringing them water from an overflowing well. In turn they primed his pump with large infusions of dollars.

Despite a gush of money, the campaign lurched to a bad start. A master of one-on-one politicking, Lyndon did not speak well before crowds. That was a serious flaw; in a statewide race, he simply could not shake enough hands or swap thoughts with enough individuals in the time available to win. He had to do better at speaking. Yet he seemed powerless to remedy his deficiencies. Indeed, he contributed to them. The folksy Lyndon charmed: he was a genuine son of the people, but running for the world's greatest deliberative body helped him decide that he should appear worthy of its higher calling. With blue suits, white shirts, ties, lengthy and complex explications of issues, he became a bore. It is worth noting that this did not go away with time. The feeling that appearing starched and stiff dignified his worthiness to be senator or president dogged him for the rest of his days. With few exceptions, so did his stilted, unpersuasive readings of prepared speeches.

Another troubling characteristic made its first appearance in 1941. As his campaign foundered, Johnson became mysteriously ill. He had to be hospitalized for a week. The public was told he had pneumonia; according to Bird, "he was depressed and it was bad." It was obvious to her he was frightened that he would lose. That had not frozen him in 1937, but his victories in that and later elections made him psychologically dependent on the people's approval. Fearful that they would reject him as unworthy of higher office, this ordinarily decisive man began agonizing about withdrawing. Bird and John Connally, the most commanding of Lyndon's young aides, brought him out by pointing to rising poll ratings and encouraging him to get active again. Soon he was fully engaged in campaigning, but dragging him out of the depths would be a recurring task for them in the years and crises ahead.

This was not the last time Lyndon rebounded from depression vigorously and creatively. His slow start strengthened his determination and sharpened his tactical brilliance, and the entry into the race of W. Lee "Pappy" O'Daniel, the hugely popular governor of Texas, inspired an imaginative and effective campaign.

Pappy was the first celebrity politician in Texas history. He became famous as the master of ceremonies for the *Pillsbury Lightcrust* radio show, which poured a mix of Texas swing music, old-time-religion hymns, and paeans of praise to Mama over a huge audience every weekday at 12:30 P.M. Encouraged by his enraptured listeners, O'Daniel ran for governor in 1938 on the Golden Rule, the Ten Commandments, and a promise to give aged mamas and daddies a good pension without raising taxes. Experienced pols scoffed at him and his impractical scheme. They scorned his campaign events, featuring a hillbilly band and collecting donations in barrels marked "Flour, not Pork," an unsubtle attack on officials bought and sold like hogs. Then Pappy won the primary without a runoff, the first time any candidate who was not an incumbent and was running against several opponents had done that. He repeated this triumph in 1940, despite not getting close to providing the "thirty bucks [a month] for Mama" he had promised to make reality.

Lady Bird aptly summarized Lyndon's strategy: "If you couldn't beat 'em, you might as well join 'em." He hired two bands and his own radio celebrity. The bands played traditional standards, interspersed with patriotic tunes. Topping the extravaganza was a drawing for defense bonds after every Johnson speech. The lucky winners got $25 worth of contributions to the nation's security. Lest Mama worry Lyndon was a warmonger, he pledged that if his constituents' sons had to fight he would leave the Senate and join them in the front lines. The isolationist O'Daniel's response to these appeals to patriotism—the creation of Texas forces to defend state and national boundaries—made him the butt of jokes.

Equally creative was Lyndon's clever appropriation of his opponent's appeal to potential pensioners. First, he convinced FDR to say he was a strong supporter of extending Social Security benefits. (That this exaggerated the truth troubled neither.) Second, he argued that the voters should keep O'Daniel governor so he could fight to raise Mama's state money while Senator Johnson added to it in Washington. To Pappy's amazed disgust, many of his firm supporters declared they would vote for Johnson to achieve this. On election eve, polls predicted Lyndon would win. He thought so, too, and his wife always recalled how that campaign's end felt: "Oh, the adventure we had. It was in a way the best campaign ever. . . . Our troops loved us, and we loved them—it was a 'we' campaign—'we're going to win.'"

But they did not win. Johnson had bounced back from depression all the way to overconfidence. Unlike 1937, he did not bend every effort to get his voters to the polls. So, though he carried San Antonio (thanks to payments to that city's political machines), his failure to make sure precinct captains exerted themselves reduced his margin considerably. Worse, he told the political bosses of South Texas—also paid off ahead of time—that they could send their official returns to the Texas Election Bureau early. This broke a cardinal rule of Texas politics: in close elections, report those counties where local bosses could "find" additional votes last. That protected against opponents "finding" enough of their own phantom supporters to surpass your majority.

Unfortunately for Lyndon, Texas's liquor and beer interests wanted prohibitionist Pappy out of Austin so they could take full advantage of the thirsty servicemen being sent to train at the bases springing up all over the state. Conservative anti-Roosevelt Democrats, such as Lieutenant Governor Coke Stevenson, wanted Pappy gone, too, so they could control state politics. Together these forces had sufficient money and leverage to steal the election in East Texas counties. Lyndon lost by 1,311 votes: 175,290 to 174,279.

Johnson was devastated. The days after his defeat were "the most miserable in my life." Feeling "terribly rejected, I began to think about leaving politics and going home to make money." While he brooded, he chewed out his staff, one person at a time, for losing the election for him. His harangues were so ugly and unjust that Lady Bird spoke words of praise and thanks to each one. Kindness moved her. So did the recognition that Lyndon would not quit politics and would need his staffers in the future.

Bird reminded Lyndon he was still a congressman. Moreover, O'Daniel's term would end in 1942; they would have a rematch then. She closed by saying "a steady diet of success isn't good for anyone" and expressing her faith that he would come back stronger and better.

Bird's gentle lecture accomplished what she had hoped. Consoled, Johnson returned to Washington, "looking very jaunty . . . and stepping along real spryly." Once more, he looked like the best congressman that ever was.

CHAPTER

3

Trying to Climb a Pole:
1941 to 1948

Franklin Roosevelt did not like losing or losers. When someone ceased to be useful, that person was cut off from the Oval Office. Lyndon had cause to worry about how FDR would react to a mismanaged election that delivered an isolationist, anti–New Dealer as Texas's senator.

Lyndon was soon reassured. The Boss was sympathetic. Roosevelt's only criticism was expressed humorously: "Lyndon, apparently you Texans haven't learned one of the first things we learned up in New York State, and that is when an election is over you have to sit on the ballot boxes." Johnson heard the warning lurking beneath the humor: he had made a stupid, inexcusable error, and if he made another, even being counterbalance to FDR's opponents in the Texas Democratic Party would not save him.

Lyndon had no intention of booting away his second chance. He looked forward to running against Pappy O'Daniel in 1942. The special election had schooled him on the need to avoid overconfidence, the wisdom of expecting attempts to steal elections, and the necessity of doing unto others as they would do unto him—first and last! It also had handed him an issue to center the next race on: he had been cheated out of victory by powerful interests and corrupt politicians. "I thought I could be elected the next year as a martyr."

No one knew better than Johnson how dubious this claim was. His staff had bought votes, too—just not enough. He had tried to get South Texas judges to fiddle the results, just as his opponents had done in East Texas; only the fact that the returns had been certified kept them from doing his bidding. When his brother advised him to protest the final count and call for an investigation, he snapped, "Hell, no! I hope they don't investigate me." None of this, though, would keep him from playing martyr.

That reveals one of the consequences of 1941: Lyndon became cynical about voters. They could not be counted on to apply common sense to deciding between policies and politicians. Why would anyone believe feckless Pappy would do more for old folks if the electorate kept him in Austin? He had not done that in the past, nor would he in the future. Yet thousands of O'Daniel's supporters had been bamboozled by Lyndon's repeating this dramatically. Thousands more Texans had been mesmerized by country bands and defense bond lotteries. Selling them in 1942 on the fable that innocent Lyndon had been martyred in 1941 by corrupt politicians and the beer and booze interests should be pretty easy.

This lesson of 1941 was reinforced by other developments. Lyndon Johnson had nothing but loathing for Adolf Hitler, but he paid close attention to how the Nazi leader brought himself to power. As Lyndon later noted, "Just repeat, and repeat, and repeat. I don't want to follow Hitler, but he had an idea that if you just take a simple thing and repeat it often enough, even if it wasn't true, why people accept it." The dictator's use of propaganda was instructive as well as frightening; Johnson adopted it for his own purposes. He intended to use it in 1942.

At closer range, he observed how FDR maneuvered the nation toward war with the Axis powers, not just by building up U.S. military forces but by destroyer deals with and Lend-Lease aid to Britain and by ordering the U.S. navy to react aggressively to German submarines in the North Atlantic. During October 1941, Johnson publicly stated that the United States was already at war. Roosevelt was never so blunt. Instead, he did what was necessary to get us there while keeping mum about his intent. To Lyndon, it was obvious we had to fight. His fellow Americans did not see this reality so clearly. As a result, it was obvious to him that the president was justified in bringing them into the life-and-death struggle against fascism by indirection and subterfuge. During 1964 and 1965, when Lyndon as president was confronted with a similar dilemma of how much to tell the American people about Vietnam, he would follow FDR's example from 1941, not his own frank talk that October. And he would suffer the consequences.

The Japanese attack on Pearl Harbor put the quietus on Lyndon's plans for 1942. Voters would have bridled at politics as usual during wartime in any case, and especially from a politician who had sworn he would be in the thick of the fight. These realities did not keep Lyndon from yearning to run; he fretted up to the last moment over the decision to file for the Senate race in June 1942, even while in the South Pacific on a fact-finding mission for FDR.

The mission was designed to cover his rear. Right after December 7, 1941, Johnson had gone on active duty as a lieutenant commander in the navy. He had not, however, joined everyone serving in combat. Rather, he inspected shipyards and war production on the West Coast. When off duty, he and John Connally partied with movie stars. Meanwhile, newspapers in his district were asking pointed questions about his promise to go in harm's way. Charles Marsh, who published the Austin newspapers and staunchly supported Lyndon, bluntly told him to get his ass overseas, hear some shots, then get back and settle down to real work helping win the war. With Roosevelt's help, he did just that.

So he could tell the voters he had been in combat, Johnson insisted on going as an observer on a bombing mission against a Japanese base in New Guinea. This was no milk run, the airmen warned him, but a highly dangerous enterprise. The B-26 he flew in was very vulnerable to superior enemy fighters throughout the long flight to the target. Events justified their warning; his plane barely survived engine trouble and several swarms of attacking Zeroes. Lyndon was cool under fire, earning the respect of the men he flew with—though they still thought he had been crazy to go along! He certainly did not deserve the Silver Star General Douglas MacArthur awarded him. MacArthur, who shared the flight crew's opinion, gave him the medal in the hope that the congressman would fight for more men, money, and machines for his Southwest Pacific command. Johnson did advocate that cause. He also wore the military's third-highest decoration for valor for the rest of his life, even convincing himself he had displayed prodigious courage over several flights.

Back home, Lyndon told the folks he knew what their boys were going through, though he did not. The men he flew with did not get medals; they got to go on more missions. He had no concept of that type of courage. Nor did he grasp the moral courage and psychological toughness that enabled officers to send their men again and again against superior Japanese pilots and planes. In fact, he downplayed the contributions of combat officers and men in the big picture of the war effort. Lyndon understood these soldiers and sailors to be, to use a term the war spawned, "expendables." Once lost, they were replaceable. Their reaction to discovering this was unknown by him. He never felt, as marine Eugene B. Sledge did, why "it was difficult to accept. We come from a nation and culture that [value] life and the individual. To find yourself in a situation where your life seems of little value is the ultimate of loneliness." Johnson saw himself as highly valuable, a life to be preserved. Rare men like him had the savvy and skills to make the crucial decisions and do what Marsh called the important work. As a result, throughout his life the appeals he made to Americans to risk being expendable in their country's cause would seem awkward, forced, and at times unconvincing.

Whatever the merits of his assumption about his proper role, it did not describe his war. After he returned to Congress, he was given no important assignments. He wanted to replace Frank Knox as secretary of the navy. Not a chance: FDR was not about to switch a prominent Republican and symbol of wartime unity with a partisan, inexperienced Democrat. He wanted to be put in charge of defense production for the navy. William Knudsen, former president of General Motors, did this for the army. Next to him, Lyndon's qualifications were nonexistent.

Around the same time, Lyndon realized he had lost access to the Oval Office. As Roosevelt became absorbed in his role as world statesman, his attention to party politics waned. It moved completely away from Johnson, whom FDR identified with party matters. Another shock followed. Faced with anti-Johnson opposition from Edwin Pauley, a West Coast oilman who controlled the party's national fund-raising, Roosevelt would not let Johnson reprise his role as the coordinator of Democratic campaigns for House seats. Lyndon was sinking into the status of just another congressman.

Before the United States entered the war, Lyndon had been certain he would play an important role in it. His frustration at having this expectation dashed probably contributed to his intensifying concentration on making money.

The Johnsons had long wanted greater economic security. The tangled mess of Sam's affairs when he died in 1937 underscored how heavily encumbered estates endangered families. Lyndon and Bird's efforts to have children heightened their concerns. Marsh and the Browns helped them invest in Austin real estate, but it was doubtful that would make them rich. (Marsh also offered to cut Johnson in on very lucrative oil deals, but Lyndon had turned him down, fearing they would ruin his prospects in national politics.) Now they looked to invest in Texas media.

The Johnsons considered buying a Waco newspaper, but the price was steep and its potential limited. More attractive was an underpowered Austin radio station. KTBC had several advantages: it was cheap, radio was clearly the wave of the future, and Johnson could use his position as congressman to get rulings from the Federal Communication Commission (FCC) to increase its power, expand its listening area, and improve its place on the dial. He could use his political clout to acquire network affiliations and popular programming. Then he could suggest to local advertisers that his activities on their behalf with federal agencies might depend on their buying commercial time on his station.

For obvious reasons, no paper trail exists to prove the extent of Johnson's role in making KTBC fantastically profitable, but contemporaries and historians never doubted he did. Again for obvious reasons, Lyndon never justified his use of his office for personal gain. Surely he figured he was just doing what other politicians did, only better because of his knowledge of the federal bureaucracy. Yet his occasional public protestations of innocence never convinced; the scale of his success was so obvious that it belied his denials and tarred him as corrupt and mendacious. These accusations would dog him throughout the rest of his career.

Equally clear is the fact that family and friends profited from his office. Lady Bird's father became richer from wartime contracts for land and services. Brown & Root, a firm that had never constructed a military base or built ships, landed the immensely lucrative contract for the Corpus Christi Naval Air Station. Alvin Wirtz's investments in providing public power for Central Texas flourished further during these years.

When need be, Lyndon protected these people from political and legal charges of corrupt dealings. In particular, he convinced FDR to influence an Internal Revenue Service investigation of George and Herman Brown for deducting illegal campaign contributions during the Senate race of 1941 as business expenses. How much the brothers were at risk of indictment for criminal fraud is uncertain; still, the Browns were clearly liable for penalties and back taxes totaling over $1,000,000. Thanks to Johnson and Roosevelt, they got off with a bill below $400,000, and Lyndon, who was increasingly vulnerable to charges he used public office to gain personal wealth, escaped with less damage from the IRS inquiry than he had feared.

The president did not intervene out of affection or gratitude. He needed Johnson to manage the Texas party. Why this was so helps illuminate Johnson's ascent to power at home and in Washington.

Horace Busby, one of Lyndon's shrewdest advisers, noted that the Depression in Texas had not been a time when business spiraled down toward collapse. Rather, the economy had been stagnant. Without the consent of the banking community, no one could start a new enterprise, and that consent was regularly withheld from those unconnected to the power structure. The New Deal had infused enough federal money to break the bankers' monopoly on start-up capital. In the old order's view, "It let people who should not do things, do things." Busby illustrated this by saying, "People who should not be Chevrolet dealers were becoming Chevrolet dealers." The local powers-that-be no longer had a stranglehold on business ventures. Threatened by this, they became "one of the places where the hard feeling against the New Deal came in." Anti-New Dealer sentiment hardened during the war as military spending put more dollars in more hands. The Johnsons were not the only ones riding this rising tide.

The spread of prosperity, however, gave a potent weapon to the old guard. With more federal money came more regulation and more resentment of "interference." Texas oilmen were incensed when Washington restricted profits on their sales. Farmers and ranchers objected to price controls on agricultural products, regarding them as denials of the full proceeds of fat times after a lean decade. Rationing chafed everyone. Washington was painted as remote, uninformed, and unsympathetic. Most ominously for FDR, conservatives appealed to the fear of rural Texans that federal assistance would mean federal control of the most intimate details of life. This is memorably captured in *The Time It Never Rained*, a novel by Texas writer Elmer Kelton. In it, a rancher rejects federal drought aid because "If you get to dependin' on the government, the day'll come when the damn federales will dictate everything you do. Some desk clerk in Washington will decide where you live and where you work and what color toilet paper you wipe yourself with. And you'll be scared to say anything because they might cut you off the tit."

That the feds would ever prescribe hues of toilet paper was far-fetched. A more likely regulation of color, and much more threatening to many white Texans, was federal action in race relations. In 1944, the U.S. Supreme Court ruled that Democratic primaries could not be restricted to white voters only. With the end of the white primary, Texas's racial status quo was jeopardized. For many, that was a powerful reason to be wary of federal power.

Also at risk was popular acceptance of the ways the old economy allocated jobs and structured classes. Millions of Americans from all economic strata were fighting for their country. They were going new places, meeting new people, reacting to military discipline, and risking their lives. What would they expect in postwar Texas? Lyndon thought he knew. As he told the legislature in 1944, "Every man who has gone through a living hell for you and me . . . shall have an equal opportunity to get a job when this is over." If free enterprise could not do this by itself, the federal government would have to act. If this meant greater centralization of power, that price would have to be paid.

Taken together, these factors constituted a crisis for the old order in Texas business and politics. Conservatives reacted by forming the Texas Regulars and seizing control of the state Democratic party in April 1944, while planning to cast the state's electoral votes for a Republican in November, even if the voters chose FDR. It was, according to historian Randall Woods, "a Republican fifth column within the Democratic Party." As individuals, Regulars gave far more money to the presidential campaign of Thomas Dewey than to FDR's coffers. Locally they worked to discourage grass-roots participation in precinct meetings. To them, Johnson was the president's "pinup boy" and "yes man," and Sam Rayburn was a "socialist" who favored the vote for blacks.

Both Johnson and Rayburn were targeted by Regulars in the Democratic primary. Rayburn won by 6,000 votes, a small margin for him. Lyndon suffered "slimy attacks," from accusations that he was a socialist and a "Negro lover," to claims that he had multiplied these sins by enriching himself in office and had sold out to Brown & Root, to charges that he was no real Texan but an Easterner. He felt endangered enough to attack the Fair Employment Practices Commission (FEPC) and to praise the poll tax as a barrier against the wrong sorts voting. He won comfortably, yet the tone of the campaign concerned and angered him.

The supple brains of Alvin Wirtz and the unyielding loyalty of moderate and New Deal Democrats helped Rayburn and Johnson fight off the Regulars' attempt to deny FDR the electoral votes. Roosevelt also got 70 percent of Texans' votes. He had been wise to keep the IRS away from Lyndon and his friends.

Johnson had no illusions about the meaning of the election. It was not a vindication of the New Deal. This vote expressed affection for FDR and appreciation for him as a wartime leader. Once Roosevelt was not president and the war was won, all bets would be off in state and nation. So they were, after Roosevelt's death on April 12, 1945, and the capitulation of Japan in August.

Rising beyond the House now would require considerable skill *and* great good luck. Lyndon joked that he had the chance of a "snowball in hell." He cited the wisdom of Sam Johnson: "Like my daddy always told me, 'If a fella starts trying to climb a pole, he usually ends up showing his ass.'" A less determined and ambitious person would have settled for the House and KTBC or retired to become richer, but Lyndon remained privately confident he could maneuver between the conservatism of Old Texas and the hunger for change to the New, and he executed a virtuoso performance.

On most matters regarding the transition to a peacetime economy, Johnson went along with Harry Truman's administration. If the private sector and state governments could not guarantee jobs, the feds had to step in; babies, he tartly noted, cannot eat states' rights. He also supported Truman's national health plan against the opposition of professions and organizations that did not deliver this basic service to all Americans.

Lyndon balanced pragmatic liberalism with conservative positions on other issues. He fought for the oil and gas industry. He broke with the administration on labor unions. He opposed efforts to organize Texas workers. Though he rejected racism, he bowed to white prejudices and anxieties by attacking the FEPC as an infringement on free enterprise, defending the poll tax as an unburdensome qualification for voting, and opposing anti-lynching bills as violations of states' rights.

Johnson summed up his vision for the future during the 1946 campaign: "where people could work; people could have a job; people could get an education; where there would be no poverty." In favor of helping all Texans economically, he was being, as George Brown said, "practical." Though Lyndon expressed sympathy for blacks and Latinos, on integration he was also ruled by practicalities. To be other than a moderate segregationist would be suicidal.

International affairs were not an issue in Texas during the early postwar period. Still, Johnson prepared himself to defend Truman's administration if and when that became necessary. Shocked by the devastation and poverty he saw in May 1945 in Western Europe, he concluded these weakened nations were very vulnerable to communist movements. A return to isolationism would be catastrophic. Harry Truman did not need to convince him that the United States had to aid Europeans and be ready to resist any attempt by the USSR to take advantage of Western Europe's distress. "From the experiences of World War II, I learned that war comes about by two things." One was "a lust for power on the part of a few evil leaders." The other was "a weakness on the part of the people whose love for peace too often displays a lack of courage that serves as an open invitation to all the aggressors of the world." These lessons had a clear relevance for the postwar world.

This did not mean that Lyndon would not seek agreements with the Soviets. Stunned by the atomic bomb, he yearned for productive talks on atomic power. He supported Bernard Baruch's plan to internationalize control of nuclear research and weapons. Although he wanted no more Munichs, he saw the need for efforts to avoid other Hiroshimas.

In sum, Johnson understood that Texans, Southerners, and, in fact, all Americans were living in a different and complex world, with serious issues that needed to be resolved in ways that mixed the best wisdom of the past with new approaches. This would require patient, thoughtful, intelligent, and flexible leadership. Lyndon felt uniquely qualified to lead this effort. However, he could not achieve this as a representative with little seniority and cool relations with Harry Truman. He would have to climb the pole to the Senate.

In 1946 Lyndon despaired of moving up in Washington and toyed with running for governor. He dropped the idea quickly. Texas governors wielded less power than legislators; they only dealt with "ticky little things." He must wait again on destiny, which arrived on schedule.

Pappy O'Daniel had not delivered federal contracts for Texas business. His repetitive anti-New Deal screeds did not mitigate that failing for the business community; instead, businessmen branded him as behind the times and threatening future funding. His reflexive isolationism marked him as out of touch with the realities of a global struggle against communism. In addition, he had speculated in Washington real estate and profited from shortages that galled Texas veterans. When pollsters matched him against Johnson in 1947, 64 percent favored Lyndon. Faced with defeat, Pappy announced he would not run.

That left Johnson facing the formidable Coke Stevenson, who had served two terms as governor and had carried all 254 counties in his second run for the office. Lyndon faced an upstream swim. Since he could not run for the Senate and the House simultaneously, his political career was finished if he lost. Weighing against this was his feeling that this might be his last chance at the Senate.

On May 12, 1948, he took the plunge. "I've hit the cold water," he told his assistant Walter Jenkins, "just like I had good sense."

The Right Place:
1948 to 1957

Millions of words have been published on Lyndon's eighty-seven vote victory over Coke Stevenson in 1948. Most have been devoted to the endgame, the ballots "found" in Box 13 of Jim Wells County that were cast by men and women who lined up in alphabetical order, had identical handwriting, and included the living and the dead.

It is true Johnson bought votes in South Texas; it is also true that, unlike 1941, he had *jefes* like George Parr hold off the official count until he could figure how many he needed to win. But these should not obscure another indisputable point: Lyndon Johnson—who began the race far behind, who lost three weeks of campaigning to the intense pain of kidney stones, who trailed Stevenson by 71,000 votes in the first primary—managed to turn what looked like a runaway rout into a photo finish that could be decided by Box 13. From start to finish, he ran a nearly perfect race.

Lyndon's basic strategy was simple. His first goal was to ensure that Stevenson would not get 50 percent of the vote in the July 24 primary and that he himself would finish a reasonably close second. He started with some edges. George Peddy, a conservative oilman, would siphon off some of Coke's votes. He could assume that Stevenson would not make a concerted effort to get supporters to the polls; the former governor relied on personal popularity, not grass-roots organizing. Finally, he could expect that his opponent's campaign, like every campaign, would make mistakes and that Stevenson's well-known cautiousness—he was nicknamed "Calculatin'

Coke" since he boasted that he always let coffee cool before drinking it—would make him slow to respond to a rival who would take
fast and ruthless advantage of them.

All that came to pass. Peddy got 237,000 votes. Stevenson did
not organize any counties, and Coke's careful reticence on questions
about organized labor allowed Lyndon to paint him falsely as
pro–AFL-CIO. To deliver this and other messages, Johnson hit
upon a device that proved as spectacular at attracting attention and
winning votes as his patriotic hullabaloos in 1941: he used a helicopter to travel throughout rural Texas. The novelty and efficiency
of the Johnson City Windmill, plus his brief, impromptu remarks
never gave the crowds, he said, "a chance to find out what a truly
bad speaker I am," and that swelled his vote.

After the dust cleared on July 24, these were the results:

Stevenson	477,077
Johnson	405,617
Peddy	237,105
Others	83,000
Total	1,202,889

This heartened Stevenson. He reasoned he would get the bulk of
Peddy's votes. He also noted that Lyndon was not a very close second, and for a time he expected his opponent would withdraw.
Supremely confident, he did not plan to do anything differently during the next race. So careless was he about organizing that he
shrugged it off when two West Texas counties strong for him decided
not to go to the expense of opening their polling places for the runoff.
That this would cost him sure votes did not worry him.

To understand what brought Johnson victory, let's skip ahead
and look at the result of the August 28 vote.

Johnson	494,191
Stevenson	494,104
Total	988,295

Comparing the two elections reveals some salient facts.

First, 214,594 fewer Texans voted on August 28 than on July 24.
Johnson's study of past runoffs had convinced him there would be a

significant decline in participation. That gave him, the much better organized candidate, a significant advantage. He could focus efforts on getting his voters to the poll again—which he did.

Second, on August 28 Lyndon gained 88,574 votes. While the total vote slumped 17.8 percent, his swelled 21.8 percent. In large part, this was because he scheduled many more events in Texas's cities and their burgeoning suburbs. During the first campaign, he and his staff heard plenty about people leaving small towns. Of the 254 Texas counties, 239 were losing population to the other 15. Johnson brilliantly recognized that the strip mall was replacing the town square as the focal point of community. He also recognized that was where he would find World War II vets and their families. That was the new Texas which, though still culturally conservative, saw the benefits of federal programs.

Third, these were the voters whose wartime experiences sensitized them to international events. Coke Stevenson regarded foreign aid as "pearls before swine"; he was an old-style isolationist. How would he deal with the Soviet threat to West Berlin? Horace Busby was certain the issue that won the election for Johnson was the Berlin Airlift. Lyndon was identified with the Marshall Plan and the containment of Communism. Coke could not be trusted to support these policies. These feelings gave credence to Johnson's claim that he was a new breed of leader for a new and vastly more dangerous world.

Fourth, Stevenson's total rose by only 17,027 votes, or 3.6 percent. He got almost nothing out of the 320,000 votes for Peddy and other candidates. Part of this was Coke's failure to organize a staff to get these folks to vote, but a larger share of the credit belonged to Lyndon, who gave the voters no cause to bestir themselves. Johnson emphasized his opposition to overpowerful unions, civil rights legislation, and Reds at home and abroad. He also quietly let the business community know he would get a lot more money from Washington for them than someone who thought the state's problems could be solved in county courthouses and Austin. He was very careful to emphasize to everyone what he felt the true role of the federal government was: "To help. That's what this *government's* for. Not 'to govern.' That's just a fancy word university 'perfessors' and knotheads use. *But to help.* . . . Government is of and for the people. People are not put here for the government to ignore and push around." To ensure this, Lyndon urged the voters to make him "your hired hand." He presented himself as "spokesman for the folks," reminding his staff to "always use 'folks,' not people." As his admiring PR man Joe Phipps pointed out, this was inspired. Johnson was promising aid without control, money without regulations on toilet paper and everything else.

Here's the bottom line: Johnson won the election by being far more aware of dramatic and permanent changes in Texas, the nation, and the world. That Stevenson came so close testifies to the grip the past still had on many in the Lone Star State. Yet this election and the future belonged to Lyndon Johnson, who straddled the divide between conservatism and liberalism, appealing to the new without being too threatening to the old.

Thanks to the skill of attorneys led by Abe Fortas, an old friend since Lyndon dealt with him during the 1930s and the epitome of a well-connected Washington litigator, Johnson fought off court challenges to Box 13. The victory of Harry Truman, who much preferred him to Stevenson, and the capture of Congress by the Democrats, guaranteed that Lyndon's win would be ratified by the Senate.

As he entered the Senate chamber in late 1948, Lyndon murmured to Walter Jenkins that it was "the right size." He would be one of ninety-six there, ideal for a man whose staff regarded him as "the greatest salesman who ever lived." "From the first day on," remembered Jenkins, "he knew he could be effective there, make his influence felt." The Senate was "his place."

To make it so, Johnson had to know the senators. He quizzed Bobby Baker, the cunning and ambitious secretary to the Senate Democrats, about his new colleagues. His frank discussion of the constraints on him—keep in mind, he told Baker, "I got elected by just 87 votes and I ran against a caveman"—and his warning that on certain issues he could not support the administration—thanks to the White House position on civil rights, President Truman was "about as popular as measles in Texas"—won him Baker's respect and allegiance. Lyndon gained an important ally, and Baker confirmed what he already suspected: to succeed, he had to impress the leader of the Southern caucus, Senator Richard Russell of Georgia.

To his peers, Dick Russell was the perfect senator. A courtly man steeped in knowledge of Senate rules and respectful of its customs, a deeply committed patriot who deserved his reputation as a master of defense and foreign affairs issues, he commanded deferential attention. That he discreetly shared many of their flaws—a taste for Jack Daniels bourbon and female company after hours—enhanced his standing. That he was an unbending segregationist and a virulent racist obsessed with miscegenation, which he was sure would threaten "white civilization," was generally overlooked by those who did not share his prejudices. Russell eschewed public race baiting, cloaking his defense of Jim Crow so artfully in constitutional arguments for states' rights that he gave everyone but the most fervent Senate liberals a rationale for letting the white South have its way.

Segregation was Russell's litmus test for senators from states that seceded in 1861. If he wanted the Georgian as friend and ally, Lyndon had to defend the cause and the South's principal weapon in the Senate, the filibuster. He measured up.

When he was president, LBJ and his defenders insisted he had gone along with Russell out of expediency, not conviction. Some contemporaneous statements corroborate this. Lyndon remarked to Bobby Baker in 1948, "If I go to voting for the FEPC and so on, they've got a good start [in Texas] toward a lynch mob." Both Luther Jones during NYA days and Horace Busby in 1948 heard Lyndon predict that something would have to be done about race relations in the South because blacks would not tolerate the status quo for much longer. That tension had increased since Pearl Harbor: "[The Negroes] fought the war, they got better jobs, they proved themselves. They want for their children the same thing I want for mine. The haters are determined to keep them down, but they won't stay down forever." Moreover, the haters were hurting whites, too. He told Busby that race is "messed up in some way in every question that comes along, and you can't get a domestic bill through" without some Southerner yelling about blacks. This stymied laws that would help everyone be more prosperous. It could not go on: "Force won't change any of it, but it has to change—we've got to get it off our backs."

These comments represented Johnson's real feelings on race relations during the 1930s and 1940s. They reflect his certainty that differences between blacks and whites were cultural and economic, not racial and perpetual. Without question he knew racial issues had warped the implementation of New Deal legislation; that had happened while he ran the Texas NYA.

Yet none of these convictions made him an opponent of segregation then and there. His views, in fact, were typical of moderate segregationists in the South at that time. He would not stand in the schoolhouse door shouting "Never!"; he would not shed tears over Jim Crow's demise once blacks got the vote and politicians started courting them. Neither was he going to do anything to hasten the day of integration. Notice his words: "Force won't change any of it." That thought, repeated like a mantra, gave him and other Southern moderates an excuse for doing nothing beyond decrying the excesses of rabid segregationists. Later, as president, he mused poignantly about how moderates were torn. "Wanting to do what's right and doing what's right's two different things. Sometimes it's a long hill to climb in between." During his early years in the Senate, he was not climbing. He had no difficulty adopting Russell's states' rights language and helping him keep civil rights bills from getting through.

Once he passed this test, nothing stopped Russell from recognizing and respecting Lyndon's intelligence, energy, and ambition. So impressed was the Southern leader that he anointed Lyndon as the best hope for Dixie.

Russell's greatest ambition was the nomination and election of a Southern Democratic candidate for president. Only this, he believed, would bring the South fully back into the Union and establish its preeminence over Northern liberals in the national party. In 1952, he ran unsuccessfully for the nomination. After his defeat, he had fastened on Johnson as the South's Great White Hope. To his Southern colleagues, he preached as gospel his conviction that getting Lyndon into the White House would defeat or defang civil rights legislation for the foreseeable future. It was a belief Johnson encouraged with words and acts from 1949 through the 1950s.

For Johnson to run for president he had to create a record of national achievement in the Senate that he could run on; if he was perceived as a regional candidate, he would never be nominated. So Russell supported Johnson's rise through a progression of Senate posts: minority whip, minority leader, and, after 1954, majority leader. He persuaded conservatives to let Lyndon appoint liberals to their committees as counters to right wing Republicans and as the means of broadening his support outside the South. He even went along with Johnson's choice of Senator Hubert Humphrey of Minnesota, the best-known advocate of civil rights in the Senate, as his link to the liberals and helper in managing them. Russell's voice on the Democratic Policy Committee, a body his colleague shaped to dominate the drafting and scheduling of legislation, was also influential. Without Dick's active sponsorship and shrewd advice, Lyndon would never have mastered the Senate as quickly and completely as he did.

Johnson's rise was also accelerated by Dwight Eisenhower. Ike's election in 1952 was regarded as a mixed blessing by Old Guard, conservative, neo-isolationist Republicans like Senators Robert Taft of Ohio and William Knowland of California. These two, who led the Senate GOP from 1949 to 1959, were convinced that Roosevelt had sold the country out at the Yalta Conference in 1945 and that Truman had threatened it with bankruptcy with the Marshall Plan and foreign aid. They condemned the North Atlantic Treaty Organization (NATO) as an entangling, expensive alliance. In contrast, Eisenhower, who had commanded NATO's military forces, agreed with the basics of the foreign policies of both FDR and Truman. He and Lyndon were one on the wisdom and necessity of military and economic containment of Communism. This common ground gave Johnson the opportunity to defend a hugely popular president against reactionaries in his own party. He presented himself and the Senate Democrats as a patriotic and responsible opposition, one that put national security ahead of partisan politics.

Democratic votes, supplemented by moderate and liberal Republicans, kept the bipartisan consensus on containment in existence. There was a moral to this, and Johnson was quick to call attention to it. The Senate was closely divided between 1949 and 1958; the majority party throughout those years had only a two-vote edge. If Democrats overlooked their differences with each other and united behind domestic bills acceptable to them all, it would be relatively easy for them to pick up some moderate and liberal Republican votes. What's more, they would usually have the tacit support of Eisenhower.

Unlike GOP reactionaries, the president had no desire to dismantle New Deal agencies. He did want to limit government expenditures and balance the budget, reasoning that America's most potent weapon in the struggle against Communism was a robust economy and that heavier taxes and/or larger deficits would weaken its performance. Johnson was committed to frugality and efficiency in government for similar policy reasons and to placate conservative Texas supporters. Starting from roughly the same place, he and Ike could negotiate levels of expenditures that were acceptable to both of them. Had the administration launched an attack on the welfare state and recruited fiscally conservative Democrats, such as Senator Harry Byrd of Virginia, Johnson could not have preserved either his position of cooperation or Democratic unity. But Ike did not do this, and the Democrats generally stuck together and followed Lyndon's lead. His reputation as a successful wheeler-dealer grew.

The issue that most sharply divided Democrats, the one they had trouble compromising on, was civil rights. Southerners had always been able to filibuster bills to death, and the frustration and anger of Northern and Western liberals grew with each defeat. Russell and his cohorts responded with their familiar vigilance and tactical mastery of Senate rules.

Then the Supreme Court ratcheted the tension even tighter. In 1954, the nine justices unanimously ruled that separate but equal facilities for schools for whites and blacks were unconstitutional. The rule of *Brown v. Board of Education,* if implemented rigorously, would have ended Southern segregation, but the court softened the impact when it ruled in a decision on implementation, known as *Brown II,* that school districts should desegregate "with all deliberate speed." Moderate white Southerners attacked *Brown* by making "deliberate" synonymous with "glacial." Hard-line segregationists went further. They formed White Citizen Councils and preached massive resistance to judicial tyranny. Meanwhile liberals outside the South urged executive action and enabling legislation to compel rapid desegregation.

Had the administration thrown the executive branch's weight behind desegregation, Johnson's chances of maintaining Democratic unity would have been zero, but Eisenhower did not believe rulings and laws could change hearts. His view was indistinguishable from moderate segregationists like Lyndon. "Any fellow," the president said, "who tries to tell me that you can do these things by force is just plain nuts." With the White House on the side of the moderate understanding of "deliberate" and effectively committed to inaction, Johnson could avoid any confrontation in the Senate over civil rights in the aftermath of the *Brown* decisions.

This respite was extended the hard way. In July 1955 Johnson suffered a serious heart attack. Doctors initially gave him only a 50 percent chance of survival. After the crisis passed, they insisted he quit smoking, lose weight, and observe a strict regimen of diet, exercise, and rest. Frightened by his brush with death, he resigned himself to obedience. For the next six months, he stuck close to the ranch he had purchased near Stonewall, Texas. He did not return to the Senate until January 1956.

While at the ranch, he contracted another kind of serious ailment: White House fever. Lyndon convinced himself that the 1956 Democratic Convention would turn to him after multiple ballots. His Senate record, he reasoned, positioned him as the only man acceptable to all factions. He did not campaign for the nomination; in fact, he seemed uncertain how to run for president, other than making it known he was available and willing. Beyond that, he simply hoped events would turn his way. Patient watching and waiting for destiny had served him well in the past. This time, though, destiny had other darlings.

Lyndon badly misjudged the depth of dislike and distrust Northerners and liberals felt for him. They still nursed grievances about his smearing prominent liberal Leland Olds as a socialist and driving him from his position at the Federal Power Commission to please Texas business interests. They remembered critically his slowness to assist in the censuring of Senator Joseph McCarthy for sensational, reckless, and largely unfounded charges about Communists in government. Johnson's record of legislative achievement did not impress them, either. To them, he seemed more interested in racking up a succession of minor victories that were the products of compromise with Ike, moderate Republicans, and the Southern Caucus than he was in confronting the major issues of the day.

Civil rights, of course, were foremost among these. Also important were issues relating to the management of the economy, with liberals questioning the use of Federal Reserve Board adjustments of interest rates to manipulate expansion and avoid inflation. Of perennial concern was the struggle with the Soviets; and liberals believed too little economic aid was being given to developing nations. Looming above everything was the sense that Lyndon was not partisan enough. He catered to the president and GOP senators friendly to him when he should have been countering and defeating them. To liberals, this revealed that Johnson was utterly unprincipled, without any goal other than self-aggrandizement.

To some extent, Lyndon was aware of this discontent. One reason he turned down the offer of Joseph P. Kennedy, Sr., to finance his presidential campaign in return for making Jack Kennedy his running mate was because alliance with a notorious opponent of FDR and a friend of Joe McCarthy would hurt him with liberals. But he was blind to their absolute determination to keep him off the ticket at all costs. When the Democrats convened, it became obvious they had the power to make his hope a joke.

Worse, bitterness toward him deepened at the convention. Liberals believed he and Rayburn, in cahoots with Russell, had convinced Adlai Stevenson to downplay civil rights during his campaign. Stevenson never had any chance against the immensely popular Eisenhower, but many Democrats saw his landslide loss as more than Americans continuing to like Ike. They also pinned it on excessive caution and too much "me tooism." Their standard bearer had not made crucial issues an important part of the campaign. No wonder Ike won big again.

Afterward, Johnson made a momentous decision. The liberals were right: Democrats could no longer dodge or postpone civil rights legislation. Also true was this: to have any chance of nomination, he must deliver a civil rights law.

The Senate had been the right place for him. His dominant performance as majority leader had raised him to national prominence, but was he in the right place to enact a civil rights law? On the answer his future in national politics depended.

5

The Riverboat Gambler:
1957 to July 1960

Lyndon did not have to bring up civil rights himself in 1957. Nor did he have to rely on those he called "red hots" to get the ball rolling. When Vice President Richard Nixon and GOP moderates studied the dimensions of Eisenhower's landslide, they discovered that Stevenson had won only 61 percent of the African-American vote. This was down 7 percent from 1952, and that year Adlai captured far fewer black votes than Roosevelt and Truman did. Pollster George Gallup concluded that in 1956 the group that "shifted most to the Eisenhower-Nixon ticket was the Negro vote." Why was no mystery to Hubert Humphrey: "The Democrats are digging their own graves in the field of civil rights." Nixon agreed. If his party could introduce a meaningful civil rights bill and pick up enough Democrats to beat the filibuster, he would gain enough black votes in Northern cities and California to succeed Ike in 1960. Some White House advisors went further. The vision dancing in their heads was a coalition of white suburbanites, fiscal conservatives, and African-Americans that would make the GOP the majority party again.

The Department of Justice did its part by crafting a bill designed to alleviate the worst effects of Jim Crow in the South and gain the maximum number of liberal votes in Congress. Its aim was to increase the federal government's power to intervene when any citizen's civil rights were denied. Specific provisions included these:

• In Part I, creating a Civil Rights Division in the Department of Justice with the power to seek injunctions against state and local officials denying the right to vote.

- In Part III, enabling the attorney general to file a civil suit in federal court against anyone depriving a citizen of civil rights.
- In Part IV, establishing that civil rights contempt charges (against officials disobeying federal injunctions) would be tried in federal courts by judges sitting without juries.

The administration introduced the bill in the House early in 1957. Debate was thorough, comprehensive, and predictable. The Republicans and their Democratic allies fought off all spoiling amendments. On April 18 they passed the bill 286–126.

When it came to the Senate, Minority Leader William Knowland happily ceded control of its consideration to Johnson. He assumed that the GOP would get most of the credit if it passed and that Lyndon would get 100 percent of the blame if it failed. A pedestrian legislator and a man of such limited political intelligence that Ike groaned, "There is no final answer to the question, 'How stupid can he be?'," Knowland could not imagine Johnson's legislative genius would turn this into his bill and his victory, catapulting himself into the race for the presidency. By August the minority leader would find out how blind he was.

Lyndon began with Richard Russell. He had to convince his friend from Georgia to agree to the enactment of a weak civil rights law. His arguments were masterful. The Republicans, he told Dick, sensed that civil rights might make them the majority party. They would be united. They would gain liberal Northern Democrats' votes for sure. They could add enough moderate Westerners to beat a filibuster. They would steamroll the bill through, and it would dramatically increase federal power over the South. Southerners had to trust that Lyndon could get them a law they could live with by using his legerdemain to break up the alliance before it was cemented. Johnson also reminded Russell that passing a law was crucial to electing him president, where he could defend Dixie against a full onslaught of laws and executive enforcement of them.

Russell took the bait. Then he helped Johnson plan by detailing what the Southern Caucus would not accept. Caucus members would never agree to Part III. If that passed, the doctrine of states' rights would be obliterated, and the federal government would compel immediate integration of schools, no matter what the cost to social peace in the South. Nor would Russell and his colleagues ever agree to federal judges determining guilt in civil contempt cases. That would elevate the power of the federal bench into the stratosphere, strengthen judge "tyranny," and impose integration by judicial fiat.

This news did not surprise or dismay Lyndon. He would find the votes to eradicate Part III and the contempt proceedings. What heartened him was the caucus's silence on one point. Once again he focused on what people did not say, and once again it proved to be more important than what they verbalized. He had already suspected that his Southern friends could not defend to themselves their states' blatant denial of the right to vote. Guarantees of the right of blacks to vote, he decided, could safely be placed in the bill. He gambled that his assessment was correct, and he won. The Southern Caucus did not filibuster against these provisions.

Amending the administration's work to fit Russell's requirements displayed several aspects of Lyndon's prowess. He persuaded some Western Democrats to help kill Part III in return for Southern support for a federal dam in Hell's Canyon, Idaho. He picked up some moderate Republican votes with a series of patronage favors. He got more by having liberal lawyers Abe Fortas and Benjamin Cohen opine that Part III was unconstitutional. At a crucial moment, he got lucky. Dwight Eisenhower revealed his lack of enthusiasm for Part III, which turned loose moderate Republicans still on the fence. Part III vanished from the bill.

Next came the removing of juries from civil contempt proceedings. Though liberals and the Republican leadership were sure they would win on this, Johnson split their forces again. Borrowing again from Fortas and Cohen, he rammed through a proviso guaranteeing jury trials for criminal contempt charges, leaving civil charges for judges to decide unaided. He also added a proviso forbidding the exclusion of anyone from federal juries on the grounds of race. These changes were shrewdly chosen to gain the support of the labor movement, which had fought for years to resist injunctions and criminal contempt proceedings against union organizers by reactionary Southern judges. Lyndon was able to win the approval of George Meany, the president of the AFL-CIO.

On this issue Eisenhower fought him. A jury trial for violators of African-Americans' civil right to register and vote would, Ike believed, enable whites to continue to keep blacks from the polls. No matter: Lyndon found the ways and means to convince enough moderate Democrats and Republicans to win passage of his amendments on contempt trials 51-42. Knowland wept in frustration; Nixon flew into a rage; Ike was appalled; liberal Democrats were certain it made the bill unenforceable. None of this prevented the full Senate from passing the amended legislation 72–18. Despite misgivings, despite fury and frustration, almost all moderates and liberals could not bring themselves to vote against a bill that made a bow in the direction of voting rights for blacks. Johnson had been right: they would not say no.

Lyndon still was not safe at home. Some liberals and African-American leaders hoped the House would reject the Senate version. Finally, after an agonizing discussion, Roy Wilkins of the National Association for the Advancement of Colored People (NAACP) recommended that the House accept it. Wilkins was persuaded by Hubert Humphrey that in politics one shouldn't disdain even a "crumb." Johnson weighed in by telling critics, "Don't worry. We've started something new. . . . [this is] only the first. We know we can do it now. We know the ropes." Persuaded by these assurances and Wilkins's approval, urged on by Sam Rayburn, the House accepted the Senate's bill 279–97.

Eisenhower thought about vetoing it, then decided that even a badly flawed civil rights bill merited his signature. Like those in Congress who held their noses and voted aye, he could not bring himself to oppose it. The cause of civil rights had its crumb. And ultimately Lyndon kept his promise. He did more. What came to pass during his presidency vindicated his prediction that the first step would be the hardest.

Lyndon regarded the Civil Rights Act of 1957 as his greatest victory as majority leader. Insofar as tactical virtuosity is concerned, it is hard to quarrel with his assessment. All his skills at maneuvering senators were on display, but insofar as causing real change in the South or increasing black political power, it failed for the reasons its critics foresaw. The act was essentially unenforceable. Lyndon hoped its passage would begin an era of progress of moderation and accommodation between the two races; hence his eloquent words during the closing debate on the bill: "Nothing lasting, nothing enduring, has ever been born from hatred and prejudice—except more hatred and prejudice," so there was "a compelling need for a solution that will enable all America's people to live in dignity and unity." Events in 1957 soon revealed this was still a long way off.

Which leaves us with Lyndon's reason for claiming its significance: It was a crucial psychological lift for liberals and moderates—for the first time since Reconstruction, they had gotten something for their efforts and witnessed encouraging signs of doubt in Southern minds about sustaining a filibuster. Was this right? Before dismissing it as self-serving, we should recall that Johnson was a master of understanding momentum in politics and recognizing fundamental shifts before others could. His career in Texas and Washington testified to his acuity at seeing the future. That he saw this act as a significant psychological boost for supporters of civil rights is reason to view it that way.

Without question, Lyndon also measured significance in terms of his personal ambitions. Did the law do what he and Russell had hoped? Did he become a legitimate competitor for the presidency? He was not disappointed. In the minds of Washington's pundits and politicians, the Civil Rights Act of 1957 made Lyndon Johnson a leading candidate for the Democratic nomination in 1960.

Almost immediately, Lyndon's prospects began to dim. He had hoped the Civil Rights Act would encourage the South away from segregation, racist rhetoric, and violence. In September, the struggle over the integration of Central High School in Little Rock foreclosed that hope. Far from reconciled to civil rights, whites there seemed ready to lynch black teenagers. Scenes outside Central High, the first of many confrontations broadcast on TV news, cast doubt on whether Lyndon's triumph meant anything at all. Misgivings deepened during the next few months as only a handful of blacks could register to vote in the Deep South.

The next month, the Soviet Union's successful launch of a satellite revealed how far behind the United States was in space exploration. It also increased concerns about the possibility of a widening missile gap between the Russians and the Americans, one that profoundly endangered U.S. national security. This was followed by the advent of a severe economic recession. What Ike regarded as the most potent Cold War weapon now appeared to be faltering. It resulted in a rapid rise in unemployment from 4.1 percent in August 1957 to 7.5 percent in July 1958. During the same months, corporate profits shrunk by 25 percent and productivity in basic industries declined to 50 percent of capacity.

This was bad news for the nation but good news for Democrats. In November 1958, after a series of campaigns focused on "time for a change," the Dems had a Senate majority of thirty. This, it turned out, was bad news for Lyndon.

When Lyndon worked with a majority of two, he could get grudging cooperation from liberals by pointing out that Democrats had to stick together to achieve anything. Intraparty quarreling, he warned plausibly, would end in Republicans "eating our lunch and

the sack we brought it in." Now there was no obvious need for
them to get along. Making his plight worse was the new senators'
politics. They were all liberals or progressive moderates. Though
Lyndon had raised money and campaigned for several, they did not
feel beholden. They came to Washington with a whetted partisan
edge and a mandate for change. The Eisenhower–Johnson bipartisan arrangement was suspect to them.

Soon most of them resented Lyndon's heavy-handed use of
patronage and power to keep them in line. His monopolization of
scarce office space and its lavish decoration—they bitterly called his
suite the "Taj Mahal"—infuriated them. Without much delay, they
accepted senior liberals' opinions: all Johnson wanted was more
laws; he would water down or gut bills to get that; he would not
fight for reform or even discuss it if he encountered the least resistance
from conservatives. "A hypocritical SOB," summed up Pennsylvania's
Joe Clark. "A typical Texas wheeler-dealer with no ethical sense
whatsoever, but a great pragmatic ability to get things done. . . . I
despised the guy."

The animus of Clark and other liberals was more than personal;
it was principled. These politicians knew Lyndon's civil rights act
had not changed anything for the better in the South. Arguably, it
had even encouraged white resistance. The Confederate battle ban-
ner was added to many states' flags and proudly displayed everywhere. Southern hoopla over the upcoming Civil War centennial
was openly celebratory, and the treatment of that war denied
Northern understanding of it. To quote the Creed of the Children of
the Confederacy (posted on the walls of the Texas Capitol in 1959):
Southerners should "teach the truths of history (one of the most
important of which is that the War Between the States was not a
rebellion, nor was its underlying cause to sustain slavery)." To liberals, Johnson's maneuvers had served the Confederate States of
America more than the United States—and himself most of all. He
had to be stopped.

Lyndon had always worked hard at running the Senate. Under
current circumstances, he had to work even harder. However productive he and the Senate were, his new colleagues remained united in
determination to keep him out of the White House. They agreed with
his analysis that his best hope for nomination was to do a fine job in
the Senate, then be rewarded for it when a deadlocked convention
turned to him after several ballots. They planned to keep him from
racking up enough successes to make this scenario plausible.

How good were the chances of becoming president for the man who now regularly referred to himself as LBJ? Here's John (Jack/ JFK) Kennedy's answer: "not very."

JFK respected the "able majority leader," but "no Southerner can be nominated by a Democratic Convention." Even if Johnson got the votes "of every Southern state, every border state, and most of the moderate and western states," the bottom line was this: "There is still too large a bloc of states with liberal and minority votes he cannot touch." LBJ was "a riverboat gambler," someone who "has no very firm principles and does not believe in anything very deeply." This passed for pragmatism in the Senate and helped him manipulate small groups. Elsewhere, it was a serious problem. Lyndon "had no popularity in the country."

In JFK's opinion, Johnson's only realistic hope of reversing these problems and perceptions was to follow his example. "Johnson had to prove a Southerner could win in the North [by winning primaries there] just as I had to prove a Catholic could win in a heavily Protestant state." He also had to borrow another JFK strategy. He had to go coast to coast, personally wooing party bosses and state delegations.

LBJ did neither. He did not even declare his candidacy until July 5, 1960, one week before the Democrats convened in Los Angeles.

One reason for this holding back was his fatal underestimation of his principal opponent. Lyndon judged Jack Kennedy by Senate standards: "a whipper-snapper, malaria-ridden, and yellah, sickly, sickly. . . . He never said a word of importance in the Senate and he never did a thing." Too late he learned it was different away from Capitol Hill. JFK "looked awfully good on that goddamned television screen." He "managed to create an image of himself as a shining intellectual, a youthful leader who would change the face of the country." How he did this bewildered LBJ. "It was the goddamndest thing. . . . His growing hold on the American people was simply a mystery to me."

No matter, Lyndon told himself, "the people" meant less at a convention than power brokers and delegates. Kennedy might win "beauty contests," he conceded to Bobby Baker, "but when it gets down to the nut-cuttin' he won't have the old bulls with him." He was indulging in wishful thinking. Kennedy was not just winning primaries; he was picking up support from party leaders and delegations. He was convincing them that this Roman Catholic had a good chance of beating Richard Nixon in November. Yet despite

JFK's successes and the momentum they generated, Lyndon did nothing to try to break that winning streak.

Robert Kennedy contemptuously explained this by saying that Lyndon did not have the courage to run against his brother. Historians have noted that LBJ had no idea how to run a national campaign for the presidency and that his ignorance and inexperience froze him into inactivity. Something can be said for both points of view.

John Kennedy had clearly become a formidable campaigner; he had his mysterious appeal and the considerable advantage of his family's wealth. To challenge him outside the South would be playing on his home field. Lose, and that was the ball game. It is true, too, that Johnson had not been able to transfer skills at organizing victory in Texas to doing the same throughout the nation. At home, those skills helped bring him out of the down times of depression, doubt, and inactivity that had spotted his major campaigns there. Remove an intimate knowledge of local politics and the inspiration of past success, and it became harder to reverse being paralyzed with worry and indecision.

The pressures on his personality help explain Johnson's strategy for victory, which seems as much the fruit of psychological desperation as rational thought. He had confidence in his unparalleled abilities to bend individuals and small groups to his will by applying what was called "the Johnson treatment": a combination of cajoling, offering favors, threatening reprisals, and appealing to compromise. The Senate was the right place for the treatment. In a presidential campaign, the closest thing to the Senate in scale and composition was the party convention. Johnson clung to the hope that he could work his reliable magic there.

Johnson's greatest strength also contributed to the 1960 downfall in another way. Staying master of the Senate imprisoned him there. He had so centralized power in himself that the assembly could not function without him. Leaving Washington for extended periods would mean standstill in the Senate. That would be followed by press criticism: either he was not as good as he claimed, or he was shirking his oft-proclaimed duty to the country. And, as he noted, the minute he announced his candidacy his opponents in the Senate would set to work stalling bills and embarrassing him. When Bobby Baker pressed him to campaign, he "swelled up like a toad and said, 'Jack Kennedy and the other senators can go gallivantin' around the country kissin' asses and shakin' hands when they want to. But if I'd done it, the Senate business would not have got done

and the press would have crucified me for running out on my job.' "
His own plan for victory trapped and defeated him.

All that remained was a series of last-gasp attempts. He and Sam
Rayburn even tried to enlist Ike's help, calling Kennedy a nobody in
the Senate who happened to have a rich father and warning, "You
cannot let that man become elected president. . . . He's a dangerous
man." Wisely, Eisenhower declined to intervene in the other party's
business.

In Los Angeles, the last spasm of the Johnson campaign, raising
questions about Jack's health, only succeeded in hardening liberal
opinion against Lyndon. In the end, JFK ate his lunch and the sack
he brought it in on the first ballot. The defeated candidate dashed
off a telegram of congratulations. "LBJ," he told the nominee,
"now means 'Let's Back Jack.' "

Historians have been obliged to concur with Robert Kennedy's
wry comment that the true story of Kennedy's choice of Johnson as
his running mate will never be told. Accounts are contradictory.
That is to be expected; contemporary explanations were made by
exhausted, emotional people. Narratives drawn from memory were
understandably colored by the tragedies of Dallas and Vietnam.

Still, certain things are clear. John Kennedy was keenly aware of
Lyndon's advantages. According to Sam Rayburn's memo of his
conversation with Bobby Kennedy, Jack thought LBJ "was the
strongest candidate; his place on the ticket was essential, especially
for carrying Texas; and of course [he] was eminently qualified to
succeed Kennedy as president."

For his part, Lyndon knew he would not have the same power
and influence as majority leader after 1960. If JFK won, he would
be following White House orders; if Nixon won, he would be working against a much more partisan Republican president. Most
important, he could read the handwriting on the wall. He would
never become president from the Senate. The only way he could
prove his bona fides to the national party was by running with
Kennedy and doing his best for the ticket's victory in November.

JFK and LBJ each had compelling reasons to run together. What
neither anticipated was the ferocious opposition to their agreement.
John Connally was so furious that he did not speak to his old
friend, who in his opinion had cast aside power for powerlessness,
for months. Kenny O'Donnell flatly accused Kennedy of betrayal
and was only partly mollified by Jack's argument that he wanted LBJ
out of the Senate so he could not strangle New Frontier legislation.

Prominent liberals in the party threatened to oppose the nomination on the convention floor. Bobby evidently tried to rescue Jack by telling Johnson that his brother was having second thoughts and that Lyndon should withdraw.

JFK and LBJ hung tough. Distraught after Bobby's attempt, Lyndon still repeated his desire to run. Jack asserted his power over the liberals and his staff by confirming the offer enthusiastically. He also convinced his running mate that Bobby had acted on his own. The day's tumult made Johnson determined to repay Jack's loyalty with complete loyalty in return. As for JFK's brother, he would keep close watch on "that little shitass."

So Lyndon embarked on another great gamble. He was betting he could carry Texas and the South. He was betting his ticket would win. He was betting he could do things in an office Jack Garner called "not worth a bucket of warm spit." He was betting he could position himself to become president in 1968. All this meant he was betting on Jack Kennedy.

A continent away from Los Angeles, Dwight Eisenhower was amused. "I turned on the television, and there was that son of a bitch becoming a vice presidential candidate with this 'dangerous man.'"

Second Place: 1960 to 1963

When Johnson got back to Texas, he quickly learned how difficult it would be for the JFK-LBJ ticket to carry his home state and the South. To difficulties posed by religion, race, regional chauvinism, and liberalism he could add suspicions about his motives for tossing aside the power of majority leader. Plus he could not rely on longtime allies for help. "Many past associates and supporters," according to Horace Busby, "were anxious to disown him in hasty, bitter terms." From Georgia came the discouraging word that Richard Russell would not campaign.

These were serious challenges for Lyndon—but not new ones. Accustomed to balancing the imperatives of Southern politics against the aims of the national party, he prepared himself to take full advantage of whatever his luck might provide him.

Almost immediately LBJ had good fortune. To bolster his sagging presidential campaign, he had arranged for Congress to reconvene in August. Kennedy decided to seize the opportunity to push through minimum wage, medical care for the elderly, housing, and education bills. Southern Democrats and conservative Republicans thwarted these attempts. Ironically, this helped Jack and Lyndon in November. A successful, rampant liberalism would have subtracted votes in several hard-fought Southern states, because it would have heightened fears that the next step would be another civil rights law. Proof that conservatives had not lost their power to defeat liberal initiatives was reassuring to white Southerners and encouraged them to retain their identification as Democrats.

This let Johnson fully exercise his knowledge and mastery of Southern politics. The region's power brokers, he knew, believed that Richard Nixon "had fluked into his prominence without being fully tested; . . . the steel essential for the presidency still was not forged in him." Kennedy was different. His relentless progress toward nomination inclined Southerners to agree with John Connally: "If it came down to protecting the vital interests of the United States, I'm certain he could be absolutely ruthless in making his choice." Lyndon stressed Jack's toughness to Southern audiences, contrasting him with Nixon and his patrician running mate. Henry Cabot Lodge, LBJ scoffed, was "just my meat."

Civil rights were also his meat. He finessed that as brilliantly as in 1957. In public, it was pointed out that "though he was a Southerner . . . he had to be more an American" and speak "as an American to Americans—whatever their region, religion or race." In the code of that day's political discourse, this signaled acquiescing in the party's platform without being committed to it. Privately, he spoke more bluntly. Republicans heard through the grapevine that Johnson exhorted Southern leaders to "vote for Kennedy and me despite all this bunk about ending racial segregation. . . . You have to elect Kennedy in order to have me in the administration so I, your fellow Southerner, can defeat his integration proposals." Lyndon had been playing this card since the 1950s. It continued to trump his opponents' tricks.

More threatening than civil rights was Kennedy's Catholicism. Johnson urged JFK to come South and talk straight about church and state as soon as possible. After Kennedy's magnificent speech to Southern Baptist ministers in Houston, Johnson missed no chance to equate prejudice against Catholicism with prejudice against the South. *We Southerners,* he would say, *know all about knee-jerk stereotyping of an entire region; we'd resist similar smearing of an entire religion. Shame on Nixon for not renouncing the support of anti-Catholic bigots!* The vice president's advisers soon noticed their man was "being religioned right out of this campaign" by LBJ.

During the campaign's last week, Johnson got the chance to display a prized virtue of Southern men—physical courage—and to reveal Republicans as discourteous, which was an awful sin in Dixie. In a Dallas hotel lobby, he and Lady Bird were confronted by angry Nixon supporters. The mob chanted obscenities, spit on Bird, and struck her with signs. Lyndon was stabbed with Nixon–Lodge buttons. Instantly aware of a golden opportunity, he dismissed his police escort and, arm around Bird, walked slowly through the crowd. The picture of the brave, dignified Johnsons contrasted with the convulsed faces around them won over thousands of voters. Johnson credited Dallas Republicans for JFK's 46,233-vote margin of victory in Texas. Russell was so scandalized by Bird's ordeal that he campaigned for the ticket in South Carolina. Boosted by Dick's speeches, Kennedy carried the state by a narrow margin.

On November 8, 1960, John Kennedy was elected president. His popular-vote margin was a slender 112,881 out of nearly 67,000,000 ballots. In the electoral college, he won 303–219. He carried seven Southern states: Alabama, Arkansas, Georgia, Louisiana, the two Carolinas, and Texas. Lyndon Johnson did not put JFK in the White House by himself, but he did play an essential part.

After victory, what? "Power is where power goes," Johnson assured the press. He planned to reprise Cactus Jack Garner's role in the passage of New Deal legislation during the Hundred Days, the wise mind and skilled hand guiding an inexperienced administration. He would still chair the Senate Democratic Caucus, and he would be de facto majority leader. "That way," he told Bobby Baker, "I can keep my hand in. I can help Jack Kennedy's program and be his eyes and ears." "Whaddya think of that?" he asked rhetorically.

Had he paused for an answer, he would have heard Baker's prediction: "a disaster in the making." Neither the red hots nor the old bulls would permit an intrusion on senatorial independence. And that was what happened. In public, Johnson joked now that he could tell a cactus from a caucus—"with a cactus the pricks are on the outside." Privately, he was furious.

Rage slid swiftly into depression for Lyndon as he realized he had been humiliated while on a bootless errand. Soon it was apparent that Cactus Jack would remain sui generis among vice presidents. Johnson recalled later, "The only vice president that I've ever looked at that had any influence was Garner," adding, "I had none because Kennedy wouldn't *give* me any." It was true. JFK never had any intention of turning legislative relations over to Lyndon. Well aware of his track record of expanding his power and dominating Congress, the new president was determined to deny him any chance to re-establish his past mastery over the passage of legislation. It helped that Senate Democrats were equally determined to nip Johnson's plans in the bud. That his former colleagues had rejected his attempt to chair their caucus served to ratify the wisdom of JFK's decision. Lyndon felt powerless. Worse, others thought he was, too. He drooped visibly. "At the weekly White House break-fasts for legislative leaders," reported Doris Kearns Goodwin, "Johnson rarely said a word. . . . He looked discontented and tired." He personified an exhausted, spent force.

Attempts to take a more active role generally ended with more embarrassing reminders of impotence. As Kearns Goodwin noted, "Johnson could not bear being treated as one of many advisers" and tried to make himself the most important. In early 1961, he sent JFK a draft order to departments to copy him on all reports they sent to the president. Jack set it aside without comment. The White House staff punished him by leaking the draft and their boss's reaction. Afterward, Lyndon saw himself as not one, but last, among many.

The most sympathetic observer of his fall was John Kennedy. The vice presidency, he believed, "was a horseshit job": the tasks vice presidents got were either unimportant or hot issues presidents want to keep a safe distance away. So it was with Lyndon.

The National Aeronautics and Space Council and the Presidential Commission on Equal Employment Opportunity (CEEO) were not among the administration's top priorities, yet each could cause trouble. If rockets blew up, someone had to take the heat. If liberals and blacks felt the government was not doing enough while conservatives and the white South raged it was doing too much, someone had to be scapegoat. Chair of both committees, Vice President Johnson was on the bull's-eye.

At first, he did not mind. The man who shepherded through the Senate the bill creating the National Aeronautics and Space Administration (NASA) was its biggest booster in the administration. When John Glenn orbited the earth in 1962, Johnson felt vindicated. Just one thing was missing, he told Kennedy: "If only he were a Negro" we'd score points on civil rights, too. This became JFK's favorite LBJ story.

That triumph soon faded. By 1963, congressmen were complaining that Johnson funneled all lucrative contracts to Southern and Southwestern companies. He had no defense; he was doing just that. A Houston space center would shore up his popularity in Texas, and he believed Yankee dollars were the best way to bring the South into the twentieth century. Fortunately, those companies were doing good work. The White House shrugged off the howls from the Hill.

The administration was less tolerant of NASA's record in hiring African-Americans, giving Lyndon more cause to wish Glenn were black. In mid-1963, Robert Kennedy discovered that in Washington, a city 37 percent black, only 1 percent of federal employees were African-American. He blamed Johnson, seizing on the space program to chew him out. When Director James Webb could not say how many NASA workers were black, Robert Kennedy blistered him and Johnson. Johnson endured the tirade silently.

For Lyndon, this was more of the same. As chair of CEEO, he could show some progress. Federal employment of minorities increased 17 percent in fiscal 1962 and 22 percent in fiscal 1963. More Southern companies with defense contracts signed antidiscrimination pledges. During 1963 the CEEO issued 1,700 orders to federal contractors to improve their hiring and treatment of blacks. The CEEO had not made much of a dent in the problems of black underemployment. Still, dismissing Johnson as "a fraud" and claims of progress as "mere words," as Robert Kennedy did, was unfair.

Tongue-lashings from the president's brother galled Lyndon. Yet he saw no point in saying he had been urging Jack Kennedy without success to treat civil rights as a moral issue. When Kennedy finally did tell the American people on June 11, 1963, "We are confronted primarily with a moral issue . . . as old as the Scriptures and . . . as clear as the American Constitution," Lyndon did not take credit for persuading him. Instead, he bestirred himself in legislative meetings in favor of a public accommodations law. He did not expect to play a role in drafting a bill or mapping legislative strategy. And he did not get one.

John Kennedy's major preoccupation was foreign affairs. To JFK the possibility of nuclear war between the United States and the USSR was very real. He was also concerned about Communist exploitation of wars of national liberation. He linked events in the Third World to tensions over Berlin, which in turn upped the chance of a nuclear exchange. That he concentrated information gathering and decision making within the White House is unsurprising.

Lyndon Johnson was excluded from the circulation of intelligence and invited to very few action meetings, except during the confrontation over Soviet missiles in Cuba in 1962. Even then JFK kept LBJ outside his innermost circle and in the dark about critical decisions.

Johnson's usual role was ceremonial. He traveled widely as a representative of the government. These visits improved his morale, one of the president's purposes. The glow always wore off when he returned.

Of greatest import were his missions to West Berlin and South Vietnam in 1961. Johnson was sent to show the determination of the United States to support allies and resist Communism. In Berlin,

Johnson borrowed from the Declaration of Independence, pledging "our lives, fortunes, and sacred honor" to defending freedom there. During his visit to Saigon, World War II memories, plus a desire to follow JFK's orders and make plain and public American support for South Vietnam's president, inspired him to dub Ngo Dinh Diem as the Winston Churchill of Asia. Hyperbole should not obscure what Berlin and Saigon tell about Johnson's views. America's allies are very important. They must be reassured about our commitment to them. That commitment must be genuine. We must protect them. The Soviets must believe we would. We must not be appeasers, nor can we appear to be. When a Wall divided Berlin and Vietcong guerrillas threatened to overthrow Saigon, we had to encourage friends and discourage enemies. And that, Lyndon told Jack, meant we had to heed the advice of our allies that "deeds must follow words, and soon."

The administration's supreme test came in October 1962. Photographs by high-flying U-2s proved that the Soviets were installing intermediate range ballistic missiles (IRBMs) in Cuba, straining to make them operational before Washington discovered them.

The military significance of strategic weapons ninety miles from Florida concerned Kennedy less than the profound political implications. In U.S. politics, he and his party would suffer. In Latin America, Cuban prestige and power would be enhanced. Our allies everywhere would be disheartened. Nikita Khrushchev would surely launch new ventures, first pressing to pry North Atlantic Treaty Organization (NATO) forces out of West Berlin, later wherever he sensed weakness. By diplomacy and/or force, JFK had to make the USSR remove the IRBMs.

How to do this consumed the attention of the president and an ad hoc executive committee (ExCom) he called together. Lyndon Johnson was a member—not because Kennedy wanted his advice or expertise but because of his office.

The crisis energized Lyndon. On JFK's secret recordings of ExCom meetings, LBJ sounds like the majority leader: forceful and urgent. When the president was not present, he assumed the role of chairman. No one called him "Lyndon." He was the vice president, large and in charge.

Like every member of the ExCom, Johnson vacillated. Initially, he believed the United States must bomb the missile sites. After hearing about the difficulty of destroying them all, he advocated a naval blockade. Once Task Force 316 was in place, he urged avoiding any action that might provoke escalation. When Secretary of Defense Robert McNamara advised using flares to help the U-2s at night, Johnson forcefully objected. Imagine "some crazy Russian captain" watching a flare go "blooey." "He might just pull a trigger. . . . I'm scared of that." Talk about night flights ended.

Soon the possibility arose of resolving the crisis by removing Jupiter missiles in Turkey in return for the Russians removing the IRBMs in Cuba. From a military standpoint, this was a good deal. Submarines with Polaris missiles in the eastern Mediterranean would be better deterrents than obsolete Jupiters. The rub was political: Jupiters demonstrated our commitment to Turkey's defense. Johnson feared that removing them would signal friends and foes that we could not be relied upon. And what if the Russians also insisted we withdraw American soldiers stationed in Turkey? Do that, Lyndon told JFK and ExCom, and "your whole foreign policy is gone." Bereft of allies, bullied by the USSR, the United States would "crumple." We should not negotiate a swap. We should pressure the Russians to take theirs out of Cuba, even though this increased the chance we would have to launch an invasion of Cuba.

Not long afterward, Kennedy adjourned the meeting. As men left, he quietly asked a smaller group to stay. They would discuss what to tell Anatoly Dobrynin, the Soviet ambassador to the United States. Lyndon was not included.

Then Secretary of State Dean Rusk proposed a plan he thought would end the confrontation: the United States would agree not to invade Cuba in the future, and the Soviet Union would remove the missiles. Dobrynin should tell Khrushchev that "while there could be no deal over the Turkish missiles, the president was determined to get them out and would do so once the Cuban crisis was resolved." This promise must remain secret. "Any Soviet reference to our assurance would simply make it null and void." The consequence of a Russian rejection of this offer should be left unsaid. Khrushchev could figure it out for himself.

Everyone approved Rusk's plan. They also decided to keep it a secret from ExCom. "Concerned as we all were by the cost of a public bargain struck under pressure at the apparent expense of the Turks," explained National Security Adviser McGeorge Bundy, "and aware . . . that for some, even in our closest councils, even this unilateral private assurance might appear to betray an ally, we agreed without hesitation that no one not in the room was to be informed of this additional message."

Another secret decision was made that night. In a one-on-one meeting, JFK told the secretary of state what to do if the Russians said no. Rusk would secretly contact U Thant, then United Nations Secretary General, and request that he propose a trade of Turkish and Cuban missiles and offer to broker an agreement. That would give Kennedy a diplomatic option to an invasion.

Matters did not come to that. Khrushchev said yes. John Kennedy emerged from the crisis with a reputation for standing firm against Soviet aggression. He was lauded for his restraint and for his readiness to fight. His strategy of increasing the pressure and raising the stakes by carefully calibrated escalations won praise as the best way to deal with crises. Meanwhile, pundits condemned Adlai Stevenson for suggesting the deal to which Kennedy had secretly agreed, and Lyndon Johnson went to his grave unaware of the real story.

This secrecy condemned him to live up to the public image of Jack Kennedy: a tough guy who used the gradual application of military pressure and the threat of further escalation to win at the negotiating table. The real Jack—who disregarded the wishes of allies, de-escalated when it served his purpose and disentangled himself from perilous situations by secret understandings—was camouflaged from Americans' view by a carefully crafted portrait of power. When he was president, Johnson measured himself against the image, not the reality. So did others.

Nowhere did this standard of comparison have more tragic effects than in Vietnam.

During 1963, Kennedy was increasingly frustrated by the situation in Southeast Asia. Could the Diem regime hold off the Vietcong? Opinion in Washington was sharply divided. Was it possible Diem might expel Americans from his country and negotiate with Ho Chi Minh? The answer was moving from "unlikely" to "more likely," thanks in part to hints that President Charles de Gaulle of France was willing to facilitate unification talks. JFK assumed a united Vietnam would be Communist. He did not want that. Nor did he want to be accused of losing Vietnam during the 1964 presidential campaign. To prevent that, he agreed to a coup d'etat removing Diem. Perhaps to salve his conscience, JFK insisted that Diem remain unharmed and be sent into exile. It was a naïve expectation; the conspirators had no intention of allowing Diem to live and foment resistance to them. The murder of the South Vietnamese president on November 1 appalled Kennedy. Still, he reassured the new rulers that the United States remained committed to an independent South Vietnam. Privately he hoped the coup had stabilized the situation enough to defer final decision on the nature and extent of that commitment till after 1964.

Speculating about what Kennedy would have decided is fascinating. Just as he did in October 1962, he might have sought a face-saving deal, confident his image as a tough guy would protect him. All we can be sure about is that on November 22, 1963, he did not know what exactly he would do because he could not foresee what would transpire in Vietnam after the coup. We do know he never discussed the possibility of withdrawing with Rusk, McNamara, Bundy, and Robert Kennedy. Indeed, in 1964 his brother said JFK "felt he had a strong, overwhelming reason for being in Vietnam and that we should win the war in Vietnam." Asked why, Bobby replied, "The rest of Southeast Asia would fall. It would just have profound effects on our position throughout the world and our position in a rather vital part of the world." When RFK was pressed if there was ever "any consideration given to pulling out, he flatly replied, 'No.'" All Jack's most influential advisers were sure the tough guy would have escalated the war rather than accept a Vietcong victory. Once more, LBJ was judged by how closely he matched his predecessor's image.

In 1963 this would not have seemed unfair to him. Johnson aligned himself with the hard-liners. He respected Diem and thought that American critics of that embattled leader were wrong to insist that he institute social reforms and expand civil liberties in the middle of a war for national survival. He also remained hopeful that South Vietnam would be able to defend itself with American assistance and advice. On August 29, 1963, when Paul Kattenburg, staff director of an interdepartmental task force on Vietnam, called U.S. policy "a garden path to tragedy," Rusk, McNamara, Robert Kennedy, and Johnson glared at him. Shaken, he still advised, "It would be better for us to make the decision to get out honorably. . . . In six months to a year, as the South Vietnamese people see we are losing the war, they will gradually go to the other side, and we will be obliged to leave." An angry Rusk snapped, "We are winning this war!" For his penance, Kattenburg was sent to Guyana.

That Lyndon confined himself to glaring at Paul Kattenburg is telling. His passivity reveals he was not the man energized by public accommodations legislation and Cuba. He was shrinking into the background again. His job was not worth a bucket of warm spit.

Staffers in the White House and on Capitol Hill, plus most of the Washington press corps, thought he was not worth the bucket. They worked over his origins, education, accent, absence of couth and class, and fall from power. Part of this Lyndon saw as prejudice against Texas. Part was glee at seeing the once mighty in the dirt. Neither, however, was the major explanation. That was Bobby.

There was cause for his conclusion. No one wondered about RFK's opinion of Johnson. Lyndon was a "phony." He was a "liar." He was so incapable of running the CEEO efficiently that it was laughable to think of his being president. During the missile crisis, he exposed himself as a "coward." Personally he was a "son of a bitch." Even his efforts to mend fences were contemptible. With a burlesque Texas accent, RFK drawled, "why don't yew lack me, Bobby," then scorned the question as a bully whining "uncle."

To Johnson, this attitude was cruelly ungrateful. He had loyally served John Kennedy, never criticizing him, even in private to intimate friends, because he liked Jack and, more important, was determined that this administration would not be riven by divisions between president and vice president. But more than Bobby's failure to appreciate this troubled him. Lyndon remembered July 1960. He believed RFK was again trying to force him out. He might not love his bucket, but he did not want to be made to put it down.

Johnson was not in the best position to defend himself. The Senate Rules Committee was planning to hear witnesses accusing Bobby Baker of influence peddling and Lyndon of profiting from it. Gossip had it that one witness would testify that the vice president forced him to buy advertising on KTBC and to give the Johnsons an expensive stereo set as the price for government deals. The same man would also claim that Lyndon had taken a $100,000 bribe to get a fighter plane contract for General Dynamics, a Texas company. That Johnson had become rich while drawing a public servant's modest salary already intrigued some newspapers. Now the Baker mess was giving that story "legs," because it raised the possibility that Kennedy might have to drop him from the ticket.

In early November 1963, Walter Jenkins told Lyndon that over forty reporters from major papers were quizzing attorneys, bankers, and businessmen in Texas about Johnson's properties and questioning his political enemies about the sources of his wealth and power. One confided, "We're here to do a job on Lyndon Johnson. When we get through with the sonofabitch, Kennedy won't be able to touch him with a ten-foot pole in 1964." The journalists were using a common list of questions. All also had a detailed file on political corruption in Texas since 1937.

To Johnson, a coordinated and informed newspaper crusade meant one thing: his enemies at the White House and the attorney general were behind it. "It's pretty, very pretty," he told Busby. "They know the president wouldn't dump me, so they're coming at him this way." When Republicans predicted he would be "purged" soon, it heightened his worry. Distraught, he convinced himself that Kennedy planned to tell him the bad news at the LBJ Ranch on November 22, 1963.

JFK laughed at these rumors. He told staff members he needed to win Texas in 1964 and could not imagine doing that without LBJ. There is no reason to doubt his truthfulness. Lyndon was not going to be hurt by Bobby Baker. The Kennedys planned to see to that.

This was done not out of love for Lyndon: what worried the brothers was the link between Baker and Ellen Rometsch, a German woman who had briefly been one of the president's paramours. On October 26 an investigative reporter published a piece about "an exotic . . . German girl" who partied with prominent men in the executive branch, adding that more on her might emerge from the Baker hearings. "More" in this case involved speculation that she was a spy for the East German secret police and the Russians, the sort of news that would finish Jack Kennedy's career. The attorney general made sure there would be no more. He informed Baker that the Justice Department had no plans to help the investigation or to prosecute. Keep mum about Rometsch and all will be fine was the subtext.

Because Johnson had cut off contact with Baker, he did not know that RFK had short-circuited the investigation. That protected him as well, thus cementing his place on the ticket. Ignorance let his paranoia run wild.

What would he do in the future? To some friends, he mused about telling JFK on November 22 that he would run for the liberal Ralph Yarborough's Senate seat in 1964. With Horace Busby he talked about quitting politics, buying a major Texas newspaper, installing Buzz as editor and himself as columnist, then crusading to improve the lives of working families. To others, he blustered about demanding that Jack do something about Bobby's behavior or he would not be vice president again.

How serious any of this was is hard to say. Those close to Lyndon could not tell whether he really planned to frankly discuss the campaign and the second term with Kennedy at the ranch. Probably he intended just to react according to the circumstances. Right before the Texas trip, Busby had "the feeling [LBJ] was wondering what might have happened to him by the time he returned again from the ranch to Washington." His parting words were "Buzz, I may stay on a few days after the president leaves and see if I can find that newspaper for us."

Even before this ordeal, Lyndon had been unenthused about this trip. Jack wanted him to use their time in the state to end the bitter fight between Yarborough and Governor John Connally before it hurt Kennedy's chances in Texas in 1964. *A hopeless errand,* Lyndon thought. Yarborough hated him. His longtime friend John was determined to keep the national party at arm's length and crush liberal Texas Democrats. Neither was interested in letting a powerless man settle their war. He was not surprised when Yarborough even refused to ride with him in the president's motorcade in Houston.

Kennedy intervened angrily: the senator would ride with Johnson in Dallas on November 22 or he would walk. He also had a firm message for Lyndon that morning: he must make peace between Yarborough and Connally. After LBJ left, Jackie Kennedy remarked that he "sounded mad." Jack smiled. "That's just Lyndon," he replied. "He's in trouble."

Six hours later John Kennedy was dead. The man in trouble before breakfast was to be sworn in that same day as the thirty-sixth president of the United States.

7

Free at Last: November 1963 to June 1964

W hen Lyndon Johnson spoke at Andrews Air Force Base in the bleak dusk of November 22, 1963, he assured a stunned nation that he grieved, too. "This is a sad time for all people. We have suffered a loss that cannot be weighed." A promise followed: "I will do my best. That is all I can do." And a request: "I ask for your help—and God's." Then he went to the White House.

Johnson's mind was already churning. He had to quickly settle on a strategy for presenting himself and execute it swiftly.

Keeping Kennedy's men with him was the first step. When Senator George Smathers urged him on November 23 to shelve JFK's tax-cut bill and focus on budget legislation, the new president exploded: "No, no, I can't do that. . . . We've got to carry on. We can't abandon this fellow's program, because he is a national hero and there are going to be those people [who] want his program passed and we've got to keep this Kennedy aura around us." Johnson knew that following Smathers's advice would drive JFK's appointees away and said, "I needed that White House staff. Without them, I would have lost my link to John Kennedy, and without that I would have had absolutely no chance of gaining the support of the media or the Easterners or the intellectuals. And without that support I would have had absolutely no chance of governing the country."

Second was defining what kind of national hero JFK was. Many already regarded him as a martyr. That suited Lyndon fine. In his speech to Congress on November 27, he inveighed against the forces of bigotry and hatred in the country that struck down John Kennedy. His predecessor's martyrdom established, LBJ moved on to answer a crucial question: what was JFK martyred *for?* "John Kennedy had died. But his 'cause' was not really clear. That was my job. I had to take the dead man's program and turn it into a martyr's cause. That way Kennedy would live on forever and so would I."

AND SO WOULD I! LBJ believed he had an historic opportunity to win immortal fame and change the country forever. The night of the assassination, as he talked with Lady Bird and two old friends who had agreed to serve on his White House staff, Horace Busby and Jack Valenti, he began calculating how to get stalled legislation on grain sales to the USSR and a reduction in the income tax through Congress by early 1964. Then he outlined further plans. "I'm going to pass that civil rights bill that's been tied up too damn long in the Senate. I'm going to get that bill passed by Congress, and I'm gonna do it before next year is done. And then I'm going to get a bill through that's gonna make sure everybody's got a right to vote. You give people a vote, and they damn sure have power to change their life for the better." Next he moved to health care. "By God, I intend to pass Harry Truman's medical insurance bill. He didn't do it, but we'll make it into law. Never again will a little old lady who's sick as a dog be turned away from a hospital because she doesn't have any money to pay for her treatment. It's a damn disgrace." His last remarks were on a subject that had been dear to him since the year in Cotulla. "We are going to do something about education. We're going to pass a bill that will give every young boy and girl in this country, no matter who they are, the right to get all the education they can take. And the government is going to pay for it." Busby guessed, "We won't be going home for a while." "Not for fourteen months," replied Lady Bird. Buzz retorted, "It is more likely to be nine years." "No!" she cried. "I'm afraid Buzz is right," Lyndon said. "At least, it may be for five years." To achieve his goals he needed—and wanted—to win election as president.

At times, this prospect exhilarated LBJ. What had tied his hands in the past—needing Texas money and Texas votes, going along with Southern politicians—was no longer as binding. He could make government more responsive and helpful to the people's needs, and he could attack the system that held down African-Americans and held back the South. He wanted, he told several people, to be "the president who finishes what Lincoln began." As he described his enthusiasm for civil rights to James Farmer, the executive director of the Congress of Racial Equality (CORE), he exclaimed, "To quote a friend of yours, 'Free at last. Thank God almighty, I'm free at last!' "

Other times, contemplation of the difficulties ahead darkened Lyndon's mood. The men with power in the executive branch were JFK's men, not his. He could not assume they would transfer allegiance to him. Robert Kennedy was still attorney general; would he command their ultimate loyalty? "That upstart's come too far and too fast. He skipped the grades where you learn the rules of life." In addition, "He never liked me. And that's nothing compared to what I think of him."

How should he deal with this? Johnson sought advice from two Washington veterans: Dwight Eisenhower, still a popular figure, and Clark Clifford, a Democratic power broker who had been Harry Truman's political adviser.

After Ike pledged his full support, he warned Lyndon about the divided loyalties JFK's appointees would feel. They would be inclined to look upon Robert Kennedy as the true heir apparent. Eisenhower also observed that RFK had wielded extraordinary power, especially in foreign affairs. He would not want to give it up. He would try to undercut the new president. Many would follow his lead. Ike urged Johnson not to rely on JFK's men, implying that it would be best if they departed quickly and voluntarily.

In a perfect world, Lyndon would have followed that advice. Not in this one. Recalling the transition after FDR's death, Clifford advised him that the best proof of continuing purpose was continuity of personnel. Keep Kennedy's people as long as you can. Take advantage of their skills. Win the respect and trust of the most valuable. Stay alert for signs of the creation of a government in exile. Many longtime New Dealers had flirted with replacing Truman as the Democratic nominee in 1948. That could happen again.

The concerns Ike and Clifford had about Bobby confirmed Johnson's suspicions. The two had already clashed over when he took the oath of office, started using the Oval Office, spoke to Congress, and moved into the White House. To Bobby, everything to do with the presidency was really Jack's; to LBJ, this proprietary attitude weakened the office and insulted him. Johnson thought he had a constitutional duty to do the most important job in the world. Treating him like a usurper, as RFK did, diminished him in the eyes of foreign enemies and domestic opponents, and it was harmful to the country. That Bobby did not care about that consequence made him dangerous. The Lyndon–Bobby relationship would be war, undeclared, but bitter and hard fought. The new president had to hold his own in this fight, or he would not meet his own challenge, "Let us continue."

What LBJ planned to continue were JFK's domestic *and* foreign policies. He was determined to fulfill the three goals of the national Democratic Party: maintaining an intelligent anti-Communism by resisting aggression and reducing the chance of nuclear war; expanding the welfare state by fulfilling the promise of the New Deal, the Fair Deal, and the New Frontier without compromising capitalist enterprise and expansion; and ending Jim Crow in the South by implementing pathbreaking court decisions without tyrannizing Southerners or causing a powerful white backlash elsewhere. He intended to reassure the country and the world that he understood the spheres of international and national politics to be overlapping and saw the policies as intertwined. Most of all, he planned to demonstrate his understanding of what was his first priority as president.

That was not domestic reform. As historian Thomas Alan Schwartz pointed out, Johnson believed this was "his central and overriding presidential responsibility: to reduce the danger of a nuclear apocalypse." John Kennedy and Nikita Khrushchev's treaty banning atmospheric testing of nuclear weapons was a step in that direction. LBJ was determined to follow it up. "I can assure you," he told Soviet Deputy Premier Anastas Mikoyan after JFK's funeral, "that not a day will go by that we will not try in some way to reduce the tensions in the world." It was therefore essential to defeat efforts to ban financing of sales of surplus wheat to the USSR through the U.S. Export-Import Bank.

This was so for LBJ not just because selling food to the enemy would give him a reason to work for more stable relations. The issue went beyond linking the United States and the USSR in a vital commerce; it impacted perceptions of whether LBJ could maintain peace. Debate over the wheat deal had stalled Kennedy's foreign aid bill for months; failure to break the deadlock would raise questions about Johnson's ability to function as president. It was not enough for him to tell European leaders that he would continue with JFK's "grand design" for a European community or to warn Communists he would resist aggression. Actions spoke louder than words. He had to prove he could deliver the goods, or he would have no credibility with foreign leaders.

After round-the-clock lobbying and appeals to JFK's memory, Lyndon kept the financing in the bill by twenty-one votes in the Senate. Then he insisted the House pass it on Christmas Eve because "the whole Communist world was watching to see any sign of weakness . . . on the part of the president." If he did not press on, they would think, "He hasn't got any steel in his spine and hell, we don't have to pay any attention to him." He won, after agreeing he must certify any Soviet sale as in the national interest. "Let me take the rap," he said. "[The Republicans] can call me a Communist all over the country—Nixon can—and that will satisfy them."

A small price to pay! Lyndon had credibility with the Russians. Wheat sales would ease tensions. Farmers would make more money. And foreign aid's passage was crucial for domestic legislation. Johnson believed if he had lost and "those legislators tasted blood, they would have run over us like a steamroller . . . in January, when much more than foreign aid would depend on their actions."

The cause of peace made LBJ take another step before the New Year. He decided a federal commission should investigate the assassination. He was worried by the possibility that Americans might conclude that Russia or Cuba was behind it and demand a declaration of war. It was essential to end such speculation and prevent an international crisis.

In contrast to his eagerness to plan domestic measures and readiness to act on grain sales and the commission, Johnson was neither eager nor ready to deal with Vietnam. He did, however, have some thoughts about that country.

Both Senator William Fulbright and President Charles de Gaulle of France urged "neutralizing" Southeast Asia. That, they argued, would prevent the United States from getting bogged down in a war. Johnson did not relish the thought of war, but he regarded talk of neutralizing Vietnam as prettifying a Communist victory. "There's no willingness on the other side," he pointed out, "to neutralize North Vietnam." That government would respond by conquering its neighbor. Johnson also suspected that the fractious president of France wanted to cause problems for his American allies, another reason to stick with South Vietnam.

Propping up the South Vietnamese, Johnson recognized, would not be easy. Privately, he understood the difficulties. Saying this publicly was another matter. As early as January 17, 1964, he complained, "We can't stand up anywhere if our own people are going to join the enemy and start putting this stuff out." For the first time, he tarred dissenters with the brush of aiding Communists.

That same month LBJ did something else that would become grimly familiar: he agreed to escalate military measures against the

North Vietnamese in the hope of dissuading them from aiding the Vietcong. The president approved Op Plan 34-A, which provided U.S. support for South Vietnamese raids against the Ho Chi Minh Trail in Laos and naval bases on the North Vietnam coast. "We're going to touch them up a little bit in the days to come," he promised on January 31. At the same time, he made sure that the touching up would not go beyond a little bit. The original proposal for covert operations had emphasized the necessity of creating indigenous resistance movements in North Vietnam to multiply the impact of attacks from outside. It urged recruiting among tribal minorities and Catholics in the north. Fearful that arousing strong reactions from Hanoi and Beijing would lead to an escalation of the war in the south, Johnson vetoed any attempt to give the North Vietnamese a taste of their own VC medicine.

And what would happen if Op Plan 34-A did not work? The president assured Fulbright it would. He kept secret word from the Joint Chiefs of Staff that it would not. On March 2, the chiefs urged destroying military and industrial targets in North Vietnam, mining the north's harbors, and blockading the coast. Even if this caused Chinese intervention and required the use of nuclear weapons, it had to be done. Johnson responded by urging support for General Khan, "our boy" in Saigon. General Maxwell Taylor, chair of the Joint Chiefs, read between the lines: "It is quite apparent that he does not want to lose South Vietnam before next November nor does he want to get the country into the war."

LBJ excused his inaction to the chiefs by telling them he needed a Congressional resolution in support of our defense of South Vietnam. Truman, he was convinced, paid a heavy political price for neglecting to get Congress's approval for the Korean "police action." Right then, he did not have a prayer of getting a resolution. "We haven't got any Congress that will go with us." What's more, "We haven't got any mothers that will go with us in a war." There was no enthusiasm anywhere for a major military intervention in Southeast Asia.

Johnson could see his dilemma clearly. Get out, and he would encourage more Communist aggression and be accused of "losing" Vietnam. Get in, and he would run into the popular desire for peace. No wonder he wanted to stall and hope for the best.

That dilemma was not entirely unique to Vietnam. Variations of it were present in all the interactions between the USSR and its client states and the United States and its allies. LBJ's reactions to Latin America paralleled his agonizing over Southeast Asia.

In the Americas, Cuba played North Vietnam's role: a Communist state bent on exporting revolution. Havana was protected by the Soviet Union, just as Hanoi was sheltered by the Russians and the People's Republic of China. Invading either country risked a wider conflict.

That was the reason LBJ insisted to Fulbright, "I'm not getting into any Bay of Pigs deal!" He ended the Kennedy administration's Operation Mongoose because he feared paramilitary efforts to destabilize Fidel Castro's government would start a perilous cycle of retaliations and perhaps lead to congressional and popular demands for an invasion of Cuba. Any responses to Op Plan 34-A were softened by Vietnam's location, half a world away. Cuba was just over the horizon from Florida, so toleration for armed clashes was far less.

Despite the end of Operation Mongoose, war suddenly seemed closer in February 1964. The U.S. navy seized sailors from four Cuban fishing boats lingering in U.S. waters, and Castro reacted by cutting off fresh water to the U.S. base at Guantanamo. Domestic politics prevented LBJ from sending the fishermen home, so he ordered Florida water sent to the base. He also replaced Cuban workers on base with U.S. citizens, thus costing Cuba's economy $7 million to $8 million dollars annually. He worried if this would placate American opinion. Richard Russell reassured him. All Congress and the country wanted was a response "within our power without involving the shedding of a lot of blood." That did not wholly soothe Lyndon, who now became concerned about the *New York Times* and the *Washington Post*. Certain that reporters in Saigon had seriously weakened Diem during 1963 and thus adversely affected U.S. policy in Southeast Asia, he worried the same might happen in this case. The papers, he fretted to his friend, thought "we ought to be feeding Cuba"; would they not object that he was hurting "a bunch of innocent Cubans"? Russell replied sarcastically, "I don't believe that even the *Times* and the *Post* could stir up five percent of the people about this."

How like Southeast Asia! Americans wanted firmness—but no bloodshed. They wanted to stand up to Communist aggression and subversion—but shrank from war. Some elite newspapers and an unknown number of citizens did not want U.S. foreign policy to adversely affect the nonmilitary population of the country's enemies—though affecting these "innocents" might be the best way of deterring enemies. LBJ had to take into account these tangled and opposed feelings. Unknotting them would require a deft hand. Many doubted he had one, and he gave them cause for concern.

When tensions rose in the Panama Canal Zone, Johnson carelessly heightened them by characterizing Panama as "no larger than the City of St. Louis." The nation's press then compared Kennedy's competence at foreign relations and LBJ's inexperience. Obscured from public view was Lyndon's doing all he could to preserve the dignity of Panama's president and government and to prevent the Cubans from taking advantage of the crisis. His success did not erase the image of a clumsy blunderer. Furious, Johnson became more determined to keep foreign affairs off page one. In particular, he kept public discussion of Vietnam at a minimum.

That was hard to do where Latin America was concerned. To Lyndon, JFK's Alliance for Progress had no clear lines of administrative responsibility and no capable management. It was, snapped Johnson, "being run by an alliance of misfits." He planned to end that by putting Thomas Mann, the ambassador to Mexico, in charge.

Mann would be more aggressive in promoting and defending the interests of American businesses and less interested in urging and expanding social reform. All to the good, LBJ thought. The Alliance for Progress, which "seemed to welcome revolution . . . at the same time we were dealing on behalf of our businessmen" was a "lot of crap." One mistake of Kennedy's was hoping Diem's removal would "make Vietnam into an America overnight"; the same forlorn hope bedeviled the Alliance for Progress. The United States could not be fastidious in picking allies or impatient with reforming them. Effective change required economic development. Its pace would be slow; the movement of prosperity would be from the top down. Accordingly, Mann informed U.S. ambassadors that this administration would not refuse to recognize military governments.

Predictably, Lyndon was sharply criticized by some pundits as illiberal as well as inexperienced. Now he had more reason to distrust the press and to feel the leadership of the Free World put him where he was damned if he did and damned if he didn't. All this fed his predilection for secrecy and inflamed his suspicion that there were conspiracies against him. Who could he trust? Precious few.

Lyndon Johnson worked on foreign affairs consistently, cautiously, and constructively. Most of the time, he also did his duty joylessly. When he turned to working on legislation, he was invigorated.

He pursued the passage of JFK's stalled programs with a happy sense of power and purpose.

First was Kennedy's tax-reduction bill. LBJ wanted to win an important victory and build up momentum for the struggle on civil rights. Before he launched a campaign for radical change in the South, he wanted to assure conservative businessmen everywhere that he aimed to help them as well. Since the late 1950s, Johnson had believed that slashing personal and corporate income taxes would prevent recessions and fuel economic expansion. JFK's proposal for a net tax reduction of $10.2 billion by 1965 had been stalled in the Senate Finance Committee since February 1963. It was high time to break that deadlock.

LBJ knew how to do that. The powerful chair of the Senate Finance Committee, Harry Byrd of Virginia, would never let the bill go to the Senate floor so long as the federal budget for fiscal 1964 stayed at $101.5 billion. Lyndon told Walter Heller, the chairman of the Council of Economic Advisers, that unless the budget was trimmed to $100 billion, "You don't pee one drop on tax cuts." He ordered Kermit Gordon, the budget director, "to go out and re-study $101.5 [billion]—through the use of gimmicks or through an actual withholding of some plans."

Gordon soon discovered that this president's expertise with federal budgets equaled his. LBJ found enough fat to shave the bottom line to $97.9 billion. Then he promised Byrd, "I'm going to give 'em hell about economy until that last budget dollar is spent, and I'm going to prove to you that I can live within my budget if something like haywire don't go wrong." Lyndon did his part, turning out lights and cutting clerical staff at the White House. Byrd did his, letting the bill go to the Senate. It passed 77–21. Lyndon urged Senate friends to reconcile differences with the House bill as soon as possible. Every day lost kept $80 million out of the economy, "and I want to have a good year, so I can get reelected." The Revenue Act of 1964 made achieving both goals more likely.

Now came the hard part.

John Kennedy sent a civil rights bill to Congress in June 1963. It ended racial discrimination in public accommodations, enabled the Justice Department to cut off funds to state and local governments practicing racial discrimination, beefed up federal protection of voting rights, authorized federal support for school desegregation, and re-authorized the Civil Rights Commission. The bill passed through the House Judiciary Committee, only to languish for months in the

House Rules Committee. Supporters of the bill began to suspect that the president was not really trying to force Chairman Howard Smith of Virginia to hold a vote on it.

Kennedy, they feared, did not want to do anything before the presidential election in 1964. Polls in fall 1963 indicated that 50 percent of Americans thought he was moving too fast on civil rights. He might be tempted to reassure white voters of his concern for their views, especially if Barry Goldwater was the Republican nominee. And Barry as opponent would ensure Jack of the Northern black vote, so he would not need action on his bill to get their votes.

Aware of these suspicions about JFK's commitment, knowing if they lingered they would be held even more strongly about him after his compromises in 1957, LBJ immediately denied that such considerations would influence him. Advised against squandering good will by pressing on civil rights, Lyndon responded, "Well, what the hell's the presidency for?" He told Roy Wilkins right after JFK was buried, "I want that bill!" Newspaper editors and network executives got the same message. So did Republicans in the House and Senate. So did Martin Luther King, with an added recommendation that the Southern Christian Leadership Council (SCLC) and the Student Nonviolent Coordinating Committee (SNCC) avoid provocative demonstrations in the future. So did Richard Russell: "Dick, you've got to get out of my way. If you don't, I'm going to roll over you. I don't intend to cavil or compromise." You may do that," answered Russell, "but it's going to cost you the South, and cost you the election." Johnson did not hesitate. "If that's the price I have to pay, I'll pay it gladly."

All who received the word from Lyndon believed that he would do everything he could to enact the bill and that he could get it done. Martin Luther King told SCLC aides, "LBJ is a man of great ego and great power. . . . It just may be he is going to go where John Kennedy couldn't." When a Southern colleague asked Russell whether Johnson would agree to weakening amendments as he had in 1957, he replied, "No. The way that fellow operates, he'll get the whole bill, every last bit of it."

That was because determined presidents had more weapons than powerful majority leaders. Among these was the power to set national agendas and guarantee something for everyone. In his State of the Union address, LBJ declared war on poverty. He followed up by assuring big city mayors that they would be beneficiaries of

LBJ and MLK. © Lyndon B. Johnson Library

Treasury largesse, civil rights leaders that a lion's share would go to the black poor, and politicians representing Appalachia that they would be pleased with the programs. He underscored this by marking the introduction of poverty legislation with a visit to West Virginia, not Harlem as originally planned. To be sure, Johnson was committed to improving the lives of America's poor. He believed this would stimulate the whole country's economy, but he also wanted to convince groups who might fear he was only willing to help African-Americans that everyone would have a piece of federal pie.

Doubters and opponents got another message: they might get a pie smashed in their faces. As British journalist Michael Davie noted, anyone who dealt with Lyndon Johnson was familiar with "the sudden alarming glint of power." He could do things *to* you as well as for you. And he would not forget which you had earned. Next to LBJ, a foreign diplomat aptly said, elephants were amnesiacs.

Lyndon's handling of moderate Republicans in Congress during the civil rights debate was a classic example of public persuasion and veiled threats. To get the proposal out of the House Rules Committee, he needed the help of William McCulloch, the ranking Republican on the House Judiciary Committee; to end a Southern filibuster in the Senate, he needed the influence of Everett Dirksen, the Senate Minority Leader. He appealed to both men's sense of justice. He emphasized that without a strong law there would be riots in the South and in many northern cities. He reminded them that theirs was the party of Abraham Lincoln. He offered to grant political favors and to agree to amendments that would not weaken enforcement of the law in the South. These were his carrots.

This was the stick: Moderate Republicans were stunned by the successful organizing of grass-roots conservatives and the rise of Goldwater. The Grand Old Party was swinging toward the extreme right. If it got there, moderates would lose control. They had to make plain their potency in national politics to maintain their position in the party. Playing a crucial part in passing civil rights would, they hoped, do this. Failing to do so would surely hurt because Johnson would blame them for lacking political muscle and nerve.

The president set up Democratic liberals in the same way. He assigned major lobbying responsibilities to Robert Kennedy, exposing him to blame if the bill stalled. Since RFK was pursuing the vice presidency, "the runt" would do almost anything to please. Hubert Humphrey was in charge of pushing the bill through the Senate. His hopes for being on the ticket hinged on success. Johnson turned up the heat further by saying that this was the type of historic moment liberals had failed to rise to in the past. They would get a full ration of blame from Lyndon if they fell short. With that message delivered, he knew they would make every effort to win.

LBJ also measured the hopes and strategy of his opponents precisely. Russell would try to filibuster through the primary season. He would hope during these campaigns that reactions against the civil rights crusade would swell outside the South. Enough senators might then shy away from voting cloture.

Governor George Wallace of Alabama was Dick Russell's Great White Hope. He lived up to expectations.

Entering the Wisconsin primary against Governor John Reynolds on the last day, so ignorant of the state some doubted he could find it on a map, Wallace shrewdly turned civil rights into an issue of federal power. "If Wisconsin believes in integration, that is Wisconsin's business, not mine. . . . And the central government in Washington has no right to tell either Alabama or Wisconsin what to do." To those whose ears were attuned to the underlying antiblack signal, the meaning was clear. At the campaign's start, Wallace's vote was projected at 5 percent, but on April 7 he racked up 264,000 ballots, one-third of the total cast in the Democratic primary. To him, these were votes against "wild-eyed, far-out pinko liberals who, under the false guise of civil rights, are trying to control your property and dictate every detail of your lives." Those results, he boasted, "have shaken the eye-teeth of every liberal in the country."

Publicly, Johnson was concerned but unshaken. When Press Secretary George Reedy asked him for a response, he noted that if he had run he would have "roll[ed] up a heavy vote." (The president had chosen not to run in any primary, claiming that avoiding partisan politics let him appeal to both parties on matters of national concern.) LBJ also coolly observed that he would settle for two out of every three votes in any contest. It was "pretty satisfactory" to him that "we got more votes than Wallace."

Privately, Lyndon wanted to end the Wallace boom. He quietly sent money and Ted Kennedy to aid the favorite-son candidacy of Governor Matthew Welsh in Indiana. And he showed up himself, ostensibly to inspect economically depressed areas as buildup to poverty legislation. After this help, Welsh got 368,400 votes, Wallace a little over 170,000.

Maryland was the climax of Wallace's foray into presidential politics. The Alabamian expected to win. Ethnic neighborhoods demographically similar to ones he swept in Wisconsin and Indiana were agitated by a new state law forbidding racial discrimination in public places; all voters were peeved at a tax hike pushed through by the Democrats. Senator Daniel Brewster was LBJ's stand-in. Once more, Lyndon privately helped all he could, funneling money and speakers to Brewster and leaking FBI investigations of possibly fraudulent highway contracts granted by Wallace to the *Baltimore Sun*. The organizing of black voters by civil rights activists was more crucial. On May 19, Wallace won a majority of white voters in the largest turnout in the history of Maryland primaries. Only the ballots of African Americans and union members held him to 43 percent.

To Senator Abraham Ribicoff, a liberal Connecticut Democrat, this revealed that "there are many Americans in the North as well as the South who do not believe in civil rights." LBJ would not have quarreled with him, but he saw no reason for despair about passing the bill. Wallace had run out of primaries. He would soon be last week's news. A Gallup poll conducted in May indicated that only 30 percent of Americans believed the administration was proceeding too quickly on civil rights. Johnson was again happy to settle for a two-thirds margin. He advised senators and representatives to explain the primary votes as suspiciousness about federal power rather than racism. Adopting, then adapting, Wallace's own tactic to the cause of civil rights proved to be important in and out of Congress.

LBJ's "no amendments to this bill" pledge in effect meant no changes weakening its enforcement or unacceptable to Kennedy and Humphrey. Within these parameters he would agree to requests from moderate Republicans, because a law produced by bipartisan consensus was much preferable to Democratic legislation. In that spirit, the White House acquiesced in a House vote to add a provision barring discrimination by sex. If Bill McCulloch wanted this, he would have it. The price of the Senate moderates was different.

Their amendments reduced areas covered by federal authority. That squared with their governing philosophy and gave them accomplishments they could point to in contests with more conservative Republicans *in their states*. The last qualifier was crucial: none of these changes aided white Southerners. For example, the bill was amended to give effective state antidiscrimination laws precedence over federal law. There were no such laws in Southern states. Now the bill required jury trials for criminal contempt defendants faced with severe punishment, except where voting rights were violated. That happened only in the South. The bill now banned bussing of students to remedy de facto segregation in schools. Segregation in the southern states was de jure, so the Department of Justice (DOJ) could mandate bussing there. An amendment eliminated the attorney general's power to initiate court litigation in individual cases of discrimination, except whenever the DOJ could demonstrate persistent discriminatory patterns. In the South, discrimination was written in the statute books. No amendments affected the bill's purpose: to end Jim Crow.

Humphrey told LBJ, "We haven't weakened this bill one damned bit." Indeed, he thought Republican amendments strengthened the bill in some ways. (They did, if "strengthened" equaled making it more palatable to whites outside the South.) RFK was also happy. As was Lyndon: that these two approved the amended bill made him safe from criticism from Democratic liberals.

Rounding up the last votes against the filibuster was the president's job. It was time for doing the "Texas twist" with Democratic senators, sweet talking appeals to past friendships and sweeter offers of favors. One example must suffice. Carl Hayden of Arizona pledged his vote for cloture if it was necessary after LBJ promised to support a multibillion-dollar plan stalled since the late 1950s to divert water from California to Phoenix and Tucson.

With Republican moderates, Lyndon was more subtle. He never called Roman Hruska or Carl Curtis of Nebraska. Instead, he made sure Curtis's Methodist pastor and Hruska's Unitarian minister lobbied them. The Catholic bishops of Iowa and South Dakota worked on Jack Miller, Bourke Hickenlouper, and Karl Mundt. In each case, the clergy's intervention was decisive. When Mundt called to announce his decision "to vote for your doggone cloture motion," he added he was glad "you didn't call me up and give me the old Texas twist." Lyndon replied, "I haven't called a human, Karl. I don't do that." Presumably both laughed.

Much less amused was Dick Russell. After the Senate voted 71–29 for cloture and 73–27 to approve the bill, he explained why Congress had passed the most far-reaching civil rights legislation since Reconstruction. "First . . . it was Lyndon Johnson." "And second," he went on, "it was the clergy." He was right.

Russell's analysis merits further discussion because it highlights one of Lyndon's principle concerns. He knew a civil rights law was not enough to achieve fundamental changes. In fact, by itself it could set back race relations for decades. On May 11, he told Humphrey, "The thing we are more afraid of than anything else is that we'll have real revolution in this country when the bill goes into effect." The way had to be prepared for its enforcement before it became law or "We'll have mutiny in this goddamn country." Remember prohibition, he urged. "It doesn't do any good to have a law like the Volstead Act if you can't enforce it." How did LBJ plan to make a civil rights law enforceable?

Lyndon was sure the men and women who opposed integration, the ones who fought the bill tooth and nail, had to be convinced to obey the law. To prepare this ground, Johnson used the same strategy Martin Luther King used: he appealed to the fervent Christianity of white Southerners. As he later told Doris Kearns Goodwin, "I knew that as president I couldn't make people want to integrate their schools or open their doors to blacks, but I could make them feel guilty for not doing it and I believed it was my moral responsibility to do precisely that—to use the moral suasion of my office to make people feel segregation was a curse they'd carry with them to their graves." It was crucially important that he succeed in doing this. "This guilt was the only chance we had for holding the backlash in check."

While still vice president, Lyndon had urged JFK to define civil rights as an issue of right and wrong. As president, he returned to this theme often. "This is not merely an economic issue or a social, political or international issue. It is a moral issue." He insisted, "The time has come for Americans of all races and creeds and political beliefs to understand and respect each other." Borrowing biblical cadences, he urged, "Let us put an end to the teaching and preaching of hate and violence. Let us turn away from the fanatics of the far left and the far right, from the apostles of bitterness and bigotry, from those defiant of law, and those who pour venom into the nation's bloodstream."

How effective was his eloquence? In early 1964, four hundred Southern Presbyterian ministers signed a petition favoring a civil rights law. "The voice of the filibuster," they wrote, "has for too long been regarded as the most authentic Southern voice. It is not. The South's most authentic voice is the voice of conscience and faith." One of those signing was William D. Russell of Decatur, Georgia.

LBJ did not expect that Reverend Russell would convert his uncle. He did hope that Presbyterian pastors would persuade their congregations to obey the law. He made this point explicitly to a group of Southern ministers whose flocks were far larger than the Presbyterian fold.

Standing before 150 leading Southern Baptist ministers he had invited to the White House, Johnson reminded them that his great grandfather had been president of Baylor. His own Baptist roots enabled him to speak truth to them. "No group of Christians has a greater responsibility in civil rights than Southern Baptists." Their people were the power structure in many communities; "their attitudes are confirmed or changed by the sermons you preach and by the lessons you write and by the examples you set." He warned them against "calling peace, peace, peace, when there is no peace." That must stop. "The cause of human rights demands prophets in our time, men of compassion and truth, unafraid of the consequences of fulfilling their faith." He wanted them to use their influence on power brokers in their pews, preaching compliance with the law as a Christian's duty.

The president also worked on his old friends in the Southern caucus. He wanted them to have their full say because he wanted to enable them to show their constituents that they had done everything possible to avoid "the rod" of civil rights. When Dirksen suggested a cloture vote in late April, Johnson said no because senators needed to deliberate and debate. This respect, plus his refusal to threaten or punish them during the filibuster, recalled his past assurances that it would be better for a Southern president to be enforcing the act. "He could have hurt us," one Southerner confidentially told Clarence Mitchell, the lobbyist for the NAACP, "in a lot of ways that [he] didn't hurt us." Said Dick Russell to Lyndon's bright young assistant Bill Moyers, "I'm sorry that it's from his hand the rod must be wielded, but I'd rather it be his hand than anybody else's I know." Johnson's heart leapt when he heard this. The Southerners would fight hard and vote no. He could not, as he told a lobbyist, make leopards change their spots. But after the battle he wanted these men to calm their people and counsel obedience.

Also crucial to obedience were the Republican moderates. The fact that twenty-seven of the Senate's thirty-three Republicans voted for the bill proved that the Civil Rights Act of 1964 was not the product of a momentary domination of Congress by liberal Democrats. This legislation could not be portrayed in the South as the work of radicals and no one else. "We've got to make this," lectured LBJ to Humphrey, "an American bill and not just a Democratic bill." Lyndon already predicted that civil rights would make the South solidly Republican. If white Southerners were going to stampede into the GOP, they must be aware they were joining a party in favor of this law. They could not hope new friends would condone efforts to flout and repeal it. By their votes, Republicans made it clear they required that the law be obeyed.

LBJ went south himself to preach this gospel. He had not been president five weeks before he integrated the Forty Acres Club in Austin by taking an African-American secretary to dinner. In early May 1964, he went to Georgia and spoke at a legislative breakfast in Atlanta and rode in a motorcade through streets lined with hundreds of thousands. His messages were straightforward: "Heed not those who would come waving the tattered and discredited banners of the past, who seek to stir old hostilities and kindle old hatreds" and "Full participation in our society can no longer be denied to men because of their race or religion or the region in which they live."

THE REGION IN WHICH THEY LIVE! Thus he displayed the fruits of obeying civil rights laws. Southerners had been denied full participation in political power and economic prosperity because the whites among them had oppressed black Americans. End that, and the sky was the limit. That message was ideally suited for Atlanta, which boasted it was too busy to hate. It was intended for the whole South.

Lyndon Johnson's shepherding of the civil rights bill through the House and Senate confirmed his reputation as a genius of the legislative process, a master politician. His pouring the foundation for Southern obedience to the law revealed something grander: his greatness as a democratic leader.

When the Senate passed the bill by a vote of 73–27 on June 19, Johnson warned Roy Wilkins, "Our troubles are just beginning." Fearful of a backlash against civil rights throughout the nation, he asked people "of goodwill and compassion" to work for "a vision of justice without violence in the streets." Soon afterward, he heard depressing news about the disappearance of three civil rights workers in Mississippi.

On July 2, Robert Kennedy urged Lyndon not to sign the bill until after the Fourth of July weekend. RFK foresaw a scene with "firecrackers going off . . . [and] with Negroes running all over the South figuring that they'd get the day off, that they're going into every hotel and motel and every restaurant." Irritated by his nemesis's pessimism, LBJ responded by signing the bill that evening, on a day with personal significance for him. Nine years ago, he reminded Bird, he had had a heart attack. "Happy anniversary!" she replied.

It *was* happy. Russell made a public statement to Georgians, telling them to obey the law "as long as it is there." So did Allen Ellender of Louisiana. So did Bill Fulbright from Arkansas. The attorney general reported, "We had a good day. . . . Savannah, Atlanta, and all these cities went along. Birmingham, Montgomery, and a lot of the cities went along very, very well." LBJ added Johnson City. Its cafes were serving black customers. "Oh, that's good," replied Kennedy. "It's been very, very good."

In a reflective mood, Lyndon commented to John Connally that the response to his July 2 speech was "just amazingly good—particularly from the South." He recalled, "I didn't cuddle up to 'em but I wasn't the least bit critical or vicious or demanding. I just appealed for us reasoning together." The president had no illusions that the millennium had arrived in race relations, but he had begun the process of freeing his home region and his fellow citizens from the bonds of the past.

8

Walking the Tightrope: July to November 1964

Less than three weeks after the passage of the Civil Rights Act, LBJ was back hustling votes from white Southerners on Capitol Hill. He claimed to Senator Russell Long of Louisiana that he had had neither any choice on the bill nor any alternative to ordering the FBI to look for missing civil rights workers in Mississippi. However, he wanted to make clear that he had not forgotten how things were in Dixie. "I've spent fifty-six years in it and living in it and I'm trying my damndest to walk the tightrope that I got to walk."

Long was understanding. "This thing had to pass sooner or later." He was also encouraging. "Momentarily it creates a big storm. . . . But it can't go anywhere but up." That someone so totally wired into the Southern power structure believed the white South would comply with the act was music to Lyndon's ears. It meant his strategy for creating conditions favorable for enforcement was working. Also, the Louisiana senator had cheering news about white backlash around the country. If Johnson could "just play it low key from here on until November it's going to get better for you."

Long's friendliness was gratifying for another reason. LBJ was buddying up to him in the hope he would support the Economic Opportunity bill. The administration needed the votes of Southern Democrats. Playing Good Ol' Lyndon was part of the campaign. When LBJ declared war on poverty, the president had no detailed plan of battle. Instead he relied on some general ideas.

He wanted an updated NYA, focusing on the young poor and providing education, training, and jobs. This would not be welfare: it would be the means for getting people off welfare. As he promised Carl Albert, the majority whip in the House, "They'll be tax-*payers* in two years, instead of tax-*eaters*."

He wanted the program to be big, with a budget of $1 billion. Anything less would delay meaningful changes, offer minimal political advantages, and cause resentment in cities and states getting nothing. Beginning with a modest budget would also bring forth unfavorable comparisons with his martyred predecessor. The attorney general had identified poverty as Jack Kennedy's major domestic concern when he died. That evidence for this was very slender did not count; Bobby's pushing of it compelled him to make a major effort.

He wanted to create new agencies. He was convinced they would pursue their missions more effectively and aggressively than established bureaucracies. He was determined the war on poverty would be creative and flexible.

He had a general in mind. Sargent Shriver had done a marvelous job as director of the Peace Corps. He and Lyndon hit it off very well from the beginning of the Kennedy administration. In 1961 the vice president urged Sarge to insist that the Peace Corps remain independent of the Foreign Service—"They'll give you a hundred and one reasons why it won't work every time you want to do something different"—and then helped him achieve that goal. It did not hurt that Shriver was married to Eunice Kennedy. This would insulate him against criticism from Bobby and Kennedy loyalists. After appealing to his patriotism and altruism, encouraging him as a devout Catholic to see this as a moral duty, permitting him to remain director of the Peace Corps, and dangling the possibility of being vice president, he landed his poverty leader.

Then began the process of making Shriver LBJ's man. There had been "opposition," he said, from "about as powerful people as we have in this government." They praised him "as a *public relations expert*" but doubted he could run large programs. The president had no doubts: Sarge had two months to plan programs and draft legislation. He also had a blank check: "The sky's the limit. You just make this thing work, period. I don't give a damn about the details." For Lyndon, "This is number one on the domestic front. Next to peace in the world, this is the most important."

Johnson was perfectly sincere when he said this. As revolutionary as civil rights were, legal equality would not eradicate poverty. He wanted a great society, one in which poverty was accidental and temporary. That was the noblest of domestic enterprises and the most beneficial.

Shriver made an impressive start. His committee devised a comprehensive bill by May. It included a jobs corps, a neighborhood youth corps, and a work-study program for disadvantaged young people. It called for Community Action Programs (CAPS), which would be energized by the "maximum feasible participation" of the poor themselves. There would be loans and grants for small farmers and loans for small businesses. There would be a work-experience program to provide job training for unemployed heads of households receiving welfare. The bill also created Volunteers in Service to America (VISTA), the domestic equivalent of the Peace Corps. All these programs would be administered by a new agency, the Office of Economic Opportunity (OEO).

Title II, the section creating CAPS, sparked the most debate within the committee. Some advisers argued that the poor should direct programs serving their community; others insisted they should simply be consulted. Because all blamed the present unresponsive, inefficient, and ineffectual performance of private and public agencies on the absence of input and direction from the poor themselves, no one felt CAPS could be cut from the draft. "Maximum feasible participation" was a compromise designed to let the poor's role be determined at the local level. No one explored the serious political problems CAPS posed. States' rights advocates would view them as dangerous elevations of federal power. Politicians controlling the patronage of existing systems would see there would be no more jobs to hand out. These obvious drawbacks were not obvious to the planners. To them, CAPS seemed "like an idea that nobody could quarrel with."

LBJ could. "You can't do it!" the president shouted at Shriver. "You can't give federal dollars to private agencies. It won't work. [Do this, and] you'll have a helluva thing on your hands. And so will I. It is just going to be awful. The people will steal the money. The governors and mayors will hate it." Shriver feared he would not send the bill to Congress. Finally Johnson agreed that CAPS could go forward, provided Sarge promised he would not let crooks, Communists, and undesirables onto the boards. The $962.5 million Economic Opportunity Act went to Capitol Hill on March 16.

Objections to CAPS arose immediately, proving that LBJ had been prescient. But he had been equally farsighted in maintaining friendly relationships with Southern Democrats. In the Senate, the White House saved the bill by adopting a suggestion of Senator Herman Talmadge of Georgia, giving governors the right to veto any poverty program within thirty days. This restored enough state power to get the bill passed 61–34 on July 23.

When the House took it up on August 5, Republicans attacked the bill. They chose arguments congenial to Southern Democrats: states' rights; integration; separation of church and state; and the morality of federally funded birth control. Johnson and Shriver realized the vote would be very close. At that moment, the entire North Carolina delegation delivered an ultimatum.

The North Carolinians objected to Shriver's proposed deputy director of OEO, Adam Yarmolinsky. Not only was he "some wild-eyed radical with a Russian sounding name"; while working at the Pentagon, he had recommended closing several bases in North Carolina. Remove Yarmolinsky—then the administration would get a bunch of "ayes." Keep him—they would all vote "no" and ask other Southerners to join them.

For Lyndon, this was easy. He did not know Yarmolinsky and wanted the bill passed. For Sarge, it was agonizing. The two men were personally and professionally close. Should he say if his friend went so would he? Johnson played him masterfully. He coolly asked Shriver what the vote looked like. Reminded of the stakes, Sarge chose ending poverty over being loyal. After Yarmolinsky was tossed overboard, the House approved the bill 226–184. When LBJ signed it, he proudly proclaimed, "Today is the first time in all the history of the human race a great nation is able to make and is willing to make a commitment to eradicate poverty among its people."

Passage of the Economic Opportunity Act capped a stunning congressional session. From the same Congress that denied Jack Kennedy a budget for fiscal 1964, Johnson had gotten two farm bills, the tax cut, a historic civil rights act, and the War on Poverty. And he topped these off with pay raises for federal employees and food stamps for those on welfare.

His record in foreign affairs, though less triumphant, pleased him. He had proved to the Soviet Union that he could be both firm and conciliatory. He had changed the direction of U.S. policy on Latin America. "The only thing we haven't yet worked out," he told the Speaker of the House, "is Vietnam." And he was not to blame! "Eisenhower got us into that. And I inherited it. And it had three changes of government before I even got in here." But he assured John McCormack, "I'm doing the best I can to work that out."

Lyndon was never shy about poorboying. When it suited, he would claim he had inherited JFK's domestic program and was forced to get it passed to keep Kennedy's people from turning on him. No one believed that. LBJ was committed to those proposals and threw himself into enacting them. His self-pity on Vietnam, in contrast, was bottom-of-the-heart real. "What the hell is Vietnam worth to me?" he burst out to McGeorge Bundy on May 27. "What is Laos worth to me? What is it worth to this country?" Was it a question of living up to U.S. treaties? "Hell, everybody else's got a treaty out there and they're not doing anything about it." That left him with one central question, which he left unspoken, but which millions of Americans would ask before he left Washington: why are we in Vietnam?

Here's his answer: "Of course if you start running from the Communists, they may just chase you right into your own kitchen." Mac Bundy agreed. "Yeah, that's the trouble. And that is what the rest of that half of the world is going to think if this thing comes apart on us. That's the dilemma."

Dean Rusk, Robert McNamara, and Robert Kennedy shared that opinion. So did Republicans in Congress. So did most Democrats on Capitol Hill, the only exceptions being the obscure Ernest Gruening of Alaska, the eccentric Wayne Morse of Oregon, Bill "Half-bright" Fulbright, and Mike "Milquetoast" Mansfield. So did the American people: polls soon told Lyndon that a majority did not like his handling of the Red threat in Southeast Asia. And if South Vietnam collapsed, Bobby would be "out in front leading the fight against me, telling everyone I had betrayed John Kennedy's commitment."

Consensus on the significance of Vietnam did not extend to what was to be done. Everyone "that's got any sense" told Lyndon, "Oh, my God, ple-e-e-ease give this some thought." Some of his oldest friends were especially wary of large-scale U.S. military involvement in Vietnam. Everyone George Smathers spoke to thought it was not a good idea to fight a war in that area of the world: "To start committin' more and more is just got everybody really worried." Richard Russell predicted it would take a million GIs and last ten years. He doubted the American people would support such an undertaking.

What to do? LBJ explored the alternatives from March through July 1964.

JFK had negotiated a neutral government in Laos. But in Vietnam, LBJ told Russell, "There ain't nobody wants to agree to neutralization. . . . They just say, 'Screw you.'" He was not exaggerating much. Remembering that the USSR had helped with Laos, Russell asked why the Russians did not do the same with Vietnam and thereby counter Chinese influence in Asia. Johnson replied that they were afraid they would lose face with all the Communist nations in the world. Besides, if Khrushchev had the will he might not have the way. The Laotians were willing to seek peace; the North Vietnamese were not.

Johnson approached Hanoi in June through J. Blair Seaborn, a Canadian member of the International Control Commission for Vietnam. Seaborn assured Ho Chi Minh that the United States had no desire to overthrow the North Vietnam government or to keep troops in South Vietnam. If North Vietnam would stop aiding the Vietcong, America would leave Indochina. The United States would also give North Vietnam economic development aid. Ho's reply was uncompromising: The United States should allow the formation of a neutral government and completely withdraw from Vietnam. Lyndon knew what that meant: a Communist nation.

In a lighthearted mood, JFK once joked he knew how to get out of Vietnam: install a government that would ask us to leave. More seriously, Russell said the same. "That's right," responded Lyndon, "but you can't do that. . . . Wouldn't that pretty well fix us in the eyes of the world though and make it look mighty bad?" It would be seen as impotence, not cleverness.

Could the United States buy time by bombing the transportation of supplies and men down the Ho Chi Minh Trail? McNamara, Russell, and Johnson agreed that would inconvenience the enemy but that it would not interdict movement enough to make a difference. American forces could not prevent the resupply of North Korea from China during the Korean War. Recalled Russell, "We had absolute control of the seas and the air, and we never did stop them. And, you ain't gonna stop these people either."

Everything pointed to one policy: the United States would have to fight a land war. That frightened LBJ. "I just haven't got the nerve to do it," he confessed to Russell, "and I don't see any other way out of it." Nor did the Joint Chiefs of Staff. Calling attention on May 24 to a rapidly deteriorating political and military situation, the chiefs said it was time to get in or get out. They thought they could win.

Johnson circled back to ask again what was at stake there for the United States. Russell had some answers. Strategically, Vietnam had no significance. "It isn't important a damn bit, with all those new missile systems" protecting the United States. Nor would losing the country have great economic or political import in Asia. Given the historic rivalry between China and Indochina, the appearance of a

Red Vietnam would not enhance Chinese influence. The only conceivable importance of Vietnam was "from a psychological standpoint." "As a practical matter," Russell elaborated, "we're in there and I don't know how the hell you can tell the American people you're coming out. . . . They'll think you've just been whipped, you've been ruined, you're scared. It'd be disastrous."

And that was true not just in domestic politics: the USSR reacted to perceived weakness by pushing, pushing, pushing—in Berlin, in Africa, in Latin America, even to another nuclear brink. At stake was more than South Vietnam. Johnson concluded, "I've got to say [to the American people] that I didn't get you in here, but we're in here by treaty and our national honor's at stake. And if this treaty's no good, none of them are any good. Therefore we're there. And being there we've got to conduct ourselves as men." Russell assured him, "They've got enough sense to realize it's just a matter of face, that we can't just walk off and leave those people down there."

Still LBJ hesitated. On May 27, he said to Mac Bundy, "It's damned easy to get in a war but it's gonna be awfully hard to ever extricate yourself if you get in." Left unsaid was another compelling reason for holding back. Mac understood. He privately told CIA officials, "We're not going to do a goddamn thing while this goddamn election is going on."

Lyndon was back on the highwire. Polls confirmed his feeling that being seen as soft on Communism would hurt his popularity. So Vietnam was one of the few issues Barry Goldwater could use to narrow the gap between him and LBJ. Seeming weak in Southeast Asia also worked to the advantage of Robert Kennedy. Johnson was sure Bobby would steal the nomination if he could. To be prepared for any tricks, he had FBI agents secretly keep tabs on the attorney general. To forestall arguments that he could not do Jack's job, he had to keep Saigon from collapsing.

But he could not be too hardline. Johnson was determined to be the peace candidate. Goldwater's proposal to give NATO commanders permission to use tactical nuclear weapons if the Russians attacked let Lyndon paint him as an irresponsible, trigger-happy extremist. Escalating American combat engagement in South Vietnam would blur that distinction. Moreover, he sensed no popular enthusiasm for that. Truman's poll ratings had dropped like a rock after a few months' fighting in Korea. That could happen to him, too.

This troubled Lyndon. He recalled the Fair Deal's fate after the Korean War began. Congress had become focused on war. Domestic reform was forgotten. He wanted no repeat in 1964. He wanted to win big and claim a mandate for the Great Society he described in a commencement address at the University of Michigan. It was a once-in-a-lifetime chance to complete FDR's mission. Right now, he told Russell on June 11, "We're just dong fine, except for this damned Vietnam thing. We're just doing wonderful." But that damned thing could cost him his wonderful opportunity.

So he had to play for time, being firm but not too firm, keeping Vietnam out of the campaign as much as he could and hiding the awful dilemma he faced and its probable resolution from the voters. It was a fateful decision.

The balancing act on Vietnam required delicate positioning. Any American military response would be limited to bombing that, as Bundy said on May 27, "shows precisely what we do and don't mean." The bombs would leave no doubt about U.S. readiness to punish specific acts of aggression. They should make the North Vietnamese draw back from future provocations. Yet air raids should be carefully calibrated in scale, scope, and damage to avoid causing enemy escalation. Bundy explained, "The main objective is to kill as few people as possible while creating an environment in which the incentive to react is as low as possible." Within ten days the policy was tested.

On June 6 and 7, Pathet Lao artillery shot down two U.S. planes over Laos. Johnson's military advisers insisted that he "notify Hanoi by taking out this anti-aircraft battery." Most political advisers agreed. So did Johnson: "My own instinct is to hit back when I'm hit." He did, and for the first time, "I stayed awake most of the night, hoping that those planes would come back." He also anguished if he should announce the raids, finally deciding not "to give any indications that we're getting involved in a war" to the public. To his delight, the North Vietnamese said and did nothing.

Perhaps this inspired him to press forward in July and August with Op Plan 34-A. Bundy had argued in May that the United States should consider doing more than just reacting to attacks. Offensive sorties against North Vietnam were "the best way of galvanizing the South [Vietnam]." He advised raids by American-trained commandos and a "show of force" by navy destroyers in the Gulf of Tonkin. LBJ agreed. He hoped the missions scheduled for July 30–31 would encourage the South Vietnamese enough to avert any crisis there until after November. He did not expect Hanoi would respond.

On August 2, North Vietnamese motor patrol boats attacked the U.S. destroyer *Maddox*. Johnson immediately concluded that this was a reprisal for the Op Plan 34-A operations. Determined not to back down, he kept the *Maddox* on patrol, reinforcing her with the C. *Turner Joy*. He also approved another commando raid for the night of August 3.

LBJ kept the National Security Council (NSC) in the dark about the raid. Only a few officials in the executive branch and on Capitol Hill knew about Op Plan 34-A, and the president planned to keep it that way. Portraying the attack on the *Maddox* as unprovoked was politically advantageous. The American public was informed he would continue the naval patrols. The navy, he promised, would destroy any attackers. Nikita Khrushchev and Ho Chi Minh were telexed the same message.

On the night of August 4, the two destroyers radioed that they were under attack. For some minutes, the ships maneuvered sharply, firing rapidly. Then the captains began to think nervous crews and freakish weather had caused a false alarm. LBJ himself later speculated in private about "dumb sailors . . . firing at flying fish." This did not make him less ready to retaliate by bombing targets in North Vietnam. That would show the enemy and our ally that the United States could not be messed with. It also helped his campaign. It showed he could respond forcefully to aggression without plunging into war. Bombing also compelled the GOP to rally round the flag. Goldwater said, "You've taken the right steps," and added, "Like always, Americans will stick together."

Other fruit was ripe for plucking. Johnson had been yearning for a resolution of congressional support. Now was the time to get it. Americans were under fire, and the impulse would be to support them. Plus debate would be short and shaped by considerations of domestic politics, since Congress was about to adjourn for the Democratic Convention. There would be little discussion of hard choices and long-term commitments.

Then "that damned fool" Hubert Humphrey volunteered on TV that "we have been carrying out some operations in the area . . . going in and knocking out roads and petroleum things." Couldn't he, raged Lyndon, "keep his goddamned big mouth shut on foreign affairs, at least until the election is over?" McNamara to the rescue! He testified that the navy did not join in or have knowledge of any South Vietnamese attacks that "might" have happened. It went unnoticed that he did not mention what Washington had done and known. Op Plan 34-A stayed buried.

The attacks were regarded as unprovoked. What prompted them concerned some senators less than that we were verging on war and that a broad resolution might be interpreted as supporting that step. A few also worried about the resolution's language. Senator Gaylord Nelson of Wisconsin pondered amending the Tonkin Gulf Resolution to oppose direct U.S. military involvement in Vietnam. Fulbright to the rescue! Lyndon assured Bill he would send no troops to fight in Southeast Asia. He also told Fulbright he needed as unanimous a vote as he could get to convince Ho that the United States would not tolerate such attacks. Armed with these comments, Fulbright persuaded Nelson to drop his amendment. He voted "yes." So did most of the other apprehensive senators.

In the midst of this, LBJ told the nation on August 4 that the navy had retaliated with bombing raids against petroleum depots and naval bases. He pledged, "We seek no wider war." A Gallup poll indicated that 85 percent of the American people approved. Their representatives were duly impressed. On August 7, the House voted for the resolution 414–0, the Senate 89–2.

Anticipating the outcome, McNamara observed on August 6 that Congress would give "near-unanimous support for everything you may do in the future, and generally a blank-check authorization for further action." Johnson chuckled. "Like grandma's nightshirt, it covered everything."

No matter what else was going on, Johnson turned frequently to thoughts about the vice presidency. Speculation about whether the president would be compelled to run with his predecessor's brother made it a preoccupation of official Washington as well.

Lyndon had firm ideas about what a vice president should be. "He'll be loyal. He'll never run against you. He'll always support you. He'll take your platform. He'll be *your man.*" In short, he would be to LBJ as LBJ had been to JFK. "If he don't want to be my wife, he oughtn't to marry me."

That was not Robert Kennedy. He would be his own man, and he would not stay hitched. Lyndon would have to clear things with him. "When I make up my mind," he told his friend Jim Rowe, "I don't want to have to kiss the ass of a vice president."

The feeling was mutual. In May, Bobby mused that if LBJ were forced to take him as vice president, "It would be an unpleasant relationship. I would lose all ability to ever take any independent position." To be sure, "His reaction on a lot of things is correct. But I think he's got this other side of him and his relationship with human beings, which makes it difficult, unless you want to kiss his behind all the time."

Why, then, did RFK encourage talk about him as vice president? In part, it preserved his ability to pressure Johnson to enact Jack's programs. But that was not the main reason. He loved hearing that the president was "hysterical about how he's going to try to avoid having me." As Evan Thomas observed, "One can only conclude that RFK's raw motivation for positioning himself as a vice-presidential candidate was perverse." Had he known LBJ suspected his teleprompter malfunctioned on May 26 because of Kennedy sabotage, he would have been delighted.

Barry Goldwater's nomination ended any chance that Lyndon would be compelled to run with Bobby. Liberals would have to vote for LBJ. And RFK would not help counter Republican appeal to white Southerners and the backlashing Northerners. Lyndon figured out a diplomatic way of breaking the news to Bobby on July 29, but he did not take the hint to withdraw. Finally, LBJ settled on the expedient of eliminating all cabinet-level officials, ostensibly so they would focus on the people's business. RFK was sorry, sardonically, that he had brought colleagues down with him.

In fact LBJ had already ruled them out. The only cabinet member he considered was Robert McNamara. Impressed by his intelligence, energy, toughness, and commitment, LBJ really wanted him, but Bob had never run for office. McNamara had probably been a Republican before 1960, and he had been a corporate executive since 1945—not the usual routes to favor in the Democratic Party. On these counts, Democratic and AFL-CIO leaders opposed McNamara. Johnson did not feel he could impose his choice on them, so he turned to the Senate.

The only two serious contenders were both from Minnesota: Eugene McCarthy and Hubert Humphrey. Each had been loyal to LBJ in the past. Each owed him for favors. Neither had any love for the Kennedys.

Hubert had the edge. He was far more popular with organized labor and rank-and-file Democrats. Gene's chief supporters were Southerners, a minus in Lyndon's opinion. When John Connally advised him to choose McCarthy, Johnson retorted, "We're not going to carry any Southern states, John, and Humphrey has a lot more appeal in the other states [particularly] in the Midwest."

Thanks to McCarthy's support for tax breaks for oil and gas producers, "He's kind of regarded as a liberal renegade." Unsaid to Connally were two other drawbacks: RFK and his friends opposed Gene strongly, and he was far less pliable than Hubert.

LBJ strung along McCarthy anyway. He always kept his options open, and this would pressure Hubert to do whatever he wanted. The wisdom of this soon became plain.

During the summer of 1964, civil rights activists in Mississippi founded the Mississippi Freedom Democratic Party (MFDP) and held an integrated election for delegates to the Democratic Convention. They planned to ask the convention to seat them instead of the regular delegation, who were white segregationists committed to Goldwater. The specter of a Southern walkout and a swelling backlash flashed before Lyndon. He told Humphrey to arrange a compromise. To inspire Humphrey and intimidate the MFDP, LBJ made it clear that the vice presidency would hinge on the outcome. Failure, LBJ intimated, would force him to chose Gene McCarthy, favorite of the white Southern Democrats.

So when McCarthy pressed LBJ to confirm he was under serious consideration, saying that he would not mind a "no" so long as he was not dumped in the end like a rejected suitor, the game went on. That this might make a bitter enemy did not deter Lyndon.

As Humphrey began wrestling with the MFDP, Johnson sank into a despondency bordering on depression. It was caused by doubts that he could be president during a period of racial crisis.

Mississippi had been a knotty problem for LBJ throughout the summer of 1964. The Ku Klux Klan did not just violate the law there; Klansmen dominated many sheriff's offices and some highway patrol troops. Yet Lyndon could not freely exert federal power to purify local law enforcement. He could not give Southerners the impression that he would create an occupying force similar to the bluecoats during Reconstruction. That would call forth last-ditch resistance to the Civil Rights Act from the class he wanted to be counselors of reason and obedience. He must use the FBI carefully and precisely to deal with violence sanctioned and directed by Klan peace officers.

To do this, he had to deal with a power he called as sovereign as Mississippi: J. Edgar Hoover. The FBI director hated Martin Luther King and never missed a chance to describe the Civil Rights Movement as Communist inspired and led. Fortunately, Hoover had only contempt for the Klan, "a group of sadistic, vicious white trash." Playing on this, Lyndon persuaded him to send more FBI agents to Mississippi, buy informers within the KKK, expose Klan members in police forces, and go to the state himself to pressure the governor to purge the highway patrol of Klansmen. Johnson even talked Hoover into assigning agents as bodyguards for King when he was in Mississippi. More outbreaks of violence were prevented.

LBJ's determination to end the horrors of Mississippi got him an important concession from the major national civil rights groups. Trusting in his support, they accepted as genuine his fears of a white backlash and agreed to a moratorium on demonstrations until after the election.

Johnson also got help from Barry Goldwater. Appalled by KKK attacks on law and order, he pledged to do his part to prevent further violence. He would not campaign in Mississippi and Alabama, and he would never directly criticize the Civil Rights Act anywhere.

These developments gave Lyndon hope that the backlash would be negligible. To his dismay, he soon discovered that African Americans in New York and Mississippi neither trusted him to deliver support for them nor cared about catering to white sensitivity on civil rights.

In late June, rioting broke out in Harlem, New York. In late July, riots occurred in black neighborhoods in Rochester, New York. Lyndon overlooked clashes between white police officers and black residents in both places. Instead of looking for local causes, he picked up Hoover's refrain, blaming the riots on Communists. Then he wrote new verses. "A Texas oil millionaire messing around up in Harlem" was financing rioters "big," even supplying them with walkie-talkies. Extremist Republicans were trying to encourage a huge backlash, first by causing riots, then by accusing LBJ of rewarding crime with government handouts. He would have to maneuver carefully, standing firm against anarchy while refusing to deny these communities their share of poverty funds.

Were Communists manipulating the MFDP? According to Hoover, yes. Nevertheless, LBJ wanted to assure the MDFP that he believed all citizens should have the vote. He was ready to promise that only integrated delegations would be seated at the 1968 convention. This year MFDPers would be nonvoting delegates and get floor passes. The regular delegates would be seated only after swearing to support the national ticket. That might make them bolt, leaving the MFDP as the forecast of the future.

No deal. The insurgents were not the ministers, lawyers, and lobbyists LBJ usually wheeled and dealed; they were working-class blacks, habituated to standing up for their rights against vicious bigots and, like their charismatic spokesperson Fannie Lou Hamer, "sick and tired of being sick and tired." They scented victory, first before the credentials committee, then in the convention itself. The president feared their count was correct. Bobby would be on the bandwagon. Liberals would be eager to shaft him as always. And Democrats running for office in the North would not want to antagonize black voters. LBJ could not risk a fight in committee or on the floor.

Time for hardball. To keep abreast of MFDP tactics and contacts, Johnson had Hoover bug their rooms and meetings. His staff told the MFDP's attorney, Joseph Rauh, Jr., that his friend Hubert's fate hung in the balance. LBJ also enlisted Walter Reuther, head of the United Auto Workers (UAW), in the cause. Reuther told Rauh he could forget his fat retainer as the UAW's lawyer if the MFDP prevailed. Then he reminded Martin Luther King that this year his Southern Christian Leadership Conference had received $176,000 from the UAW. That would sink to nothing with no compromise.

Carrot and stick. Threat and promise. Lyndon's tactics worked—on Rauh and King but not on Hamer and her friends. Hoover's bugs revealed that Rauh and King could not move them. Humphrey and Reuther also struck out. What should have been a week of triumph for Lyndon, crowned by his nomination, had become a time on the cross of race and politics.

It got worse. Convinced that LBJ was toying with him, McCarthy gave notice that he was withdrawing from vice-presidential consideration. News of this would loosen Lyndon's hold on Hubert and his liberal friends. He pleaded with Gene not to tell the press. McCarthy made no promises. Everything was falling apart. Anguished, Johnson drafted a statement announcing he would not run for president.

After McCarthy broadcast his decision, a dispirited LBJ read his draft to George Reedy, his press secretary. "The times," he intoned, "require leadership about which there is no doubt and a voice that men of all sections and color can follow. I've learned, after trying very hard, that I am not that voice or that leader." He launched into a rambling list of reasons. He did not "want this power of the Bomb"; he did not "want these decisions I'm being required to make"—presumably a reference to Vietnam. Being president without carrying his own state and home section would be agony. Plus, "The Negroes will not listen to me. They're not going to follow a white Southerner."

The United States needed someone else. Reedy retorted that he must bear these burdens, because withdrawing "just gives the country to Goldwater." Replied Johnson, "I don't care." Then he went into a rant against the press, topping it off with charges that the South, the North, and the Negroes were against him.

During the next few hours, staffer Walter Jenkins, family friend A. W. Moursund, Dick Russell, and Lady Bird heard the same words. Russell bluntly told LBJ to stop acting like a spoiled child; he thought Johnson was more likely to swim the Atlantic Ocean than quit the race. The others feared that he would act impulsively and read his statement to the press. Bird's diary entry called these the hardest hours of her life. She assured him he would be a great leader, she forecast disaster for the country if he withdrew and Bobby or Barry became president, and she predicted he would be miserable if he left without achieving the rest of his domestic agenda. Unmoved, he told Moursand he would tell reporters he was quitting at 3:00 P.M.

At 2:31 P.M., Humphrey and Reuther called. They had a deal—not with MFDP delegates but with Rauh, King, and Roy Wilkins. Aaron Henry and Ed King, who had run for state offices in the MFDP election, would get at-large seats and votes. The rest would be nonvoting delegates. The regular delegation would have to sign loyalty oaths to be seated. Humphrey and Reuther rushed the deal before the credentials committee, implying that LBJ had approved it. Committee approval was rapid and unanimous, foreclosing a floor fight. Once this was a fait accompli, they let the MFPD delegation know.

The MFDP delegates were furious. Bitterness over what Robert Moses called "a back of the bus deal" sped many in the Movement on their way from civil rights to Black Power. Also embittered were most white delegates from Mississippi and Alabama; they walked out rather than swear loyalty. (Some of the members of the MFDP staged a walk-in and occupied vacant seats.) So what! To Lyndon what mattered was this: both groups were off center stage and other Southern delegations stayed put. Reinvigorated, he looked forward to accepting the nomination.

First, though, LBJ indulged in two vindictive acts. Angry at Humphrey's getting the glory for resolving the MFDP controversy, he anointed Senator Thomas Dodd of Connecticut as a possible vice president. Hubert twisted in the wind for two days. When his ordeal ended, the humiliation of McCarthy began. Johnson ordered him to nominate Humphrey. Gene never forgave Lyndon, and not long afterward, he told a close friend he might run an insurgent campaign in 1968.

Lyndon would not have cared. He had his party's nomination. Humphrey was under his thumb. Bobby would be preoccupied running for the Senate in New York. The poverty bill had passed. The Civil Rights Act was starting to work; the Deep South had settled into a sullen calm. South Vietnam, he hoped, would survive the next few months. Relations were stable between the United States and the USSR. He was running against a man who had eschewed civil rights and Vietnam as issues while still sounding like a dangerous extremist. There was a real chance for a monstrous landslide and monumental change.

The campaign was almost anticlimactic. Lyndon's margin in the polls never sunk lower than 60 percent for him and 40 percent for Goldwater. What concerned him was not whether he would win but by how much and how many Democrats he would sweep into office. LBJ needed an overwhelming mandate to dislodge Medicare from the House Appropriations Committee and cut federal aid to education free from entangling issues of federal–local and church–state relationships.

How could he secure this? He had two options: he could emphasize accomplishments since last November and pledge more ahead, or he could attack Goldwater as an extremist. Polls, his own and Gallup's, guided the decision.

Those filling out a White House survey in August had mixed feelings about Johnson's legislative record (especially civil rights) and lukewarm enthusiasm for Great Society plans. Thirty-four percent doubted the poverty program would work well; 38 percent felt his administration was doing only a "fair to poor" job; only 9 percent rated the administration as "excellent," with 44 percent grading it as "good." Other polls revealed that prospective voters had serious doubts about Goldwater's fitness to be president. Twenty-four percent described him as "reckless"; only 2 percent called LBJ that. Johnson's advisers were sure that echoing attacks Republican moderates had already made on Barry would widen that split. "Our main struggle," they argued, "lies not so much in the *for* Johnson but in the *against* Goldwater." "We ought to treat Goldwater not as an equal, who has credentials to be president, but as a *radical,* a preposterous candidate who would ruin this country and our future."

Lyndon applied this strategy with a vengeance. So did other Democrats. The Goldwater slogan "In your heart you know he's right" became bumper stickers reading "In your guts you know he's nuts" and "In your heart you know he might."

What Barry might do was shown in a series of TV ads. One became an instant classic. A young girl was tearing petals off a daisy and counting them. When she reached nine, another voice began counting down. A close-up of her eye became a mushroom cloud enveloping the screen. Then LBJ claimed we could live or we could die. "Vote for President Johnson," an announcer intoned. "The stakes are too high to stay home." The ad ran only once—as a paid commercial. Republican protests guaranteed it would be shown many times on news shows. LBJ complained piously about overzealous staffers who had approved it. Privately, he loved it.

Less notorious ads were as effective. A young woman was shown licking an ice cream cone, while the voice-over said that should Goldwater become president future cones might be radioactive. Less subtle were hands tearing up a Social Security card, as well as a cross burning while a Klansman said, "I like Barry Goldwater. He needs our help." Brilliantly shot, the ads were hugely successful. They were also something new.

Before 1964, presidential ads were upbeat, positive, and devoted to the man who paid for them. Opponents were never mentioned; their proposals were never directly attacked. LBJ pioneered the attack ad on the national level. His successful wielding of this weapon convinced others to do likewise.

Lyndon's speeches were more circumspect. The rhetorical question—"Whose thumb do you want on the button?"—was his specialty. His special emphasis was on mixing firmness and prudence, befitting a man of peace who would not give in to the Reds. On domestic matters he spoke glowingly but vaguely about an America where children would be safer, better fed, better educated, and would have more opportunities and where people of all regions, religions, and races would live together in productive unity. Specifics were usually avoided.

One exception became legendary. Lyndon was never reluctant to send Bird into a heckler's way; he reaped political advantage from her calm endurance. On a whistle-stop tour through the South, catcalls and signs like "Black Bird" marred her speeches. He met her train in New Orleans, then spoke to a large crowd. Inspired by her courage and commitment, he tossed aside prepared remarks, shucked his coat, loosened his tie, and launched into a stem-winding address. With sweeping gestures and fierce looks, LBJ laid bare how racism had held the South back politically, economically, socially, and culturally. That had to stop. He would do all he could to stop it.

When he sat down, his audience was silent for a long minute. Then the applause began, swelling and lasting as the crowd stood, cheering the president of all the people of the United States. Reporters judged it the greatest stump speech they had ever heard.

Ultimately, Lyndon did not carry Louisiana. He knew why; the place was "corrupt." But in the larger arena of the campaign, speaking heartfelt truths to white Southerners meshed with his more cautious addresses and his attack ads to serve his larger purpose.

Johnson's negative campaigning was aimed at winning moderate Republicans, who were receptive to attacks on Goldwater in particular and extremists in general. These voters, LBJ believed, would cancel out the white backlash against civil rights. Whenever he was asked by the press about it, he countered by referring to his "frontlash." As the race approached November, he realized that the frontlash could do more than just compensate for the loss of white votes; it might overwhelm the backlash. He kept accentuating the negative.

Meanwhile, Goldwater was frustrated by the lack of serious discussion of philosophical differences. He had important points to make about the burgeoning size of the federal government and the implications of its expansion for the American economy and the lives of individual citizens. His criticisms of the Tennessee Valley Authority (TVA) in Tennessee and Social Security in Florida were not quixotic foolishness or outright cruelty; Goldwater was straining to point out that the Democrats were corrupting the body politic by buying the votes of interest groups. As time grew short, he introduced an argument by conservative economist Milton Friedman: cutting federal taxes would stimulate more business activity and generate more than enough revenue to fund Social Security, balance the budget, and increase defense spending. When an actor named Ronald Reagan trumpeted this plan, he raised so much money that Goldwater could not spend it all before November 3. In contrast, coming from Goldwater it sank without a ripple—because, he bitterly realized, *he* had said it. Johnson had made him the issue.

At the end, Goldwater's campaign began to make coded warnings about the future of race relations. It also tried to return the favor by making Lyndon an issue. The most effective ad followed a white Lincoln Continental with Texas plates careening down country roads, beer cans flying out the driver's window. This recalling of press criticism about Lyndon's driving-and-drinking ranch tours stung the president. So did allusions to Bobby Baker and KTBC. Johnson hit back by telling journalists about two nervous breakdowns

Goldwater allegedly had, plus a paternity suit supposedly filed against him. He also leaked material from Goldwater's income tax returns, suggesting he had his elderly mother on the federal payroll.

The slinging of mud was already fast and furious when D.C. vice cops arrested Walter Jenkins on a morals charge on October 7. By October 14, major newspapers were ready to publish the details. Lyndon's first reaction was stunned disbelief. Then he wondered if the Republicans had entrapped Walter. The political implications were obvious: the Soviets had blackmailed gays in Britain, so his opponents would ask about possible breaches of national security as well as saying that here was more proof of corruption and immorality in the White House. Walter had to resign, for reasons of politics as well as for his health. Johnson also insisted that the FBI do thorough background checks on other presidential advisers. He sighed relief at the news that no one else was homosexual.

LBJ did not have to worry long about any major political fallout. Soon after the bumper stickers "Johnson for King Jenkins for Queen" appeared, the Politburo ousted Nikita Khrushchev. Then the Chinese detonated a nuclear device. Wryly, Johnson said, "The last piece of good news I've had, I guess, was . . . the Chinese Bomb." There was more truth than poetry in those words. Events in the USSR and the People's Republic of China brought the question of who should be in charge of foreign relations back to voters' minds. Walter's resignation also occurred, luckily, during an exciting World Series. When the nation went to the polls, LBJ's ordeal did not have a significant effect.

LBJ won big: 43,130,000 votes to 27,178,000 for Goldwater. The margin was the largest in history. In the electoral college, he got 486 votes to his opponent's 52. Barry Goldwater won only Arizona, his home state, and five Southern states: Alabama, Georgia, Louisiana, Mississippi, and South Carolina. He carried only 60 of the 435 congressional districts in the country. The Democrats gained two seats in the Senate, for a majority of 68–32. In the House, their bulge increased by thirty-eight, for a margin of 295–140. These gains and that mandate, according to White House congressional liaison Larry O'Brien, "provided us with an opportunity to move much more aggressively. . . . The road was just made much smoother."

On Election Day, LBJ could feel the tide rising and see the Great Society arriving. Surrounded by family and friends, getting and making phone calls of congratulations, he was exhilarated. Next came a sobering thought: "God, I hate for it to be over, because the hell starts then."

Living in the Middle of It: December 1964 to April 1965

Hell was located in Southeast Asia. Since early September, LBJ had been hearing that the North Vietnamese were stepping up aid to the Vietcong (VC). More bad news followed. A Defense Department estimate warned, "The odds are against the emergence of a stable government capable of effectively prosecuting the war"; constant threats of coups, plus rioting by Buddhists and student demonstrations continued to destabilize South Vietnam. "If you have a government that can't protect itself from the kids in the streets," mused Johnson, "what the hell can you do about an invading army?"

On November 1, VC attacked the Bien Hoa air base, killing five servicemen, wounding 76, and destroying 27 planes. The president chose not to respond on election eve after pollster Lou Harris assured him a majority of voters would approve of his delaying any retaliation. Afterward he did nothing because he feared the North Vietnamese would retaliate against other American installations and perhaps push the shaky government in Saigon over the brink.

This excuse would not work much longer. Doing nothing kept Americans targeted and let South Vietnam's decline continue. Decisions were overdue. Lyndon began the process by forming a National Security Council Working Group, chaired by William Bundy—Mac's brother and the Assistant Secretary of State for Far Eastern Affairs—and tasked with determining the U.S. options.

This working group did not consider negotiations viable. Nor did it scout the possibility of getting a government in that would invite us out. All alternatives were military. On November 21, they reported. The United States could retaliate by bombing North Vietnam for any spectacular Vietcong attack; or systematically and rapidly increase air strikes against the North; or gradually bomb first the Ho Chi Minh Trail and then targets in North Vietnam.

On December 1, the president heard from Mac Bundy, Rusk, and McNamara. Massive bombing was their solution. This offensive would have two phases: first, against infiltration routes in Laos and against North Vietnam as punishment for dramatic VC attacks; then gradually extended raids against targets in the North.

LBJ chose none of the above. During the campaign, he had secretly agreed to bombing infiltration routes. That could go forward. He would not approve anything else. Reasoning as he had after Bien Hoa, he forecast that the North Vietnamese Army (NVA) would strike back hard in the south against sustained attacks. Escalated conventional warfare might lead to Saigon's military and political collapse. South Vietnam had to bring order to the cities and fight insurgents in the country before intensive bombing of North Vietnam could begin. Once more, Johnson shied away from tough choices.

How much freedom of choice did he have? According to the vice president, he had a stunning amount. In January 1965, Hubert Humphrey told LBJ that his landslide left him in that rarest of positions, where one can do as one pleases. That being so, Hubert urged negotiations leading toward American withdrawal. In retrospect, his opinion is arresting. Lyndon said during the campaign that he did not think "we were ready for American boys to do the fighting for Asian boys. What I have been trying to do . . . [is] to get the Asian boys in Vietnam to do their own fighting with our advice and our equipment." Time had passed, with no signs that the South Vietnamese were doing any better—or that they would. If LBJ was as unconstrained as Humphrey believed, why did he not point out to Americans that the Asian boys were not defending their nation and announce that he was going to take the United States out of Vietnam?

The answer is that LBJ did not feel free to do whatever he pleased about Vietnam. It takes two willing participants to negotiate anything but unconditional surrender. Lyndon asked McNamara, rhetorically, why Ho Chi Minh would want to negotiate when he was winning. When Ho said "talks," his "terms" equaled immediate U.S. withdrawal. The Chinese fully supported his position. The

Johnson and McNamara. © Lyndon B. Johnson Library

Russians felt compelled to do the same. Lyndon's choice was limited and stark: fight or give up.

What would happen if the United States gave Indochina to the Communists? Here's Johnson's judgment: "There would follow in this country an endless national debate—a mean and destructive debate—that would shatter my presidency, kill my administration, and damage our democracy." To Lyndon, this was inevitable. He would have rejected the advice of all Kennedy holdovers in his administration and the Joint Chiefs of Staff. The spin Washington would put on this was already apparent in columns and cocktail party talk: he would "lay Vietnam off onto Kennedy's inexperience [and] immaturity." RFK would lead the charge against him. The battle following would doom the Great Society.

These were only the consequences for domestic politics and policies. More compelling to LBJ were concerns about the catastrophic impact on international relations. It would profoundly discourage our closest allies and dangerously encourage our most powerful enemies. Russia and China would try to take immediate advantage of our weakness. The result could be nuclear war. Thus Johnson could not let Ho unify Vietnam.

What remained open was the nature and timing of American involvement. What held LBJ back was his hope that he could still delay. The longer he could focus Congress on his legislative proposals, the better. Convinced that Capitol Hill could handle only one big issue at a time, and certain that war would take precedence over reform, he kept Vietnam on the back burner. The window of opportunity for a Great Society was small; it would close soon. He gambled that Southeast Asia would wait while he seized that chance.

The first Congress Lyndon served in had large Democratic majorities. Franklin Roosevelt had just been reelected by the greatest landslide in American history, yet by 1937 FDR's programs were stymied. Political capital could be gone with astonishing speed. "I've got a 16 million vote majority right now," Lyndon remarked, "and after one good fight in Congress, it would be down 2 million. Within a month, I could be at 8 million, and falling rapidly." Legislation had to be proposed and passed as soon as possible. After six months, he predicted, Congress would be sick of its rider and looking to buck him off. By the end of 1965, his capital would be spent, but the country would have gained the 105 bills he would introduce.

Another concern spurred him on. Lyndon respected the power of the Right. When the first teach-ins against the war began in April 1965, he told Undersecretary of State George Ball, "Don't pay any attention to what those little shits on the campuses do. The great beast is the reactionary elements in the country. Those are the people we have to fear."

Ball did not ask Johnson to explain who he was referring to, and the president chose not to flesh out his comments. It is worth filling in this blank. LBJ was not referring to extremist groups like the Klan or the far-Right John Birch Society. To him these were on the fringes and had only limited and local power. Nor was he thinking of those who voted for Goldwater. Grass-roots conservatives were in the minority in the country and would be preoccupied by their efforts to maintain control over the Republican Party. What Lyndon was talking about were powerful economic interests who were used to throwing their weight around and practiced at arguing that foreign and domestic crises were reasons to avoid expensive domestic reforms. He had listed some of these when he mused about publishing a Texas newspaper to Horace Busby right before JFK's murder. That night in Brussels he promised, "We'll take on the oil crowd, and the utilities, and the TMA [either the Texas Manufacturing Association, or the Texas Medical Association, or both, each of which had consistently opposed him], and all the fat cats," a category that included insurance companies, realtors, truckers, and highway contractors. These were the people who had stymied progressive legislation in Austin and had often succeeded in doing the same in Washington.

Recent proof of the power of these reactionaries could be found in California. LBJ had carried the state by nearly 1.3 million votes. That same day, Pierre Salinger, a staunch liberal, had lost the Senate race to Republican George Murphy, a Right-wing former actor, by 215,000 votes. Governor Pat Brown had campaigned long and hard to defeat Proposition 14, an initiative repealing California's Fair Housing law. Anyone who voted for Proposition 14 was a bigot, claimed Brown. Proposition 14 passed by 2 million votes, and the governor predicted, understandably, that he would have a tough campaign for reelection in 1966. Frontlash had worked for Lyndon against Goldwater in California. Backlash had swept aside fair housing. If California realtors could muster such a majority, other powerful interest groups might do the same against the Great Society.

The Right's potency meant that Lyndon could not rely as much on moderate Republicans. They were locked in combat with conservatives overrunning the GOP. Too much cooperation with LBJ on domestic matters could weaken them. They had to be more partisan and less liberal. This would make passing reforms more difficult.

The situation of Southern Democrats in Congress vis-à-vis the Right also complicated matters. Johnson had lost Alabama, Georgia, Louisiana, Mississippi, and South Carolina. He had won Arkansas, Florida, North Carolina, Tennessee, and Virginia only because of a record-setting 90-percent-plus black turnout for him. The only Southern state where he carried the white vote was Texas, where he had the home-field advantage. Southern Democrats had powerful enemies to their right, and Johnson was identified in Dixie with liberalism and civil rights. It would be tough for them to stick with him on Great Society votes.

Giving moderate Republicans and Southern Democrats the chance to focus on a war and put civil rights and the Great Society aside would have predictable results. They would do it. The same could be said about powerful interest groups, who had seen what California realtors got done during peace.

So Lyndon stalled all he could on Vietnam. If he had to commit American forces to Southeast Asia, he resolved to do it as quietly and as gradually as he could manage.

In February, news about Vietnam got worse. An attack on a U.S. base at Pleiku cost the U.S. army eight dead, over a hundred wounded, and ten helicopters. The president felt he had to retaliate. The target, an army barracks in North Vietnam, had been prese-lected, suggesting that the Pentagon felt an attack on Americans was inevitable. LBJ's response had the same inevitability. He told himself, though, that this was tit for tat, not the prelude to sustained bombing.

Concerned that the country was sliding into war, Mike Mansfield urged Johnson at a briefing of Congressional leaders on February 7 to negotiate rather than retaliate. He was the only one there who did. LBJ sought to isolate him further by identifying opposition to retaliation with placing troops in jeopardy. "They are killing our men while they sleep. . . . I can't ask our American sol-diers to fight with one hand tied behind their backs." Reprisal would show Hanoi that it "could not count on continued immunity if [it] persisted in aggression." He underscored his point with a Texas metaphor: "I have kept the shotgun over the mantel and the bullets in the basement for a long time now, but the enemy is killing my personnel and I cannot expect them to continue their work if I do not authorize them to take steps to defend themselves." He closed by saying the Soviets and the Chinese wanted no direct involve-ment in the conflict.

One day after ripping into Mansfield, Johnson escalated. He agreed to a series of bombing missions code-named Rolling Thunder. "We face a choice," he said, "of going forward or run-ning." The only question was how fast U.S. forces would go for-ward. House Minority Leader Gerald Ford pressed LBJ on whether raids would be restricted to retaliation for VC attacks. LBJ said no. He still claimed that this was not escalation and requested those present to avoid referring to Rolling Thunder as "broadening the war," even though it was. Keeping mum did not change the truth. All silence did was sow seeds of future credibility problems when other escalations followed.

Humphrey saw this danger and felt duty bound to spell it out to LBJ. He also thought the president might be receptive. As the two men talked on February 11, Lady Bird was surprised to hear Lyndon say something she thought he would confess only to her: "'I'm not temperamentally equipped to be Commander-in-Chief. . . . I'm too sentimental to give the orders.'" Hubert hoped to play on those emotions.

On February 15, Humphrey wrote the president a heartfelt letter. Since this could be among "the most fateful decisions of your Administration," LBJ must make "a cogent, convincing case if we are to enjoy sustained public support." In the two world wars, well-informed support had been essential. The people also understood about Korea. That just was not so now.

The vice president was pessimistic that even full discussion of the issues would help if "we find ourselves leading from frustration to escalation and end up short of a war with China but embroiled deeper in fighting in Vietnam over the next few months." Then "political opposition will steadily mount." It would spring from "Democratic liberals, independents, [and] labor." It would spread "at the grassroots across the country."

This was unwelcome advice. Then Humphrey made things worse for himself. He spoke publicly about the hope for negotiations. He also told Fulbright that military advisers should be replaced with civilians helping villagers. Fulbright passed this on to Lyndon, who tartly replied, "In a choice between Humphrey and General [Maxwell] Taylor as our major strategist I am disposed toward Taylor." Humphrey was ordered to speak only on domestic reform. LBJ went on to exclude him from important deliberations on Vietnam, limit his access to the Oval Office, and let him know his opinion on any subject was now suspect. Lesson learned, the vice president toed the official line.

Punishment was only one reason for putting Hubert into "limbo." Johnson wanted to point to him as an example. The president believed he had to discourage dissent in his administration. Though he boasted that he wanted to hear what his people believed "with the bark on," in truth he craved unanimity. "A government that's divided" is, he told Mac Bundy, "the greatest danger we face here." When internal debates leaked out, they would inspire questions in the United States about his policies and encourage North Vietnam's expectations of victory.

Silencing Humphrey did not, however, make the warning unfounded. LBJ remembered that popular discontent with Korea came about because of a bloody military stalemate. He anticipated that this might also be the result in Vietnam if, as he suspected, fighting dragged on for an extended period. Humphrey was predicting the spread of antiwar sentiment much more quickly. Was he right? Did it matter?

Polls in February showed that 75 percent of Americans favored a negotiated settlement. The clarity of this finding was blurred by other results: 68 percent felt the Vietcong would violate a ceasefire, 93 percent approved of air raids on North Vietnam, and 79 percent believed American withdrawal would lead to a Communist Vietnam and that it was very important to prevent that. Almost half supported sending a large number of troops if necessary; 60 percent approved of LBJ's handling of the situation. The American people were as conflicted about Vietnam as he was. Telling them more would not resolve these conflicts. They would lean toward the conclusion LBJ described to McNamara on February 26: "I don't think anything is as bad as losing, and I don't see any way of winning." Such national irresolution would impede the country's foreign policy while a Great Society went by the boards.

Lyndon did make one bow toward providing more details. On February 27, he had the State Department issue a white paper entitled *Aggression from the North: The Record of North Viet-Nam's Campaign to Conquer South Viet-Nam*. The report included some bogus evidence of arms shipments by sea cooked up by CIA agents. LBJ did not check the sources. He wanted the white paper to show his willingness to explain why we were in Vietnam.

Still, that was not his major preoccupation. He would put his hand to the plow, whatever the public reaction might be. "Now we're off to bombing those people," he said on February 26. "We're over that hurdle." Four days later Rolling Thunder began.

The Pentagon wanted a "swift squeeze": massive raids destroying all targets before the NVA organized defenses. The president opted for a "slow squeeze." Gradual escalation made Soviet or Chinese intervention less likely. It had worked in Cuba in 1962; perhaps it would work again. Also, wholesale destruction might cause continued resistance and aggression, while limited damage might lead Hanoi to back off to avoid losing its "ten years of work" reconstructing the country since the French left. It was a slender hope, but one Lyndon felt he must pursue.

Another advantage to squeezing slowly and carefully was the preservation of control over sorties in Lyndon's hands. Military historians have criticized his close involvement in tactical decisions on targets and missions as intrusive and inappropriate. LBJ saw this differently. He remembered how in November 1950 the Truman administration had paid no attention to Chinese warnings about American military operations close to the Yalu River. The price paid for that had been massive attacks by the Chinese army and a stalemated war. Johnson was determined to avoid giving China any provocations whatsoever in this war; thus, he had to be in complete charge of the squeeze.

Whatever the squeeze, the Joint Chiefs wanted part of a marine expeditionary brigade moved to Danang to protect U.S. aircraft from a "fairly substantial" number of VC nearby. Lyndon resisted at first and asked McNamara if helicopter patrols and fighter strikes would protect the base. Bob did not think so. "I'm scared to death of putting ground forces in," responded Johnson, "but I'm *more* frightened about losing a bunch of planes from lack of security."

Ambassador Maxwell Taylor cabled his opposition from Saigon. Once troops were "in country," resisting reinforcements would be very difficult. The protectors themselves would need protecting. That would include offensive operations. The United States could get in the same fix the French had.

Two weeks earlier LBJ had preferred Taylor over Humphrey. Now Taylor was displaced by William Westmoreland, the general commanding the Military Advisory Command, Vietnam (MACV). On March 8, 3,500 Marines landed. Lyndon had McNamara minimize press coverage to gain a day or two before "a lot of headlines" appeared. He unburdened himself to Bird: "I can't get out, and I can't finish with what I have got. And I don't know what the hell to do!"

To Lady Bird, it was obvious that "foreign affairs devour [Lyndon's] days and nights." She was not surprised. "The problems are harder to solve than domestic affairs." Then she added a telling insight: "He takes less joy" in foreign policy.

LBJ was a happy warrior during legislative campaigns. Decisions on Vietnam were avoided or approached with trepidation; in contrast, he told domestic aides not to party too long on inauguration night because they would be hitting the ground running in the morning. "Do it now. Not next week. Not tomorrow. Not later this afternoon. Now." His chief domestic adviser, Joe Califano, observed later that his assistants internalized this attitude or they left.

Decisions on Vietnam were the exclusive province of a few advisers deliberating in secret. Not so domestic matters: When LBJ began orchestrating the Great Society, he created fourteen task forces. These were composed of academics from leading universities and people from business, labor, and community-interest groups. He wanted, recalled assistant Marvin Watson, those who "were powerfully influential and who were not afraid to request as much funding as the legislation required." As they deliberated, Johnson prodded the federal bureaucracies for input. They were also responsible for drafting bills.

By early 1965, Johnson's commissions began reporting to the congressional leadership and to chairs and ranking members of committees. At these meetings bills were finalized. Watson explained the purpose of this. Before bills reached Capitol Hill, there was agreement among "significant national constituencies as well as powerful members of Congress."

Next came the discussion of bills by other senators and members of Congress at the White House. This let the president construct a broader consensus and learn who would oppose and why. That prepared his staff to lobby bills through to passage.

During this legislative stage, LBJ limited his direct involvement, reasoning he would be more effective if reserved for crucial moments. This did not mean he had no contact with most members. To the contrary: each session, he worked his way through the entire membership of the House and the Senate, staying in touch on matters of patronage and favors. Whenever he needed to intervene with someone, he already had a personal connection. In most observers' opinion, no president ever worked harder than Lyndon Johnson at maintaining close business and social relations with Congress.

Johnson insisted that his staff do the same. They had these orders: "Become their friends. Socialize with them. . . . Let them know that you are their man in the White House. Be ready and willing to do favors for them: to help them get an answer for any problem they might have with any agency . . . ; and to be there for them whenever they need you." Then "they will always know that you are their friend and whether they realize it or not, they will feel beholden to you." This did not always mean a "yes" vote, but they might not work to oppose a measure and they might be absent at crucial times. "Believe me," LBJ closed, "it works."

Making nice did not mean Lyndon and his men would not play hardball. "Politics," Califano learned, "was not Ping-Pong." It could be a street fight, and the president was the toughest guy on the block. "The applicable moral maxim then became not simply whether the end justified the means, but rather what means did a particular end justify." LBJ once had the Department of Justice string out a secret grand jury probe of two senators until he got their votes. And when Senator John McClellan held up the bill creating the Department of Transportation, Johnson told Califano to leak that he was doing it for personal gain. It was untrue, but "you just let [him] deny it." The bill went to the floor.

Johnson pressured Congress in other ways as well. He always beat the hyperbolic and informational drums for his legislation. Get a simple message on radio and television and in the newspapers: "Then that will help us when we are going to shove through in the end." So "compensatory education"—federal funds for poor schoolchildren—would do wonders for fighting poverty. Medicare and Medicaid would bring "the healing miracle of modern medicine" to all Americans, not just the elderly. A federal guarantee of voting rights would give blacks the "most powerful instrument ever devised by men for breaking down injustice." Americans were in the dark about conditions in Vietnam and alternatives there. LBJ put them there, and kept them uninformed. On domestic matters, if he had his way every citizen would know the details of pending legislation and all the reasons to want it enacted.

In both foreign and domestic affairs, the president believed people paid attention to results rather than the tactics used to achieve them. According to Mac Bundy, this was one of "the extraordinary qualities of Lyndon Johnson." He thought "It's nobody's business what you have to do to get a law; if you get the law, that does the job." But, added Bundy, "that isn't true really, and he found it out to his great pain later."

So focused was LBJ on official Washington that he did not feel a seismic shift in attitudes elsewhere. On campuses and within intellectual elites, he would discover an insistence on pure means as well as noble ends. He would also find a feeling that wheeling and dealing—the "old" politics—corrupted the best of goals. His greatest strength was about to become a significant weakness.

To the extent that Lyndon was aware some questioned his ideas about ends and means, he dismissed it as the resentment that those who could not showed toward those who could. To refute them, he would point to the accomplishments of the first session of the 89th Congress.

The record is stunning. LBJ's achievements defeat biographers who write volumes much longer than this; there is no way they could receive full description and analysis. For example, discussing the Elementary and Secondary Education Act (ESEA) only scratches the surface of what his administration did for American education. There were funds for scholarships and work-study programs for college students. There was an act improving health professions education. Another benefited medical libraries. A third and fourth created the National Endowment for the Humanities and the

National Endowment for the Arts. Head Start, a program for poor preschool children, was founded and funded.

Take health care. Medicare and Medicaid loom largest, but other legislation funded research into the causes and cures of heart disease, cancer, and strokes. Another act expanded basic research on mental health and facilities for treatment. Another provided for children's medical assistance. Another increased vocational rehabilitation programs.

LBJ persuaded Congress to commit $1.75 billion to the War on Poverty for fiscal 1966, a sum that seemed sufficient to him (though not to Shriver, who estimated the program would soon need $10 billion a year). In addition, Congress raised Social Security benefits by 7 percent. It funded programs for Appalachia and for regional development. The Housing and Urban Development Department was created. An Omnibus Housing Act funded rent supplements and assisted the construction of housing for persons with low and moderate incomes. To make Americans safer, the administration won passage of the Law Enforcement Assistance Act, a law creating the National Crime Commission, and one stepping up federal involvement in drug control.

Lyndon and his staff shepherded through Congress pathbreaking environmental legislation. Lady Bird inspired the Highway Beautification Act. The White House developed legislation on air pollution—imposing restrictions on auto exhausts, funding research into smog reduction, and allocating more money to mass transit—and on water pollution—devising federal standards and extending them to local and state governments.

LBJ also took up immigration reform. The initiative for this came from urban Democrats in Congress, who wanted to lower discriminatory quotas on immigration from southern and eastern Europe. The president seized the opportunity. The administration's bill reduced the number allowed yearly from most countries in the Western Hemisphere to 120,000, while raising quotas from parts of Europe, Asia, and Africa to 170,000. More people from Mediterranean countries and eastern European nations and significantly greater numbers from Asia immigrated. Close relatives of native-born and naturalized citizens were permitted entry without counting against the statutory limit of 290,000 immigrants per year. This jumped annual legal immigration to the United States to around 400,000 and increased the diversity of the nation's population.

All these acts were designated "landmark achievements" by Johnson's staff. They omitted foreign aid and general operating appropriations, regarding as routine what JFK had trouble getting through. The staff also left out the Freedom of Information Act. They did not guess that granting citizens easier access to federal files and limiting government wiretaps would be among LBJ's most enduring legacies.

President Johnson regarded the 89th Congress as the most productive and consequential in American history and boasted, "They've done more than they did in Roosevelt's Hundred Days." Three laws were dear to his heart. "Every guy that votes for Medicare and education. . . . his grandchildren are going to say, 'My grandpa was in the Congress that enacted these two.'" The Voting Rights Act of 1965 was the third. The enactment of these three acts fulfilled the promises he made to Lady Bird, Horace Busby, and Jack Valenti during the first twenty-four hours of his presidency.

Mention education and health, and Lyndon stomped on the verbal accelerator. "I'll go a hundred million or a billion on health or education. I don't argue about that any more than I argue with Lady Bird buying flour. You got to have flour and coffee in your house. . . . I'll spend the goddamned money." He could see cutting back on "some tanks" but not on education and health.

Federal aid to education had been on liberals' minds and on every president's agenda since the Second World War. The three R's—race, religion, and Reds—prevented action.

Thanks to the Civil Rights Act of 1964, race was no longer a factor. Northern congressmen had balked at funding segregated schools in the past; the law now excluded all such from federal funds, so none of Washington's money would find its way there.

Parochial schools had also vexed proponents of federal aid to education. Johnson had two advantages. Unlike JFK, he was not Catholic, so he could not be accused of trying to favor his religion's schools. He and his staff also saw the opening presented by a series of Supreme Court decisions approving aid to *parochial* students. Shrewdly, Lyndon mandated in this bill that only *poor* students would receive federal individual funds. He could then argue that this was equitable and beneficial for the whole society. This cancelled out the objections to religion.

"Reds" was shorthand for interference by federal bureaucrats in matters traditionally left to local independent school districts. Often, "interference" was replaced by "dictation"—of curriculum, classrooms, buildings, construction, boundaries, and whatever else excited apprehension. Johnson and his advisers disarmed this opposition by letting the school districts spend the grants as they saw fit. Liberals objected, arguing that this put the solution of the problem in the hands of the institutions that caused it. They wanted to amend the bill, either by restricting aid to poor districts or by allowing expenditures only on poor students. But LBJ was doubtless correct when he reasoned that even this Congress would see these changes as attacks on the autonomy of local districts and refuse to pass the bill. The House and Senate endorsed his strategy by approving ESEA by comfortable margins.

Elated, the president traveled back to Johnson City to sign it at his grade school, in front of a few of his teachers and some of his students from Cotulla and Houston. They listened while he repeated a lesson he had often taught: "As the son of a tenant farmer, I know that education is the only valid passport from poverty."

Schemes for helping the elderly pay for hospital care had been kicking around Congress for nearly three decades. Harry Truman had introduced legislation; so had liberal Democrats in every session since 1957. Polls showed that adding hospital insurance to Social Security was popular, but no bill came close to passing. The American Medical Association (AMA) stigmatized this as "socialized medicine." This was AMA shorthand for government control over doctors and hospitals leading directly to a sharp decline in the quality of treatment and a drastic diminution of American freedom. Large insurance companies added their own adjectives. It was unwarranted interference with private enterprise and market imperatives that would drive them out of business without assisting the elderly. Representative Wilbur Mills of Arkansas, the chairman of the House Ways and Means Committee, and his conservative colleagues stressed another drawback. They buried the bills because they feared the program would be ruinously expensive. Liberal eloquence and popular approval for the principle could not overcome the opposition of powerful interest groups and Mills's fiscal objections.

November 1964 changed the odds. The presence of sixty-five more Democrats in the House, most of them liberal, convinced LBJ that some Medicare bill would pass. Wilbur Mills could count, too. The chairman became a proponent of Medicare. Both favored a conservative approach to legislation, limiting coverage and eligibility rather than pushing for a comprehensive plan.

The initial bill covered only hospital care (60 days), nursing home care (180 days), and home health visits (240 days) for recipients of Social Security over age sixty-five. A small payroll deduction, plus employer contributions, financed it. Doctors' fees remained uncovered. Paying those, the president reasoned, would call forth AMA charges of socialized medicine. Insurance companies would object, but the limited plan would make them less vociferous.

What LBJ and Mills did not expect were Republican and AMA alternatives. Taken together, these two proposals covered both doctors' and hospitals' fees, either by federally paid voluntary insurance policies (the Republicans) or by an expansion of an existing welfare program administered by the states (AMA). Neither required the creation of a new fund because both restricted eligibility to the low-income elderly. Most on Social Security would not receive anything, but the poorest would get more than from the administration's bill. This alternative was unacceptable to Johnson. Backed by a majority swelled by fifty-eight votes from new Democrats, he defeated it.

Now Mills became Medicare's hero. Lyndon was cheerleader, urging him to speed up. Delay, LBJ warned, would "get the *doctors* organized. Then they get the *others* organized." Bills that lay around in committee were like dead cats on the porch: "They stink and they stink and they stink."

Mills responded by devising a three-tier system: hospital insurance would be covered by Social Security; voluntary insurance policies to pay doctors' fees would be funded out of general revenues; and those who already received welfare payments would be covered by Medicaid, a program run by the states. The federal government would match each state's funding for Medicaid. That gave the administration the advantage of not having to seek appropriations for it each year, but it injected an element of budget uncertainty. Lyndon shrugged off fiscal concerns. Told insurance for doctors' bills would probably cost $500 million a year, he reacted, "Is that all? Do it. Move that damn bill out now, before we lose it."

The president worried more about keeping certain provisions out of the bill. Some congressmen feared doctors and hospitals might use guaranteed payments to raise their charges. They proposed a schedule of fees. That, Lyndon knew, would spark desperate resistance from the AMA and jeopardize the bill's passage, and a ceiling on fees might cause doctors and hospitals to refuse to treat Medicare/Medicaid patients. Medical participation in the programs was voluntary, and Johnson did not assume compliance. His bill allowed hospitals "reasonable costs." Doctors could charge "customary fees," based on "billing history." That should stifle fears of the impact of "socialized medicine" on incomes and profits.

Medicare passed the House by 110 votes. Its progress through the Senate was more protracted. The White House had to deal with about 500 amendments. Ultimately, Medicare became law. Lyndon signed it at the Truman Library. His predecessor received the first pen he used to scrawl his name.

Work on the Voting Rights Act did not start with the appointment of a task force. LBJ simply picked up the phone on December 14, 1964, and directed Acting Attorney General Nicholas Katzenbach to draft a bill without delay.

This news dismayed Katzenbach. His staff was preoccupied with figuring out enforcement procedures for the Civil Rights Act of 1964. Besides, the U.S. Constitution assigned determination of who could vote to the states. A constitutional amendment federalizing voter registration, he suggested, might be best. Lyndon's reaction was swift: "How can we beat it? Can we beat that some way?" A constitutional amendment was not his preferred strategy. Nevertheless, he asked Katzenbach to draft one. The acting attorney general formed two committees: one drafting a law with an amendment, the other one without.

The next day Martin Luther King pressed for voting rights legislation in 1965. He would soon begin demonstrations in Selma, Alabama, a small city with a black majority where only 1.9 percent of adult African-Americans were registered. This would make the case for federal intervention. The president replied that his first priority was Great Society laws: "I think in the long run they'll help Negroes more, as much as a voting rights bill." Eventually he would present such legislation to Congress, but not during this session. "I need the votes of the Southern bloc to get these other things through. And if I present a voting rights bill, they will block the whole program. So it's just not the wise and the politically expedient thing to do."

Considered together, these conversations reveal LBJ's preparations on civil rights for 1965. Given his sense that the clock was ticking on reform, he would not risk a filibuster and the consequent delays that would narrow his window of opportunity for the Great Society. He did not want to promise MLK that voting rights would come up late in the session; that might not happen, and he did not want to be wounded politically by appearing to break his word. He was willing, however, to commit himself in principle to guaranteeing black citizens' right to vote in the State of the Union address.

The Justice Department had to have bills ready to send to Capitol Hill so LBJ could respond to any crisis without delay. Fire hoses and police dogs in Birmingham had led to the 1964 act. It was possible that the SCLC could manage events in Selma in a similar fashion. Lyndon even suggested that King try to do this. "If you can find the worst conditions you can run into," and broadcast them widely through the media, and from the pulpits, and in meetings, "pretty soon the fellow that didn't do anything but drive a tractor will say, 'That's not right. That's not fair.'" When that happened, it "will help us when we are going to shove it through in the end." That "will be the greatest breakthrough of anything. . . . It'll do things that even that '64 Act couldn't do."

Selma was the worst. That no one was killed in early March by the savage beatings given demonstrators by Dallas County deputies and state policemen was miraculous. James Rebb, a Unitarian minister from Boston, was murdered as he walked to a meeting one night. Selma pushed the Marines landing in Vietnam to page two. The reaction was what Johnson predicted: polls indicated that men and women all over the country responded by saying, "That's not right."

This did not impel Johnson into an immediate response. Aware of how potent the enduring resentment among white Southerners of the role the occupying Union Army played during Reconstruction, he was determined to give present-day demagogues no opening to claim he was reprising policies of the 1860s and 1870s. If he simply ordered federal troops to Alabama to restore order and protect demonstrators, Southern whites would resent and resist racial reconciliation for decades. LBJ had to avoid letting George Wallace pose as a martyr to federal tyranny. At the same time, he had to warn Martin Luther King against defying a federal court's injunction prohibiting a march from Selma to Montgomery. Lyndon and his staff had a series of tense conversations and meetings with all parties to the Selma struggle.

As days slipped by, pressure mounted. Congressional Republicans threatened to introduce their own legislation; so did Mike Mansfield. Pickets circled the White House chanting, "LBJ, just you wait! See what happens in '68!" The president saw the justice in one complaint: "If we can send [troops] into Vietnam, we can send them in to protect Americans . . . who are being beat up here." He was willing to talk with young SNCC demonstrators who were sitting in at the White House. To his dismay they did not want to speak to him.

Patience finally bore fruit: King obeyed federal injunctions, and Wallace asked for federal troops to protect the marchers. Feeling that the moment was right, LBJ asked to address a joint session of Congress on March 15 to describe his bill and comment on Selma.

That speech was the best of his life. Drafted by Richard Goodwin in less than twenty-four hours, edited by the president, who mastered it so fully he was untroubled by the absence of a teleprompter, it was the quintessence of American ideals. Equal rights for African-Americans were central to "the values and the purposes and the meaning of our beloved nation." That was more important than "our growth or abundance, our welfare or our security." Using the cadences of St. Paul's letter to the Corinthians, he exhorted, "Should we defeat every enemy, should we double our wealth and conquer the stars, and still be unequal to this issue, then we will have failed as a people and as a nation." There could be no arguing with the right to vote. "Yet the harsh fact is that in many places in this country men and women are kept from voting simply because they are Negroes." That "is wrong—deadly wrong." And "their cause must be our cause too. Because it is not just Negroes, but really all of us, who must overcome the crippling legacy of bigotry and injustice." Then Lyndon Johnson paused, riveting attention on him. He spoke four words slowly, precisely, and strongly, chiseling them into national memory.

"And—we—shall—overcome."

The chamber exploded in applause. Hundreds of miles away, Martin Luther King cried. Even farther from Washington, Richard Russell felt the rod of history, yet thought it was the finest political speech he had ever heard.

Lyndon was not finished. Rights just started the struggle for national redemption. Opportunities must be created, too. He recalled those he taught in Cotulla: "You never forget what poverty and hatred can do when you see its scars on the hopeful face of a young child." At that time, he had not guessed he would have the chance to help their sons and daughters and others like them. "But now I do have that chance—and I'll let you in on a little secret." Once more he paused. Again he spoke slowly, precisely, and strongly.

"I—mean—to—use—it!"

The hall erupted once more. When he got back from Capitol Hill, there were no more pickets around the White House.

Encouraged by the overwhelming applause for his speech, Lyndon tried to hurry Congress along. That sixty-six senators were willing to be cosponsors suggested that the filibuster would be a small bump in the road. He hoped for a law by Easter Sunday.

Those expectations were dashed. Senate Republicans were tired of Everett Dirksen's bartering their votes for favors for him from Johnson. That slowed things down. House Republicans, urged on by Minority Leader Gerald Ford, spent days attacking LBJ as a hypocrite who had built his career opposing civil rights until it was expedient to switch sides. The president publicly shrugged off these attacks: past mistakes he had made were hardly an issue in 1965. Privately, the charges of dishonesty and deviousness were troubling because they echoed a rising chorus on Vietnam. Lyndon was too intelligent not to grasp how much trouble distrust could cause. He was concerned that the moment of outrage at Selma would fade and that passing legislation would become much more difficult.

Meanwhile, liberal Democrats wanted to add provisions outlawing state and local poll taxes. In the House they were successful. In the Senate the administration beat them 49–45. Johnson sighed with relief. He feared that intruding on state and local taxing powers might be ruled unconstitutional, and he worried that it would fuel anger against Washington's centralizing and "tyrannizing" tendencies. The Senate and House conference to reconcile differences dragged into the summer. A new fear troubled LBJ: what if riots like last summer's erupted in cities? That might jeopardize voting rights. Finally, he persuaded a reluctant Martin Luther King to support the Senate bill. King preferred legislating against poll taxes, but he was moved by Lyndon's concerns about the possible consequences of delay. By a vote of 328–74, the House removed the poll tax clauses from its bill; the Senate approved the changes 78–19. The president signed the new law on August 6, praising it as "a triumph for freedom as huge as any victory that has ever been won on any battlefield."

For the South these words were true. By the end of 1966, the only states with less than 50 percent of their black citizens on voting rolls were Georgia, Louisiana, and Virginia—each with 47 percent signed up—and Mississippi with 33 percent. A year later, only Mississippi fell below 50 percent, and there the total had reached 45 percent, a level unimaginable during the Freedom Summer of 1964. By 1968, Mississippi was at 59 percent, and the average for the eleven Confederate states was 62 percent. The crumb of 1957 had become a whole cake. Lyndon Johnson, accused then of gutting that law to serve his own ends, fulfilled his promise to return to the issue and delivered a law that lived up to expectations.

One morning in February 1965, after Lyndon stayed up late to learn how a bombing mission went, Lady Bird wrote in her diary, "It was a tense and shadowed day, but we'll probably have to learn to live in the middle of it—for not hours or days, but years." By August 1965, the Johnsons had lived in that tense middle for half a year. LBJ's record on domestic legislation was beyond triumphant. To him, it was unequaled. When historian William Leuchtenberg said that the 89th Congress was arguably the most significant ever, LBJ retorted, "No it isn't. It isn't arguable." Observing her husband as he contemplated the Great Society legislation of 1965, Bird recorded Lyndon was "like a man riding on a crest of achievement and success."

Beneath that wave LBJ felt Vietnam's undertow. Did he foresee the tide turning? Did he fear it would keep receding for the rest of his life?

10

Looking for Light:
April to September 1965

Lyndon Johnson simply did not know how to deal with the North Vietnamese. He hated facing this fact. So he often tried to shoehorn them into familiar categories.

In April, LBJ offered Hanoi a chance to stop more suffering and death and avoid the destruction of what it had achieved since the Geneva Conference of 1954. If it guaranteed South Vietnam's independence, the United States would spend $1 billion to develop Indochina. "The vast Mekong Delta," he rhapsodized, "can provide food and water and power on a scale to dwarf even our own TVA. . . . The wonders of modern medicine can be spread through villages where thousands die every year from lack of care. Schools can be established to train people in the skills that are needed to manage the process of development." Caught up in the majesty of bringing the Great Society to Vietnam, Lyndon predicted to Bill Moyers, "Ho will never be able to say 'no' to this offer."

That assumed Ho Chi Minh was like American doctors, opposed in principle to "socialized medicine," yet willing in practice to settle for guaranteed fees they had the freedom to raise. It guessed that Hanoi's Politboro would be like local school districts, fuming about federal interference while drooling at the thought of the money. Johnson even wishfully likened the North Vietnamese to senators filibustering: they began with strong, principled words and put up resistance during long sessions, then resolve weakened and negotiation, compromise, and acquiescence followed. Maybe, he speculated, the same would happen in Vietnam.

It did not. Ho said "no." His price for peace was the evacuation of U.S. troops and the termination of American influence. He would not settle for less than a unified Vietnam under a Communist government.

LBJ claimed not to be surprised. When he looked back on 1964 during a press conference in late April 1965, he observed that it was clear "our restraint was viewed as weakness; our desire to limit conflict was viewed as prelude to our surrender." And in early June he pointed out to Mike Mansfield, "We think they are winning. Now, if *we* think they are winning, you can imagine what *they* think." A week later, he told Senator Birch Bayh of Indiana he did not blame Ho for rejecting the offer. After beating Goldwater by 15 million votes, he was not going to let him name half the cabinet. "They're winning. Why would they want to talk? All the talk would do is get them to give up something they're going to win."

Therefore, the United States would have to convince the North Vietnamese that they were not going to win. That seemed obvious, yet Lyndon shrank back from saying this to himself or others because what he had learned about the enemy gave him no cause for optimism about military victory. Sometimes he admitted to despair. "They hope they can wear us out," he told Bayh. "And I really believe they'll last longer than we do." He had reasons. "One of their boys gets down in a rut and he stays there for two days without water, food, or anything and never moves. Waiting to ambush somebody. Now an American, he stays there about twenty minutes and, God damn, he's got to get him a cigarette!" Soon afterward, he returned to the theme of North Vietnamese toughness with McNamara. Nobody, he complained, could come up with a plan "that gives me much hope of doing anything, except just praying and gasping to hold on during monsoon [season] and hope they'll quit." That was not enough, because "I don't believe they're *ever* going to quit." So somehow the United States had to win, although "I don't see . . . that we have any . . . plan for a victory—militarily or diplomatically."

Confronted with powerful and uncompromising opponents on Capitol Hill who welcomed the chance to beat his brains out, Lyndon would have shrugged, accepted defeat, and moved on to another bill. But that he could not do in this case. Aggression had to be resisted, or there would be more, this time from the much more formidable Russians and Chinese.

At the same time, though, Vietnam could not be a no-holds-barred fight to the finish. That, he was certain, would bring the

Chinese for sure and the Russians perhaps into the conflict. He could have a nuclear confrontation on his hands, like the one three years earlier over the missiles in Cuba. The insertion of American troops and the application of military power must be gradual and restrained. That dovetailed with the imperatives of domestic politics. Any rapid, obvious escalation would finish any chance of adding to the legislative triumphs of the 89th Congress's first session.

When the Joint Chiefs pressed LBJ during early summer to dramatically raise the number of troops in Vietnam, go on the offensive, and activate units in the Army Reserves and the National Guard, he responded cautiously. Putting Reserve and Guard units on active duty was too politically controversial; by signaling we were in a war that act would jeopardize the prospects for domestic reform. For similar reasons, he refused to countenance a swift, massive reinforcement of American troops. He limited the augmentation to numbers that would increase the MACV's strength to 125,000. When he permitted offensive operations, he did it with little fanfare and no great expectations. Far from predicting progress toward victory, he explained his decisions this way: "If you *don't* put them in, you're going to lose substantially what you have. . . . This is . . . a holding action." And it was a holding action he had to execute. A deserter from the 325th NVA regiment had revealed the presence of that elite force in the south and enabled CIA analysts to predict accurately the timing and location of a major offensive in late summer. U.S. troops would have to be ready to help Army of the Republic of Vietnam (ARVN) forces to repel these attacks. But while LBJ was willing to add more soldiers and approve their involvement in defending themselves and counterattacking in force, he went no further. Calling up the reserves was out; the USSR and China would feel compelled to respond, and the domestic political fallout would be toxic. LBJ had no option but heavier draft calls and gradual escalation of force. As he bitterly recognized, he did not know how far he would have to go. Nor did McNamara or the Joint Chiefs. "What human being knows?" The answer: nobody.

Others would answer Lyndon's poignant question another way. To "how many," they would respond "none." Johnson and his advisers were surprised and dismayed by the vocal opposition to United States fighting in Vietnam that swiftly arose on U.S. campuses during March. They worried about an echoing chorus from senators, congressmen, and some pundits. Robert Kennedy's private and public reservations were especially troubling.

Lyndon could explain RFK's opposition: the New York senator was undercutting his brother's successor to serve his ambitions. For the others, he had a different explanation. In early April, he observed to Katzenbach that "a bunch of Communists . . . is going to picket my ranch." In May, Lyndon and Moyers raged against "kooks," "zealots," and "Communists." Later that month he vowed to resist "a bunch of little yellow pinkos." In mid-June, he assured Birch Bayh that he knew who was behind the small number of Americans raising hell about the war. "We read the Communist bulletins. Their orders [are] go out to do it." Protests on campuses, sit-ins at the Pentagon: "They're all led by Communist people." And "If I get out and go talking about the Communists, they say, 'Oh, he's a McCarthy!'. . . . But . . . they're stirring up this agitation." The Soviet ambassador was convincing senators at cocktail parties that "I'm a warmonger." LBJ honestly believed antiwar protests were designed by the nation's enemies to weaken U.S. will to oppose aggression in Southeast Asia and to encourage the enemy to fight on.

In fact, criticizing military intervention in Vietnam or questioning unbending anti-Communism did not mean these people were Communists themselves, or dupes, or unopposed to Russian or Chinese aggression. What that signified was their refusal to view the war in Vietnam as part of a worldwide Communist offensive or to predict countries all over the globe falling like dominoes if the Vietcong prevailed.

Why did LBJ not grasp this? He was intelligent and well informed. He knew Communism was not monolithic; there were obvious tensions between the USSR and the People's Republic of China (PRC). In theory, he believed the United States should recognize the PRC, though he saw no practical way of doing this. He also realized the Soviets and Chinese could not dictate to North Vietnam, and he was capable of conceding that "It's going to be like the Yale professors said: it's going to be difficult for us to very long prosecute effectively a war that far away from home with the divisions we have here—and particularly the potential divisions." So why did he persist in calling criticism of his Vietnam policy Communistic in origins and nature?

The origins of LBJ's charge were the divisions to which the professors referred. "I'm very depressed," he told McNamara, because divisions were "very potentially dangerous to our general cause in Vietnam." Lyndon was hoping the enemy would become discouraged and then quit—and sooner, quicker, and cheaper than he anticipated.

Domestic dissent encouraged Hanoi and prolonged the war, which, in turn, would call forth more opposition at home, with a snowball effect on the intensity and duration of the conflict. To him, protesters and critics were objectively aiding and abetting Communists in Vietnam. It was only a small intellectual jump for a frustrated, harried president to characterize them as Communists, too.

Even when he conceded that domestic critics probably were not Reds, Johnson still was furious about their failure to take the Communist threat seriously. The domino theory was so obviously right to him, he could hardly conceive how anyone could in good faith doubt it. If South Vietnam fell, North Vietnam could and would intervene with covert action and conventional operations in Laos and Cambodia. Hanoi and Beijing would bully Thailand diplomatically and compel the Thais to defer to them. North Vietnam and China would encourage indigenous Communist insurgents in Malaysia. They would use these successes and the huge Communist Party in Indonesia to intensify Premier Sukarno's flirtation with China. "More," warned Dean Rusk in January 1964, "is involved in Indonesia with its 100 million people, than is at stake in Vietnam"; Johnson concurred. Finally, the Communists would cap their victories by pressuring Japan to move into their sphere of influence. LBJ believed even the most cursory knowledge of Asian politics made this scenario not just plausible if South Vietnam disappeared but inevitable. "We know from Munich on," he said on February 17, "that when you give, the dictators feed on raw meat. If they take South Vietnam, they take Thailand, they take Indonesia, they take Burma, they come on right back to the Philippines." Those who did not agree must be knaves or fools.

Also infuriating to Johnson was the inability of his critics to comprehend how potent anti-Communist feeling was among most Americans. These feelings surfaced in late April and early May as LBJ struggled to comprehend and respond to events in the Dominican Republic.

On April 24, supporters of Juan Bosch staged what they called "a constitutional coup" to restore him to the presidency of the Dominican Republic. At first, U.S. Ambassador Tapley Bennett advised that there was no cause for concern, even though Bosch was a leftist in Dominican politics and had aroused enough opposition from the military for them to depose him from office in 1962. Then Bennett decided the rebels possibly had Cuban aid. What if they did? As the ambassador contemplated this, the realization that he might be blamed for the rise of another Cuba transfixed him. Washington caught the contagion from Bennett.

LBJ got it bad. Soon he was running "the Dominican intervention like a desk officer in the State Department." His intimate knowledge about the situation did not help in decision making. He could not bring the small details to bear on his view of the big picture; the desk officer and the chief executive could not reconcile their roles. Desk Officer Lyndon knew that evidence for Communist involvement was ambiguous. President Johnson agreed with McGeorge Bundy that a Communist takeover would be "the worst political disaster we could suffer." Desk Officer Lyndon understood the relevance of another of Bundy's points—"to quash Castro in DR we need above all else to get hemisphere public opinion on our side"—and realized unilateral political and military intervention would turn attitudes hostile. President Johnson fretted that the Organization of American States "couldn't pour piss out of a boot if the instructions were written on the heel."

The debate was won by the president. By early May, 14,000 American soldiers and marines were in the Dominican Republic with more on the way.

Liberal Democrats expressed concern over a return to "gunboat diplomacy" and characterized a State Department list of fifty-four "Communist and Castroite" rebels in Santo Domingo as reminiscent of Joe McCarthy's wild accusations. RFK chimed in with criticism. Bob McNamara told LBJ he doubted that fifty-four or fifty-eight or any number of Cuban sympathizers were fomenting revolution.

Privately, Johnson spoke harsh words against "the sob sisters and . . . some of the extreme liberals" who thought "we are throwing our weight around." "I don't believe," he told sympathetic Senator Dirksen, "you ought to wait and have a Cuba and then try to do something about it." Press coverage was hopelessly slanted: "We're just mean sons of bitches and outlaws, and they're nice, virtuous maidens." He decided to correct this picture.

Although he knew better, LBJ inflated possible Red involvement into "what began as a popular democratic revolution . . . was taken over and really seized and placed into the hands of a band of Communist conspirators." Sporadic sniper fire swelled into "firsthand evidence of the horrors and hardship, the violence and the terror, and the international conspiracy from which U.S. servicemen have rescued the people of more than 30 nations from that war-torn island." This rhetoric won the support of 69 percent of the American people. The same survey revealed that 20 percent did not believe him, and influential members of the media and Congress sided with them.

Violence in the Dominican Republic soon ended. The political situation stabilized. The bad news was that the damage to hemispheric relations endured. Sending in the marines cost LBJ Latin American opinion. He regretted that but claimed he had no choice, and not because of the Cubans. Now he blamed his decision on American public opinion.

The polls, he claimed, proved that relying on diplomacy would have ruined him. This was disingenuous. While Lyndon never questioned the fundamental anti-Communism of the American people, he was convinced that leaders had to mobilize them before they acted on their conviction. The 69 percent were largely his creation, the result of his incendiary language. His interpretation of the polls also was misleading: it implied he did not care that 20 percent believed he was misinformed or lying—but he did.

LBJ understood that doubts about his handling of foreign crises could have serious consequences. They would make his relations with allies and enemies more difficult. Assuredly, doubts would not help him deal with Ho Chi Minh or Congress. He must restore his credibility.

On May 4, Johnson sent Congress a request for $700 million more to pay for rising expenses in Vietnam. Added to that was a warning that this was not routine. The president prompted George Mahon, chair of the House Appropriations Committee, on how to spin this: He did not have to ask; Congress had given permission in the Tonkin Gulf Resolution. He thought, "This would be a masterstroke . . . to show them I was frank and candid, and when I needed something, I would put it right in their belly, and if they didn't want to give it to me, they'd say so." If they agreed, "Why, they'd say, 'We can trust this guy. Although he's got authority, he didn't write his check. He let us in on it.' " So, "We'll see whether they believe in the Executive being frank and candid and open with them."

It was a clumsy tactic—one that critics resented because they knew what was going on. As LBJ gleefully told Humphrey, "To deny or to delay this request means you're not giving a man ammunition he needs for his gun. . . . You've got him standing out there nekkid and letting people shoot at him. And we don't want to do that." It was coercion, not candor.

The president also claimed this would send a message to Hanoi. They say, he told Senator John Stennis of Mississippi, "if they can hold out two or three weeks longer, we're liable to quit. And we want to show them that we got the money and the Congress is behind us." A yes vote "is worth more to me than a division psychologically." Then he asserted, "If we can just let them know in forty-eight hours that we're in the thing to stay, I think they'll fold."

·This verbal overkill was unnecessary to persuade hawks like Mahon and Stennis. With those inclined to be doubtful or dovish, his words stored up trouble for the future. They did not swell the number of yeses; reluctance to jeopardize the troops did that. Instead, they increased suspicions of LBJ.

Publicly, the president interpreted the House (408–7) and Senate (88–3) votes as proof that Congress was committed to fighting aggression. Yet he confessed to Adlai Stevenson that even his decision to halt bombing on the Buddha's birthday would not win over critics. "The liberals are not going to be with us anyway. They're going to be raising hell around all over the lot." The North Vietnamese would stay hell-raisers, too, he glumly continued. "We don't think they're going to call off anything." He was praying they would back off a little, then the United States would "work ourselves out of it, like we did [in] Cuba [in 1962]." More likely, he would have to resume bombing again "pretty strong." The latter proved to be correct, and questions about the effectiveness of his prosecution of the war and the truthfulness of his words mounted.

The scale, boldness, and success of attacks by the NVA and the VC increased, too. During June and July, some in the MACV feared that the Communists were beginning the insurgency's final stage: conventional warfare. The South Vietnamese military reacted not with better defenses but with another coup in Saigon. The new leaders, Nguyen Van Thieu and Nguyen Cao Ky, were described by William Bundy as "absolutely the bottom of the barrel." That Ky seemingly admired Adolf Hitler did not help LBJ's cause in the United States. That neither Thieu nor Ky had any answer for the NVA threatened his position in Vietnam.

To Republicans in Congress, it was clear that Johnson must send more troops to Vietnam to take up the principal burden of combat. They asked if the additional $700 million would cover the cost of an expanded war. This, Lyndon realized, could be prelude to a battle over the whole federal budget. The GOP would emphasize balancing the budget and defending freedom over funding Great Society programs. Nervously, he asked McNamara on June 17 how to respond.

"The answer," McNamara replied blithely, "is we don't need more." *What if they say more troops are going?* LBJ asked. McNamara had an answer: "The number of men we have is the number of men we planned for in the budget. We have to feed the men, house them, equip them . . . whether they are in the United States or South Vietnam." Dubiously, Johnson responded, "Well, in light of the president's decision to escalate the war. . . ." McNamara cut him off. "I don't know that you *made* any decision to escalate the war." Back to the point: "Do we need more in the budget for '66? And the answer is 'not now. . . . [though] we may later, depending on what happens in the next thirteen months.' " Thus primed, the president staved off congressional inquiries.

He could not keep from deciding about escalation for long. Gathering his closest advisers around him, reaching out to old friends Abe Fortas and Dick Russell, powwowing with Dwight Eisenhower, LBJ rehearsed the pros and cons in anguished and repetitive meetings. Not much new could be said. Typical is a conversation between LBJ and McNamara on June 30. The president asked him to speak with RFK and other Senate critics of his policy, then veered off to his problems.

LBJ: You just can't find anybody who thinks we ought to leave these boys out there and do nothing. And we can't give up. I don't see anything to do except give them what they need, Bob. Do you?

McNAMARA: I'm very much of that frame of mind. . . . It is a very heavy risk. But that's my vote.

LBJ: I don't believe it is as big a risk as walking out.

McNAMARA: Neither do we.

LBJ: Now, what are the alternatives?

McNAMARA: The alternative is to go in a half-assed way.

LBJ: I think we'll be wrecked doing that.

McNAMARA: I went through the Bay of Pigs. . . . And we were wrong not because of what we did. We were wrong because we failed.

LBJ: That's right.

Given this attitude, it is not surprising that Johnson listened courteously to Undersecretary of State George Ball's arguments for negotiating withdrawal, then rejected them. He was not going to pull out.

Yet he was not quite ready to put in. He wanted to be reassured that the United States could win. And McNamara, though never guaranteeing victory and always anticipating a tough fight, exuded confidence that American power would force Hanoi to negotiate. He also advised that this could probably be done with fewer men than the army wanted, remarking that in his experience military men asked for the maximum while preparing to do the job with less.

Two issues remained. Should the reserves be called up? How should LBJ inform Congress and the public about his decision to escalate?

Lyndon was most concerned about the second matter. "We know ourselves, in our own conscience, that when we asked for [the Tonkin Gulf Resolution] . . . we had no intention of comitting this many ground troops. We're doing so now, and we know it's going to be bad. And the question is, 'Do we just want to go out on a limb by ourselves?' "

McNamara said no. He urged Johnson to call up the military reserves and ask Congress for the authority, though he could legally do it by presidential fiat. There would be a debate, one that McNamara believed the administration would win. In fact, he thought they would do better than merely an overwhelming majority for escalation. He believed they would persuade critics to support their definition of victory, a negotiated political settlement. There was no reason to shrink from a national debate on Vietnam.

LBJ totally disagreed. That debate would threaten passage of more Great Society legislation. Besides, it would not end with a unified Congress and country. The chances of bringing on board Bobby Kennedy, with his own fish to fry, and the intellectuals, who seized on Lyndon's invitation in the spring to come to the White House to celebrate the arts to scold him on Vietnam, were slim and none. Since everyone who advised him to call up the reserves urged him to seek Congress's approval, this helped decide him against it. He would increase draft calls, something he could do more quietly by himself. Announcements about troops would be made in televised addresses where there would be no direct questions.

On July 28, LBJ told the country that he was raising U.S. forces in Vietnam to 125,000 men and ordering doubled draft levies. More troops would be added as Westmoreland needed them. Left secret was his commitment to have 200,000 soldiers in Vietnam by 1966.

Lyndon had shoved his chips in, and it is informative to reflect about why.

Robert McNamara played a major role. According to Lady Bird, LBJ fretted about the dangers the defense secretary ran on trips to

Saigon, claiming that he did not believe he could do without him. When McNamara advised on July 21 that reinforcing the troops and letting General Westmoreland take the offensive would, "if the military and political moves are properly integrated and executed with continuing vigor and visible determination . . . stand a good chance of achieving an acceptable outcome within a reasonable time," he sealed the deal.

Other advisers stuck the same oar in, and the skeptics undercut their own doubts. Richard Russell could see no realistic alternative, absent an invitation from a Saigon government to leave, which would itself have bad consequences. George Ball's lone voice was not raised persistently in front of Johnson, and the undersecretary was unwilling to resign over policy. When LBJ quizzed him on the damage a withdrawal would cause the United States, he replied that a worse humiliation would be defeat by a few guerillas. Matched against McNamara's confidence in American forces, this was not compelling.

Still, Lyndon knew if the fight went badly, it would not be "McNamara's War." It would be all his. That was just. The decision to escalate or not was his. He was not the utter captive of the defense secretary: witness the refusal to call up the reserves and insist on congressional approval. Although McNamara and others had an impact on his choice, their advice was not the ultimate reason why he chose.

Later, Johnson claimed that the Vietnam War was a price he had to pay for the Great Society. No doubt he believed that when he said it. But historian Fredrik Logevall makes a significant point about that: preserving the prospects of the Great Society determined the *timing* and *tactics* of escalation, slowing it down and muting public announcements in 1965, but did saving domestic reform compel the decision to adopt the *strategy* of escalation?

Of much greater import for the strategic decision was Johnson's belief in the necessity of resisting Communism and preserving America's credibility in the contest for hearts and minds throughout the world. The president was a Cold Warrior. He believed defeat in Vietnam would lead inevitably to probing attacks elsewhere and from these to dangerous, perhaps nuclear confrontations. Once the United States was perceived as so weak-willed it could be bullied and backed down by some guerrillas and the army of a "pissant country," it would be in grave jeopardy. That is why fighting a hard war in a faraway country was better than accepting national humiliation. Lyndon Johnson believed he had no choice.

The president's lack of options was fundamentally owing to considerations of geopolitics, not partisan, domestic politics. Obviously, he needed no instruction on the dangers of appearing "soft on Communism." But when he later whined that he would have been impeached if he pulled out of Vietnam, he was talking nonsense: political impotence, perhaps; impeachment, no. Beyond the self-pitying exaggeration, though, lurks an important revelation of his inner thoughts. He would have believed he would have deserved such a fate for not doing his duty. Of course, he would gladly reap what benefits he could glean from his anti-Communism. But he also would grimly endure attacks by critics from both parties.

Historians have also speculated that Johnson was swayed by the effect defeat in Southeast Asia would have on his historical reputation and his masculine identity. He did once describe his view of international relations by saying, "If you let a bully come into your front yard one day, the next day he'll be up on your porch and the day after he will rape your wife in your own bed." One need not practice psychoanalysis on the dead to see this implication: was he man enough to stop this in Vietnam? As for history's verdict, he did vow later in his term that he would not be the first president to lose a war.

What is crucial in assigning significance to these remarks is the *time* they were made, late in his presidency, when he was frustrated over stalemate in Vietnam and on Capitol Hill. In 1965, Johnson believed he would receive his share of credit for the greatest congressional session in history. He was much more sure of his place in history when he made the decision to escalate. And in 1965, LBJ did not use macho words to discuss Vietnam with advisers and members of Congress.

Such words were also absent in his bedroom. On June 22, Lady Bird woke suddenly to hear her husband say, "I don't want to get in a war and I don't see any way out of it. I've got to call up 600,000 boys, make them leave their homes and families." "It was," she realized, "as though he were talking out loud, not especially to me." Hoping "the refrain hadn't been in his mind all night long," trying not to disturb him, she crept out. When she tried to sleep in another room, her rest was "fitful and unsatisfactory."

Bird's attempt at sleep mirrored LBJ's tossings and turnings. That refrain was there all night long. Soon it would become the same old song.

Escalation was not the only threat to the Great Society during the summer of 1965. Three other problems imperiled it. One was constitutional: LBJ had to ensure favorable Supreme Court rulings on federal aid to education. A second was financial: he had to protect the dollar and the pound sterling against devaluation. The third was social and political: he had to deal with the consequences of rioting in Watts, a black neighborhood in Los Angeles.

Asked if he believed in the separation of powers, Lyndon would have repeated textbook theory and answered "Of course." In real-life Washington, politics suffused everything, including the Supreme Court. He intended to insert a reliably pro–Great Society justice into it. He also planned to choose a man who would be privy to his innermost thoughts, then would work to shape the court's deliberations to match them. Adding Abe Fortas would be tantamount to giving LBJ a vote, plus enabling him to lobby other justices. Plus his old friend and confidante would provide accurate intelligence about his colleagues' inclinations and biases. This might be vital in shaping future legislation.

There was no danger that Abe would become committed to judicial independence. The two would have described their attitude toward that principle as "realistic"—others would say "cynical." Added to this bond was Fortas's joy in using his extraordinary intelligence to advise Lyndon on policy issues. He was not going to give that up.

So the two maneuvered to get their way. LBJ began by persuading Arthur Goldberg to resign from the Supreme Court and become ambassador to the United Nations (UN). He played upon Goldberg's ambition to be the first Jewish nominee for the vice presidency. He could not expect this should he remain a justice, but at the UN he would be ideally placed, if he played a vital role in a negotiated settlement of the Vietnam War. The president dangled this bait by insisting there was a real possibility of talks—something he did not believe—and hinting that final decisions on escalation were being further deferred—something he knew was a lie. Goldberg explained his agreement by asking wryly, "Have you ever had your arm twisted by Lyndon Johnson?" In truth, LBJ did not have to twist much. Hungry for higher office, ready to believe he would move Johnson toward a negotiated settlement, in mid-July Goldberg promised to resign, whereupon Lyndon and Abe played two elaborate charades.

As historian Robert Dallek astutely observed, the two men acted out a scenario in which Johnson forced Fortas to join the court by announcing his nomination in public after Abe had declined privately. This let him claim to his wife, who violently opposed the appointment, that he had no choice. During the Senate hearings on his confirmation, Fortas testified that reports about how close he was to LBJ were "exaggerated out of all connection with reality." The Senate swallowed this whopper. Only three senators voted no. Lyndon had Abe on the Supreme Court, and the Great Society had a powerful protector.

Since 1944 the world's economy had been under the financial system created by allied finance ministers at Bretton Woods. There the United States had insisted upon free trade and stable currencies. To aid the first and achieve the second, every country pegged its money to the constant value of the dollar, set at $35 per ounce of gold. Any institution or individual could exchange dollars for gold if they chose to do so. To increase confidence further, FDR let it be known that the United States had $25 billion worth of gold in Fort Knox, Kentucky.

Bretton Woods worked very well while America dominated international trade. Foreigners did not have dollars to exchange because the balance of their trade with the United States was against them and they made up the difference with their own currencies. As the economies of Germany, Japan, and other nations began to grow, and as American soldiers and tourists spent more in foreign countries, the balance of trade and payments swung the other way. The spectacular economic "miracles" of former enemies decisively reversed the situation. By the 1960s, the balance of trade was against the United States. Its gold reserves had shrunk to $15 billion. That foreigners held billions more dollars than this made a troubling situation even darker.

Johnson pressed the Germans and Japanese to buy more American goods as quid pro quo for our defending them and stationing troops in their countries. He also launched a "See America First" advertising campaign to convince citizens that patriotic duty demanded staying in the country on their vacations. He used "moral suasion" to convince U.S. businesses to invest less capital abroad.

This combination of jawboning and public relations succeeded in reducing the payments deficit to $1.3 billion in 1965, its lowest level in eight years, to the president's delight. He would not have to tighten the money supply and raise interest rates to slow the outward flow of dollars. Doing that would have cooled off the economy and jeopardized creating the Great Society. Affluence, optimism, and expansion were, Lyndon was sure, absolute political prerequisites for continuing the impetus of reform.

Another crisis threatened to cancel out the president's successes. Compared to other European nations, the British economy was stagnating with no recovery in sight. Harold Wilson's Labour government had recently won power by a commitment to expand social services. To afford this, it had to raise taxes, increasing the price of British goods and depressing further the country's ability to compete in international trade. LBJ and his economic advisers feared that Wilson would feel compelled to respond to the lethal combination of expensive commitments and deepening slump by devaluing the pound sterling. This could trigger a run by international financiers on dollars, which, unlike the pound, were "good as gold." That could end by forcing Johnson to devalue the dollar to protect Fort Knox. The resulting recession would shrink Great Society funding, end hopes for more reform, and make the cost of Vietnam harder to meet and impossible to hide.

This looming crisis coincided with other tensions in Anglo-American relations. In 1963 and 1964, the Tory government infuriated Lyndon by trading with Cuba. In 1965, Labour opposed U.S. military action in Southeast Asia and offered to mediate between the United States and North Vietnam. Some in the administration urged LBJ to link economic assistance from Washington to participation by London in the war. "A British brigade in Vietnam," noted McGeorge Bundy, "would be worth a billion dollars at the moment of truth for sterling." When George Ball recoiled at trading financial support for the pound for British troops in Vietnam, Bundy told him the Brits had to understand the price of doing business with Lyndon Johnson.

Lyndon, however, knew business much better than Mac. Wilson would never cave in to this. Asked to choose either losing face first and then office or devaluing the pound, he would opt for the latter. The president commanded Bundy to keep "the pound sterling and Vietnam completely separate." American negotiators on the fiscal crisis did as they were told.

Ultimately, Wilson delayed some expansions of the welfare state and restrained British labor unions from immediate wage increases. He pledged to keep sterling at the then current exchange rate of $2.80 per pound, and he agreed to maintain a British military presence east of the Suez Canal, while reserving the option to reduce or end a more expensive commitment in West Germany. In return the United States brokered an international credit of $925 million to support the pound, to which the United States committed $400 million. LBJ was happy. With good reason: as historian Thomas Alan Schwartz noted, "At relatively little cost, the Johnson government avoided a major international financial crisis at the same time as the escalation of the war . . . that might have exacerbated the politics of both Vietnam and LBJ's real love, his Great Society."

Rioting in Watts began five days after Lyndon signed the Voting Rights Act. That left him so depressed he would not answer urgent calls from Joe Califano pleading for orders to send troops to restore order in Los Angeles. Califano finally made the decision himself, claiming he had presidential approval. LBJ never explained why he had stayed incommunicado. He just said Califano was right to insist that the soldiers keep a low profile and defer as much as possible to local authorities. He would send more troops if necessary, and he wanted Joe to investigate whether a "Communist conspiracy" had incited rioters.

Johnson never said Watts totally surprised him. He had periodically worried about a reprise of the riots of 1964, and he had eloquently expressed his understanding of the causes of black discontent in a commencement speech at Howard University in June. "You do not wipe away the scars of centuries by saying 'Now you are free to go where you want, and do as you desire, and choose the leaders you please.' " No one could fairly say, " 'You are free to compete with all the others,' " either. Next came "the next and most profound stage of the battle of civil rights." What LBJ sought was "not just freedom but opportunity . . . not just equality as a right and a theory but equality as a fact and equality as a result." Black leaders like Wilkins and King had been enthusiastic about his scheduling a fall White House Conference to plan how to take affirmative action to achieve equality. LBJ thought his Howard speech heralded a "second Emancipation." Obviously that had not been enough for Watts.

It was equally obvious that Watts might end the president's noble plans. Blacks, he told Califano, were acting like "fools" out of "frustration, impatience, and anger." They might be dooming any chance of further civil rights legislation. Many whites believed rioting in LA was the direct result of the Voting Rights Act. Lyndon's own cousin said as much to him. William Parker, the Los Angeles Police Department's chief, fanned these flames by saying that unrestrained violence inevitably happened "when you keep telling people they are unfairly treated and teach them disrespect for the law." Lady Bird was afraid that "It's exactly what millions of people are thinking."

Lyndon shared her fear, so he made strong public statements condemning the riots and describing rioters as exactly like the KKK. He postponed the White House Conference until spring of 1966; too many would see discussing black rights and poverty as appeasing violence. Then he told Califano to maneuver Hubert Humphrey out as chair of the President's Council of Equal Opportunity; Johnson feared he would say things that would add to the backlash. Califano bore the blame for that decision. Civil rights leaders would protest the removal of their longtime champion, and the president wanted to hide his role from them and the vice president. Humphrey never suspected who fired him.

With similar stealth, Lyndon privately assured Martin Luther King that he would do his best to improve conditions in Watts. He appointed a White House Commission on the riots and quietly told its chair, John McCone, which findings he wanted. The president approved a $25 million aid package for Watts. King was told to keep it secret so that LBJ would not be charged with caving in to looters and encouraging more rioting. Such accusations would threaten poverty program funding and end initiatives on equality of opportunity. King kept his mouth shut, and this assistance—which, conceded Johnson, was not nearly enough—flowed into Watts. The Great Society, he hoped, still had a fighting chance.

August 27, 1965, was LBJ's fifty-seventh birthday. To Lady Bird's delight, there was a joyful party. Lyndon was "a happy and relaxed man." "I shall remember," she promised her diary, "his fifty-seventh birthday with happiness."

One year earlier, Johnson had agonized to George Reedy, "I do not believe I can physically and mentally carry the responsibility of the bomb and the world and the Negroes and the South." The next 365 days proved he could.

LBJ would be challenged again. He knew Vietnam would require far more men and cost much more than $700 million. It would be a long struggle, one fraught with peril for the Great Society and the nation. Though he strained to see a pinprick of light in the blackness, there was no flicker yet.

On the home front, Lyndon had not merely looked for light. He had lit up the darkness of poverty and racism; he had blazed new trails in housing, education, health care, and a cleaner environment. He had fired the hopes of millions with his masterful management of the 89th Congress. But would the flame gutter out? Could he stave off a backlash? That he had to help the people of Watts surreptitiously was not a good omen.

11

Impatient People: Fall 1965 to December 1966

During the spring of 1965, Hanoi's leaders predicted a significant American military intervention would be forthcoming. Debate over how to respond ensued.

Vo Nguyen Giap, the architect of victory at Dien Bien Phu, advised ending the conventional battles now being fought against the Army of the Republic of Vietnam (ARVN). The struggle should return to the smaller-scale fights and guerrilla warfare that bedeviled the French. The United States would have to be worn down. Nguyen Chi Tranh, who directed the VC struggle against Saigon, argued for major attacks on American forces before their numbers and firepower peaked: hurt the Americans bad enough, and they would be gone quickly. Lyndon Johnson would stop the buildup and look for a way out.

Each believed the United States would not have the will to prosecute this war to victory. The records of their debate reveal why. They were heartened by signs of opposition to the war in the United States. More important than this, though, was LBJ's comments that he sought no wider war when he sent the Tonkin Gulf Resolution to Congress and the assurances he gave through Blair Seaborn that he did not plan to try to overthrow the North Vietnamese government. Historian Mark Moyar summarized their conclusion: North Vietnam "could send more troops to South Vietnam and take other provocative actions without endangering their existence." The father of their country agreed and added another reason. "Don't worry,"

Ho Chi Minh told his generals. "I've been to America. I know Americans. They are an impatient people. They will leave."

Tranh prevailed. In August, the 1st Vietcong Regiment fought a savage battle with the marines at Chu Lai. The Americans counted 573 VC dead, while suffering 46 killed in action (KIA) and 204 wounded (WIA). The kill ratio was roughly 12 to 1, without including a probable equal number of enemy deaths from wounds. During November, the North Vietnamese launched their own offensive. The 66th NVA Regiment attacked American forces in the Ia Drang Valley. For the first time massive U.S. firepower was brought to bear, with B-52 bombers providing tactical support. Four days later, 1,800 NVA were confirmed dead—the MACV estimated the actual number was twice as high—as were 244 U.S. troops.

General Westmoreland applied the adjective "only" to the 244. In Washington, different modifiers were chosen. LBJ sent McNamara to Saigon to assess the situation.

McNamara came back with a somber report. The defense secretary had thought bombers, fighters, helicopters, rockets, and artillery would minimize American deaths. The Ia Drang Valley shattered that expectation. The president should prepare for 1,000 KIA a month for the near future, and he should not assume that number would decline later. "The odds are even that we will be faced in early 1967 with a 'no decision' [in the war] at an even higher level [of casualties]." He did not need to add that this would pose political problems for LBJ.

McNamara then turned his formidable intelligence to asking what should be done. The way he approached answering the question made his report a turning point of the war—not because of what it said but because of what he left out and Lyndon did not insist on including.

Westmoreland had sold LBJ, McNamara, and the Joint Chiefs on a strategy of attrition. To grind down the NVA and VC, he would mount massive offensives called "Search and Destroy" missions. There would be a price: GIs would die, but so long as the ratio of battlefield deaths favored the United States by substantial margins—and the MACV calculated it during fall 1965 at forty enemy deaths for each American—the United States would be steadily, inexorably winning.

For attrition to work, however, the enemy had to engage continuously in major battles. Would they? Or would the NVA and the VC scale down their attacks, nibble away at American forces, and reduce the kill ratio? McNamara understood that this war could become a race between military attrition (our enemy) and political attrition (us). So did LBJ, but neither insisted that Westmoreland answer these questions.

They left another fundamental query unasked and unanswered. How many NVA and VC had to be killed each year to have the desired effect? The secretary of defense had made his reputation as a numbers cruncher, but instead of aiming at precision, he indulged in prediction.

McNamara told Johnson he could expect huge enemy reinforcements. The United States must react by sending more troops— 400,000 by the end of 1966, perhaps 600,000 by December 1967—and more ordnance. This would cause protest and criticism at home and abroad. So "we must lay a foundation in the minds of the American public and world opinion for such an enlarged phase of the war." Throughout, Vietnam would remain a brutal slugging match, highlighted by large conventional battles.

That combat forecast was the result of wishful thinking, not hard analysis. Its attraction was this: it gave McNamara hope that the North Vietnamese would predict the same future and would back off from a fight to the finish. This hope fathered another wish posing as well thought-out policy. Since Hanoi would not want to appear to be giving up, "We should give [them] a face-saving chance to stop the aggression." He recommended a pause in bombing the north and a renewed expression of willingness to negotiate.

Johnson's coolness to this agitated McNamara. The more he thought about what lay ahead, the more desperately he sought an escape route. The defense secretary interrupted a vacation to fly to the LBJ ranch right before Christmas and plead for a suspension of sorties to the north. Before he went, he shared his thoughts with Robert Kennedy. Had Lyndon found that out, McNamara's tenure might have been over.

LBJ suspected disloyalty and conspiracy after other casual contacts his men had with RFK. This particular meeting would inform RFK's criticism of the administration's conduct of the war. Clearly McNamara doubted that he could convince Johnson to negotiate without a strong push from Kennedy.

Risking his job proved unnecessary, as McNamara talked a reluctant president into a bombing pause that stretched from Christmas until January 31, 1966. LBJ sent diplomats seeking mediation to several nations. He did not expect any results. Nor did he change his position: the North Vietnamese must withdraw from

Johnson making notes in Cabinet Room meeting. © Lyndon B. Johnson Library

South Vietnam. The enemy did not change, either, and insisted the United States leave. The war itself seemed unchanged too.

Appearances deceived. The North Vietnamese had switched to Giap's strategy. With the return to sharp, short fights between platoons and extensive use of mines and booby traps, enemy casualties declined and the kill ratio shrank. These tactics had a profound effect on American soldiers' morale and their relationship with civilians. During World War II, only 3 percent of U.S. fatalities were caused by mines; in Vietnam, the percentage was one-third. GIs moved through populated areas at a half mile per hour and still were killed by snipers and traps. Where was the enemy? *Who* was the enemy?

Westmoreland interpreted the end of conventional battles as a favorable sign. The troops were fighting by his "Search and Destroy" book, and it was working. But as one grunt remarked, "Charlie doesn't read English." Victor Charlie (the VC) ran his own missions, which GIs named "Find and Kill" because they realized what the brass first did not see, then denied, then tried to cover up. The enemy had the initiative. It chose when contact would occur, breaking off when the odds were not good, attacking when they were, fighting at close range by "grasping the American's belt" to reduce U.S. advantages in artillery and air power. The enemy controlled the rate of attrition. Hanoi figured that for American strategy to succeed the NVA and VC would have to lose a minimum of 250,000 men a year. They kept losses well below that.

It is incredible that LBJ did not press the Pentagon or the CIA for a reliable estimate of how many KIA and WIA were required for attrition to work. It is also incredible that he did not question whether it could possibly succeed if there were no infantry attacks on North Vietnam and no blockade of Haiphong harbor. Westmoreland, the architect of Search and Destroy, asked for both, because these operations would really squeeze the enemy. Johnson vetoed both because they might bring the USSR or China into the conflict. Why did he not seriously consider that failing to execute them would make wearing the enemy down much more problematic? And why did the president or his advisers not notice that the NVA and the VC initiated most combat in Vietnam—and think about the implications of that for attrition?

Lyndon Johnson did not apply his incisive intelligence and shrewd realism to military options at the strategic level. Sure, he kept close control over bombing targets and agonized over American deaths, but that was tactics and tragedy. All his obsessive worrying did was convince him that he was not a good commander-in-chief. Then he fulfilled his own prophecy by not using his brains to examine the actual situation and the proposed solution closely and clearly.

Did LBJ flinch from focusing on these issues because he feared the answers? Suppose he determined the war was unwinnable. How would he extricate the United States without destroying his presidency and the Great Society? Suppose he determined the United States had to win the fight but that it would be years before any light could be perceived at the tunnel's end. What would that do to domestic reform? Stuck between rocks and hard places, it is possible that LBJ did not want to take a searching look at military strategy. It was easier by far to rely on others' expertise and brainpower.

That left the man Lyndon told Lady Bird he could not do without: Robert McNamara. No question, McNamara was forcefully bright and wonderfully persuasive. At the Pentagon he was in charge; on Capitol Hill, he was a force with which to reckon. That had been the case from November 1963 well into 1965. The appearance was still there as 1966 began, but it belied an underlying reality: LBJ's secretary of defense was freaking out.

A colloquial term coined in the late 1960s, *freaking out* is an imprecise though still useful description of certain types of reaction to perceptions of potential disaster ahead. Those who freak out do not respond by composing themselves, clearing their minds, considering the future without self-accusation for past errors, and acting with a clear understanding of the situation. Instead, they are consumed by worry and self-doubt. As psychologist W. Timothy Gallwey notes, "When action is born in worry and self-doubt, it is usually inappropriate and often too late to be effective."

So it was with McNamara. He hid his anguish and despair from his boss when they talked before Christmas. Had he been thinking clearly, he would have realized that the North Vietnamese were not going to be interested in saving face. Lyndon was right: Ho had no reason to withdraw and negotiate. Another sign of McNamara's discombobulation was sharing his doubts with RFK: had the defense secretary been thinking clearly, he would have known that pressure from Bobby would cause LBJ to dig in his heels. So, if the United States was not going to get out, the most effective thing McNamara could do was to come up with a better way of fighting; he could not get himself to do that.

Not until 1967 did McNamara order a study of who began battles in Vietnam. Nearly 80 percent of the time it was the enemy. During the early months of escalation, such findings might have had a critical impact. For instance, the administration could have reconsidered marine general Victor Krulak's proposal to establish a series of strategic enclaves and pacify them politically and militarily, thus forcing the NVA to try to dislodge Americans where they were strong. But in early 1966 the secretary of defense was too distracted by worry and self-recrimination to advise Johnson to consider carefully how the war should be fought.

McNamara also did not examine how LBJ should prepare the American people and Congress for a long war. In the past, he had argued for a major presidential address describing the difficulties, explaining the need for patience and fortitude, and inspiring the audience. Right now, Lyndon would not find this advice helpful.

For starters, he had to consider whether a speech would imply that he had developed doubts and was uncertain about how to proceed. Johnson had determined that he had to hide those feelings. His assistant Marvin Watson understood his thinking: "All presidents in all crises harbor some doubts about the wisdom of the course they choose. But having chosen, they know that they must rally the country behind that choice. . . . One never hears the President speak of his doubts. The reason is simple: if he does so, he inevitably dilutes the strength of his leadership in the course he has decided to take." LBJ had to be particularly careful about this, because he was widely perceived as unsure about foreign affairs.

Moreover, critics on Capitol Hill were already asking whether taxes should be raised to finance the war. Lyndon did not want a protracted debate on taxes. As he told McNamara, the possibility of a tax hike would give many congressmen and senators the excuse to deep-six the Great Society. No matter what, Congress would balk at raising taxes in 1966—a judgment McNamara confirmed by talking with Wilbur Mills—so he would not get the trade-off of higher revenues for the end of domestic reforms.

A tax increase might be attainable if Lyndon acted like Harry Truman and "scared the hell out of the American people." Doing that would risk creating a "war psychosis." That, he reminded McNamara, must be avoided. Firing up the nation for a crusade against Vietnamese Communists might do worse things than destroy his domestic agenda; it could convince the Soviets and the Chinese that the administration was thinking of measures against them and could lead directly toward a confrontation between the Great Powers. It was essential to keep U.S. involvement in Vietnam as limited and low-key as he could manage.

A major presidential effort to prepare the country for a long, difficult war would also inspire more speeches like Bill Fulbright's in September against the administration's actions in Vietnam and in the Dominican Republic. Critics would see it as implicit admission that their doubts were well-founded. Those sitting on the fence about Vietnam, like Martin Luther King, might be tipped onto the side of opposition. These developments, Johnson was certain, would increase North Vietnamese optimism, call forth more enemy resistance, and lengthen the struggle.

The bottom line was this: LBJ must prepare the nation for the ordeal he and McNamara believed lay ahead, but he had to do it very subtly and almost surreptitiously.

To accomplish this, LBJ had to dominate the flow of information available to the public. The main emphasis would be on managing, manipulating, and (occasionally) bullying the media. He knew editors and publishers of newspapers throughout the country; as KTBC's owner, he had long-standing business and political ties with owners and operators of electronic media. He took advantage of his contacts, criticizing some reporters' work, praising others, suggesting positive stories about progress in South Vietnam, and protesting the absence of stories on VC atrocities. Nothing escaped his attention, and a telephone was never far from his hand. Offending reporters, such as Morley Safer at CBS and the *New York Times* correspondents in Saigon, he suggested be reassigned or fired. Pro-war columnists and stories were touted.

The impact of Lyndon's interventions is hard to gauge. It is clear that the nation's journalistic establishment essentially supported the war until the Tet offensive in 1968, although not as unanimously or as enthusiastically as he wished. Could he have done it, he would have removed reporters he labeled as Communists and columnists he scorned as enemy supporters. Still, he got good press. If journalists influenced opinion, they moved it in pro-war directions. At the end of 1965, a poll revealed that over 90 percent of Americans opposed withdrawing from Vietnam. More than 60 percent felt the administration was doing a good job.

That was not enough for the president! He always suspected that commitment to the war was not deep and might not be abiding. The usual treatment for this was whipping up patriotic enthusiasms, but Johnson's concerns about the threat of a war psychosis held him back from full doses of this remedy. Discrediting and discouraging opponents of the war were safer approaches.

Johnson's tactics with his former Senate colleagues were well-known. He froze out staff members and spouses of critics at White House receptions. He spread the word about telling Frank Church that the next time he wanted a dam in Idaho he could go ask Wayne Morse, another opponent of the war. That gossip warned others and their constituents about the practical consequences of calling for a negotiated withdrawal. Lyndon did draw the line at saying these senators had Communist connections, though Everett Dirksen told him they were deeply influenced by leftists. He contented himself with accusing them of encouraging the enemy.

Senatorial courtesy did not apply to Martin Luther King. Thanks to FBI wiretaps, LBJ knew a week before King made public his plan to urge the United States to stop bombing and to write all the combatants appealing for negotiations. J. Edgar Hoover seized the chance to tell the president once again that King was the cat's-paw of Communists. Before, Johnson had shrugged off Hoover's accusations about King and his adviser Stanley Levinson; on Vietnam he gave them credence.

An attempt to persuade King to back off was unfruitful; he made a statement calling for the United States to include the VC in negotiations, end the bombing of North Vietnam, work for a seat for the People's Republic of China in the United Nations, and reassess American foreign policy in general. Seeing this as a personal insult. Lyndon took off the gloves.

First, he got Thomas Dodd to flay King as an ignorant *appeaser*— a word deliberately chosen to recall surrenders to Hitler. Dodd also speculated that this adventure had cost King most of his support in Congress. Simultaneously, Johnson orchestrated sharp criticism of King from a variety of newspapers and Whitney Young of the Urban League. Unused to attacks from liberal senators, friendly media outlets, and mainstream movement leaders, frightened by the raw power of a few LBJ phone calls, shaken and "emotionally fatigued" (according to FBI reports), King dropped plans to oppose the war on moral grounds. Lyndon had won—*for now!*

Dueling with King depressed the president. MLK's intentions were more proof to him that Communists were behind criticism of the war and would not give up easily. That conclusion fueled private outbursts like "the Communists are taking over the country" and "Communists already control the three major networks and the forty major outlets of communications." LBJ's staff tried to dismiss these as letting off steam with a stream of colorful expletives; they hoped his success at shaping media responses to the war would in calmer moments temper his concern about Reds. But LBJ viewed his inability to completely freeze out criticism as confirmation of Communists' power. He would have steady work marginalizing the war's critics.

The campuses concerned Johnson less than Congress or the media. His reaction depended on whether he saw the glass that day as half full or half empty. Protests occurred on a tiny percentage of American campuses in 1965; numbers of faculty and students participating were quite small. In contrast, he received a telegram of support from the University of Michigan, the site of the first teach-in on Vietnam, with so many signatures it stretched thirty feet.

To see the half-empty glass, Lyndon recited where the protests were: elite private institutions and some of the nation's greatest public universities. That demonstrations were happening there gave them a cachet. Status attracted press attention. And these protesters were not only questioning the war's expediency; they were challenging it on principle and morality. Would their ideas spread further? How could he keep the majority behind him? Beyond dispatching prominent members of his administration to campuses, LBJ was stumped.

Due to his fear of inciting so much patriotic fervor that it would endanger relations with China and Russia, he could offer no antidote of patriotism to counter young male students' resentment at the prospect that an expanded draft might interrupt their plans or threaten their lives. He provided no sense of duty and mission to fortify young men against fear, resentment, an emphasis on self rather than country, and the temptation to justify these feelings by blaming them on Lyndon Johnson.

Foreboding signs began surfacing on the domestic front in September 1965 when LBJ suffered his first major defeat in Congress. When a bill granting home rule for the District of Columbia stalled fatally, he warned Joe Califano, "It only takes one [defeat] for them to see they can cut us and make us bleed. Then they'll bleed us to death on our other legislation." Still, he continued to press an ambitious agenda, including creation of a Department of Transportation, a Model Cities bill to improve urban conditions, and a bill guaranteeing fair housing for African-Americans. Johnson had always believed the opportunity to enact reforms would be brief. Watts and war meant he had to move faster to maintain the initiative.

He also had to avoid shifting the momentum to the Great Society's opponents. When Gardner Ackley and the Council of Economic Advisers (CEA) argued for a tax hike to cool off inflationary trends, Johnson pointed out that Congress would not pass it. Proposing such a hike would cut the administration again, and the blood would be smeared all over LBJ's legislative agenda. No matter how persuasive arguments for a tax increase were from a fiscal and economic standpoint—and Johnson admitted they were probably correct—the politics of the situation forbade it. When Ackley hinted that the president could get an increase if he put all his energy behind the effort, LBJ was furious. *Go talk to people on the Hill,* he commanded. There Ackley swiftly learned that the master of congressional relations was right. There was no chance.

This still left Johnson and his advisers with the likely possibility of inflation and a decision by the Federal Reserve Board to respond by raising the prime lending rate. The president wanted neither. His only alternative was to strongly recommend that no wages or prices be raised by more than 3.2 percent, the average annual increase in productivity between 1957 and 1962. He had administration officials apply pressure to unions and corporations when they bargained on wages and prices. This intrusion of the federal government into negotiations, called *jawboning,* frequently involved Ackley and the CEA, occasionally McNamara (because of his experience as president of Ford Motor Company), and in crucial cases LBJ himself.

Johnson pulled out all the stops during the steel negotiations in late 1965. He succeeded with I. W. Abel, the Steelworkers president, by appealing to his sense of patriotism and pointing to the sacrifices of young men in Vietnam. Then he turned to the chairman of U.S. Steel. Roger Blough never finished explaining why he had to raise prices more than 3.2 percent. LBJ cut him off and, in Ackley's words, "just started working him over and asking him questions and lecturing him . . . [about] what kind of a low form of human being would ever stoop to that kind of behavior when we were at war, and people were dying in Vietnam, and the economy could be so prosperous if people would not be so selfish." "I have never seen a human being reduced to such a quivering lump of flesh," recalled Ackley. The price of steel did not rise more than 3.2 percent.

That success was typical. Throughout the private sector increases in wages and prices stayed at or below 3.2 percent, but jawboning did not work at all on the chairman of the Federal Reserve Board. During late 1965 and early 1966, Lyndon and Ackley worked over William McChesney Martin, pleading and blustering against raising the prime rate. Finally they gave up. Ackley "found Martin one who—quite surprisingly—was pretty much immune to 'The Treatment.' " Interest rates went up. The president took solace in the fact that economic expansion continued and that the gross national product grew during 1966, but he worried that he could do nothing to deflect Martin from following the conclusions of his icy intellect. Would others follow this example?

The economy continued to boom, but would expansion benefit the poor? Those in the administration who focused more on the War on Poverty than prosperity fretted about the funding for their programs. Liberals in Congress worried, too. LBJ had different priorities. He planned to keep budget requests low and uncontroversial. He wanted Congress's attention on new legislation, not on costs. Create more agencies and programs, let them win constituencies of their own, and fight for adequate funding later. That was his modus operandi.

When Sargent Shriver suggested that $11.25 billion for the Office of Economic Opportunity (OEO) would end poverty by 1975, Johnson dismissed it as utopian. Back came Shriver with a $2.5 billion request, twice the then-current budget. Johnson's response was $1.5 billion, a flat budget. He had "troubles in Vietnam. We couldn't lose there. It would take American boys and arms to turn it around." Then Sarge proposed $1.75 billion, which he said would give the OEO room to grow and the poor reason to hope. Reluctantly, LBJ agreed.

Settling on a budget did not free him from concerns about the OEO. The Community Action Program administrators and their antagonists did not keep disputes quiet. Nor did they accept Shriver's arbitration. The side that did not get its way went public. Charges of mismanagement were rife. LBJ was forced to appoint an investigative commission directed by Bertrand Harding, deputy director of the Internal Revenue Service. The commission's report, which was kept secret, pointed out hundreds of inefficiencies and made an equal number of recommendations. Then Harding was named the OEO's deputy director in hopes he could control its agencies.

It was soon apparent that Harding was not the cure-all. Lyndon looked for other ways to make the swelling Great Society bureaucracies more accountable and efficient. As during the New Deal era, jurisdictional disputes between agencies proliferated. These became protracted due to struggles over scarce fiscal resources. The president approved a new process for improving the assessment of programs and making intervention to change their internal budgeting easier. In theory, the Program Planning Budgeting System (PPBS) did that; in practice, an office charged with coordinating agencies and programs should have supplemented its efforts. After toying with creating that office, Johnson scrapped the idea.

Politics explained his retreat. LBJ kept his investigations of the poverty agencies as far under Congress's radar as possible; he did not want to be charged with interfering with the Civil Service for partisan advantages. Creating a new agency designed to help him intervene would be controversial. Moreover, it would be public, and Congress would want to know its findings. That would be dangerous. To Lyndon, "The president's real problem is with the Congress, not the bureaucracy. It is the Congress that demands numbers from us, insisting that we handle the most people at the least cost. If we went around beating our breasts and admitting difficulties with our programs, then the Congress would immediately slash all our funds for next year." Discretion was the best part of budgeting. "Better to send in the reports as they are, even knowing the situation is more complicated than it appears, and then work from within to make things better and correct the problems."

Another reason for keeping problems out of sight were those in the voting middle class who did not view ending poverty the way they saw going to the moon. In space, "They accepted mistakes and failures as a part of the scientific process." On Earth, it surely would have been better to experiment freely with different approaches, "admitting some were working better than others. . . . But I knew that the moment we said out loud that this or that program was a failure, that the wolves who never wanted us to be successful in the first place would be down among us at once, tearing away at every joint, killing our effort before we even had a chance." Lyndon had to prettify the Great Society up front. He did. He promised he would work offstage to correct its deficiencies, but he never did.

As Doris Kearns Goodwin noted, LBJ never rode herd over the bureaucracy as he did the Texas NYA. He had no appetite for the task. He wanted new programs. He wanted quantity. Quality could wait.

Bureaucrats soon figured out that LBJ wanted good reports and no problems from them. The poor soon grasped that no one in the agencies made waves by pointing out and solving difficulties. The white middle class's discovery that all was not perfect in the Great Society came close behind. The perception grew that Johnson was concealing problems with sleight of hand and lying about their existence. The Great Society was sliding into the credibility gap he was digging around Vietnam.

More legislation. More programs. That is what Lyndon wanted from Congress during the session that stretched from the fall of 1965 until the end of 1966. While Shriver struggled to do good with less money, Joseph Califano shot for the moon.

Califano hit the target more often than not. Despite LBJ's worries that he was daily losing clout on Capitol Hill, the administration did succeed in getting a Department of Transportation and initiating programs for dealing with the problems of poverty, rage, and despair in American cities. Over the next two years, Model Cities allocated $900 million in matching grants (80 percent federal, 20 percent local) for urban efforts to improve neighborhoods. Some programs aimed at providing better housing with low-cost apartments and rent supplements for qualified poor people. Others strained to improve ghetto schools. Crime prevention and reduction programs were implemented in inner cities. More parks and recreational opportunities were created. LBJ could justifiably claim that he had done a great deal toward bettering life in the city.

With progress came criticism. Proponents of Model Cities correctly observed that $900 million was a drop in the bucket. Some suspected that money would fund patronage jobs for Democratic machines; time proved them right. Others wondered if these programs would generate more jobs in the cities. Soon it was apparent that the principal beneficiaries were middle-class blacks hired to staff the bureaucracies managing the programs, not the unemployed poor. These were troubling weaknesses, but LBJ did not look beyond the triumph of getting a law. Instead of improving Model Cities right away, he wanted more laws.

As was the case with the 89th Congress's first session, the breadth of Great Society legislation is stunning. Consumers received the benefits of the Truth-in-Packaging and Truth-in-Lending Acts. Underfunded urban school districts got assistance from a Federal Teaching Corps. The Child Safety Act imposed nationwide standards on producers of cribs and clothing; other legislation set federal guidelines for children's nutrition. Laws tightened safety standards on highways and in coal mines. Congress revised and extended existing legislation on water purity and passed a clean water restoration bill. The Johnson administration also succeeded in pushing through the first Endangered Species Preservation Act.

Any of these would be seen as a major achievement in a twenty-first century congressional session. Enactment of one might now consume almost the entire session. Clearly the huge partisan majority LBJ enjoyed was crucial to his success. Equally so were the ideals and the personality of the president. Lyndon believed the federal government could identify and solve major national problems. He believed Washington had the duty to do so. He believed those involved should rejoice at the chance to help all Americans, especially the poor and minorities.

When he could do so without going through Congress, he did. LBJ seized the opportunities presented by Title VI in the Civil Rights Act of 1964, which let the executive branch deny federal funds to discriminatory state and local programs, and by the money allocated to Medicare, which allowed him to attack segregation in hospitals effectively. "We're not going to lock the barn door after the horse is stolen," he ruled. "We're going to desegregate first," before billions of Medicare dollars watered Southern hospitals. Holding funds back did the trick. Within nine months virtually all Southern hospitals were desegregated.

Another example was Johnson's expansion of birth control. Part of the burden of poverty, he believed, was the size of poor families. Determined "not . . . to deny contraceptives to any poor person who wanted them," he ordered Califano to make their provision part of the War on Poverty. That devout Catholic dutifully obeyed. Next Lyndon assigned him the job "to make peace with the Catholic bishops, because before long they may be the only allies we have on Negro rights and the poverty program." Califano brokered this agreement: in government announcements, LBJ would remove "birth control" and "population control" in favor of "population problem" and the bishops would stay mum about it and remain hitched to the Great Society.

When new laws were required, Johnson pulled out all the stops. He had the advantage of preaching to a large choir. A majority of the House and Senate shared his creed and adopted his urgent impatience. Time-consuming debates over the cost and effectiveness of various programs were avoided by Johnson's keeping budgets underfunded and difficulties under the rug. Another factor was his determination to fend off detailed discussion of Vietnam's fiscal cost. Guns *and* butter, he assured Congress, could both be afforded.

The beat went on, with one significant exception: the civil rights bill of 1966. That failure did more than break the momentum behind Great Society legislation: it signaled the arrival of forces threatening to drive LBJ and his party out of power.

None of LBJ's advisers was sanguine about passing a fair housing law in 1966. Victory would be very difficult, because the votes of Dirksen and moderate Republicans were in doubt. Nonetheless, Lyndon plunged ahead. As he told Congress, "Negro ghettos indict our cities North and South, from coast to coast. . . . [They] represent fully as severe a denial of freedom and the fruits of American citizenship as more obvious instances. As long as the color of a man's skin determines his choice of housing, no investment in the physical rebuilding of our cities will free the men and women living there."

What moved him to go forward was his conviction that fair housing was absolutely necessary. Riots in more than ten cities during the summer of 1966 persuaded him that something must be done to bleed off tensions in the ghettos. Beyond that concern lay another. The rise of the Black Power Movement and its critique of integration depressed LBJ. He told Whitney Young that he had no brief for white or black power; he was for "American power and democracy with a small d, the fellow armed with the right to vote or armed with a job, a fellow armed with a house to live in, armed against discrimination." A fair housing act would help drown out Black Power's siren song.

Lyndon knew that only the federal government could bring about fair housing. The passage of Proposition 14 in 1964 and the violent reaction in Chicago's suburbs and ethnic neighborhoods to Martin Luther King's marches there in 1966 proved realtors, landlords, and homeowners were not going to be moved by calls for brotherhood. A series of Gallup polls during the early summer revealed that 52 percent of white Americans thought the administration was going too fast on civil rights. Local and state governments would not take measures against this backlash, and a mayor like Richard J. Daley of Chicago was a much tougher opponent than George Wallace. Even Lyndon paid homage to the Boss. When federal officials cut off funds to Chicago's public schools on the grounds that they were de facto segregated, Daley protested and Johnson restored the money. The president's only hope was to persuade a much smaller community: a majority of the House and enough senators to end a filibuster. Back to his old stomping grounds he went.

To the surprise of many, fair housing won a narrow majority in the Judiciary Committee and later was approved by the whole House. The Senate would be tougher. Some senators and staffers urged separating housing discrimination from sections of the bill aimed at Southern violence. The sponsors of the House bill refused to agree to this, as did King and other civil rights leaders. LBJ wanted no compromise either, reasoning that removing the housing provisions would heighten black rage, despair, and separatism. He called on Dirksen for help. The minority leader would not support fair housing, adding that even if he changed his mind Lyndon still would not have the votes. He did not. Johnson could only get fifty-two votes for cloture, well short of the sixty he needed.

Soon afterward, a Gallup poll found that a majority of Americans believed "racial problems" were the most important domestic issues. LBJ was not heartened. He recognized that this grouped together those who thought he was going too far and those who were sure he was not going far enough. He was stuck in the middle—and not just on race relations: no victory in sight in Vietnam, and no negotiations either; no stopping inflationary trends; no new taxes ahead to slow the rise of prices; and midterm congressional elections were just around the corner in November.

Hubert Humphrey was assigned responsibility for planning the 1966 election in April 1965. He soon discovered why. LBJ had little interest in the reelection campaigns of Democratic senators and congressmen. He excused this as bowing to the inevitable future and concentrating on the potential present. Some Democrats would be swept away in the usual reaction against the party in power at midterm elections. Moreover, narrow winners in 1964 would not be running against Goldwater in 1966. Given predictable shrinkage of Democratic majorities in the House and Senate, making hay while the sun shone was Johnson's rule. He focused on lawmaking, not politicking.

By 1966, the Democrats at risk were reversing the order of these priorities. Rumblings reached the media about their discontent with LBJ's inattention to the election. The president was not even posing for photos with them, let alone raising money and committing to campaigning.

Their complaints did not move Lyndon to action during the first half of 1966. That his staff thought this was unwise did not sway him. Only Bill Moyers's suggestion that if prospects in Vietnam brightened he should get out on the hustings tempted him. If that happened, he would be willing to take the credit, then use it to help other Democrats. Otherwise, he would lie low. His decision revealed that events in Vietnam were determining his acts in partisan politics.

Next Tommy Corcoran, a friend of Lyndon's since New Deal days, tried to get him into the campaign. To Corcoran, this was a chance for him to barnstorm across the country with the slogan "A vote against Lyndon Johnson is a vote for Hanoi." Why LBJ rejected this strategy is easy to understand: he remained wary of encouraging war psychosis and risking a Great Powers confrontation. What he overlooked or dismissed was that he did not have to be as crude as Corcoran advised. Campaigning was a chance to explain why the United States was in Vietnam and what it would take to defend its ally. Audiences would likely be receptive, for polls indicated a majority supported the war. The moment might not be perfect, but the opening to inform and rally was there. Instead, Lyndon waited for just the right time.

No time ever qualified, though some seemed right to others. In February 1966, Johnson met with President Nguyen Van Thieu and Premier Nguyen Cao Ky in Honolulu. Talks on pacification programs, termed by him "the other war," went smoothly. The Vietnamese leaders pledged to win hearts and minds in the countryside. Delighted, Lyndon portrayed this as a "Southeast Asian War on Poverty." The public response was heartening, and he cited it as an antidote to doubts raised by Fulbright's hearings on the war, but he did not follow up. Then events overtook him once more.

In April and May, Ky took advantage of Washington's approval of him to strike with ARVN forces against Buddhist demonstrators in provincial cities. Johnson watched the potential start of a civil war helplessly. Fortunately, the North Vietnamese and the Vietcong were surprised, and took no action. The crisis was over soon; its consequences lingered. The end of the Buddhist movement removed any intermediate group between Ky et al. and the VC; the United States had no options in South Vietnamese politics now, which put a major crimp in pacification. Stateside, it raised more questions about the legitimacy of South Vietnam's government. Lyndon responded by shrinking back into a shell of near silence on Vietnam.

The president also had to escalate. For months, the air force and the navy had been urging attacks on storage tanks in North Vietnam that were holding petroleum, oil, and lubricants (POL). The president had resisted on the grounds that the Chinese might use them as a pretext for intervention. With declining prospects for pacification, he felt he had to authorize the raids. The tanks were destroyed. The Chinese did nothing. His poll ratings went up. Then he learned that the North Vietnamese had long ago dispersed and concealed their POL in the countryside. Their war-making capabilities had not been diminished. They could fight for years with what they had.

This convinced Robert McNamara that bombing had no strategic military significance. The North Vietnamese could overcome it. It was also a political advantage for them. Civilian casualties from bombs gave protestors a potent argument against the war; Martin Luther King found these attacks especially immoral. The North Vietnamese improved this advantage by inviting Western journalists to see the damage. In late 1966 the *New York Times* highlighted a series by Harrison Salisbury on the bombing. The president could only fume again about Communists running the media; he had no other response.

Though LBJ saw the harm that bombing was doing to support for the war, he believed he must continue it. The Pentagon insisted that the raids were essential to military operations in the South. He still hoped that the cumulative damage of air attacks in the North would compel Hanoi to negotiate. McNamara's alternative—building an anti-infiltration fence around South Vietnam—was impractical. So LBJ stuck with a policy that armed dissenters with arguments without inspiring more support from other Americans. By early fall his approval rating slumped to 48 percent. Pundits and politicians predicted massive Republican gains in November.

Looming defeat convinced Johnson to keep a low political profile. He asked cabinet members to serve as surrogates. Instead of his getting contributions with public appearances, he commissioned Arthur Krim, the president of United Artists, to quietly raise several hundred thousand dollars in cash. Marvin Watson dispensed it in increments of $1,000 (for unopposed elections) and $2,000 (for contested seats) to all Democrats in the House and Senate running for office. He claimed they were all grateful; more likely, their reaction was grudging.

Moyers hit upon a solution to defuse criticism of LBJ as party leader: the president should take a seven-nation trip to Asia from October 7 to November 2. This would give LBJ a legitimate reason for not campaigning. He could highlight progress in Vietnam and focus attention on a president abroad. Johnson agreed enthusiastically. Hopeful that the trip's afterglow would help Democrats, he asked Watson to investigate the wisdom of his making a whirlwind tour of twenty-two cities in seventeen states between November 4 and 7. Watson urged him to do it and thought LBJ said yes. While the president traveled, his assistant began making arrangements. Democratic candidates were pleased; community leaders were excited. Word leaked to local and national media, who geared up to cover the president.

Everything fell into place. After LBJ's return, his approval rating skyrocketed to 63 percent. Photographs of him with troops at Cam Rahn Bay in Vietnam got great play. That he urged them "to nail that coonskin to the wall" was widely reported. Buoyed by meeting soldiers, Lyndon blurted out in South Korea that his own family had always fought for freedom, including at the Alamo. Again his words were featured. Before long he would be under fire for both statements.

What ignited criticism was not his words. It was his refusal to campaign. His doctors, he told the shocked Watson, wanted to remove a polyp from his throat and repair a hernia surgery incision. *Can't it be postponed,* he asked. *No,* replied Lyndon. Watson pointed out that thousands of people would be disappointed and furious. The press would claim that he was afraid of the response of crowds and the results of the elections. Tired from traveling, concerned about his health, Johnson erupted, claiming he had never agreed to it, accusing the staff of leaking their own scheme to make him campaign, and refusing to bail them out. What Watson predicted came to pass.

The press flayed LBJ alive. Once more, his credibility became a central issue. Adding fuel to the fire were the alleged tastelessness of the "coonskin" remark, which smacked to many of racist and imperialistic sentiments, and the outright falsity of the Alamo claim. That none of his relatives had fought there for Texas inspired jokes that his kin must have fought with the Mexicans.

Whether or not this brouhaha had a significant impact on the elections is unclear. Republicans were already poised to take advantage of disquiet about Vietnam, misgivings about the Great Society, and the white backlash against civil rights. Still, it did squander whatever boost Lyndon's trip might have given Democrats. The combination of emotions and events climaxed with the GOP's winning forty-seven more congressional seats and electing four new senators and eight more governors.

On the morning after, LBJ told Watson, "What this means is that all of us—and that includes me—must simply work harder." Not different. Harder. He would have to encourage an impatient, increasingly concerned country to stay the course. And he would have to urge patience and persistence in the face of an inclination by his fellow Americans to regard his concealing actions and thoughts as a major national issue.

Waist Deep in the Big Muddy: 1967

It did not take political genius to see trouble ahead in 1967. The genius resident at the White House had no difficulty picking out the challenges.

THERE WAS VIETNAM   The United States and South Vietnam were not losing the war, but they were not anywhere near victory. On January 1, 1965, about 184,000 American soldiers were there. A year later, almost 385,000 were in country, and the MACV was asking for more.

Because the U.S. army was composed principally of drafted men in 1965 and the soldiers who survived would return to "The World" when their year in Southeast Asia ended, heavier draft calls were needed in 1966. So, inductions during 1966 produced a 250 percent increase over 1964, for a total of a little over 300,000 men. Projections indicated that at least an equal number would be inducted in 1967. More and bigger demonstrations protesting the draft could be expected.

LBJ could also look forward to Vietnam's testing the patience of all citizens. Polls said that most Americans continued to approve of U.S. presence there. Even larger numbers disapproved of antiwar demonstrations. Lyndon hoped to intensify this negative reaction. Convinced that Communists were funding and leading the peace movement, he secretly ordered the FBI and the CIA to spy on its leaders. When these efforts bore no fruit, he leaked phony rumors to friendly congressmen so they could make public these bogus claims. These tactics gave him limited comfort, though, because popular disapproval of peace activists did not translate into support for him. The voters' estimation of *his* performance bounced up and down, rarely crossing 50 percent approval. In January 1967 the number was 43 percent. At the same time, a majority favored escalating the conflict. Under attack already from the antiwar left, now LBJ was the target of a frustrated right, who wondered why we were not fighting to win.

These crosscurrents in public opinion were roiled by another development. In 1964, only 16 percent of those polled agreed that the nation "should mind its own business internationally and let other countries get along as best they could on their own." By early 1967, 27 percent favored a return to isolationism. Even more were applying neo-isolationist nostrums to Vietnam. The feeling that "we ought to win it or get out" became more pronounced as 1966 turned into 1967. The consensus on containing Communism—so universal during the early Cold War—was tearing apart.

There was Europe   The Cold War consensus was unraveling even faster in Europe. Efforts to ease tensions between the United States and the USSR depended on Russian perception of U.S. strength. The North Atlantic Treaty Organization (NATO) had been the chief bulwark against the expansion of Soviet Communism. Now President Charles de Gaulle was pushing for the removal of U.S. forces from France. Embittered by memories of the U.S. failure to back France during the Suez crisis in 1956, de Gaulle claimed that America could not be relied upon to defend Europe in any major confrontation. The West Germans worried that the cost of Vietnam might compel LBJ to withdraw American soldiers from their country; they were aware how unprecedented the U.S. level of military commitment in Europe and Asia was. Britain's pound sterling was again in peril; if Harold Wilson's government had to devalue, the consequences for the dollar and for international financial markets might be serious. A rush by foreign investors to convert dollars to gold had shrunk Fort Knox reserves to $12.5 billion, and the outflow was multiplied by a growing trade deficit with Europe. The unfavorable balance of trade was worsened by stalled negotiations on the reduction of tariffs. LBJ had until the end of June 1967 to produce agreements before the authorizations for tariff reductions approved by Congress during Kennedy's administration expired.

After that, he would have to ask Congress for new authorizations. Who knew what would happen then?

Results might not be good. Congress might be inclined to walk away from the political, diplomatic, military, and economic problems in Europe, despite the impact it could have on Soviet relations. In August 1966, Mike Mansfield persuaded the Senate to pass a nonbinding resolution recommending substantial cuts in U.S. forces in Europe. Some were concerned about the balance-of-payments deficits; others thought we should allocate more troops to Southeast Asia. Mansfield believed that Europeans were starting to be irritated by the size of the American presence. By 1967, Congress and the general populace might let impatience with the troubles these allies caused ruin trade talks.

THERE WAS INFLATION In 1966, the rate of inflation was 3.4 percent, the highest since 1951. That inflationary cycle had caused Harry Truman's popularity to slump and ended his hopes for the Fair Deal. That could happen to this presidency. The Department of Housing and Urban Development isolated and highlighted problems faced by the 23 million families of "working Americans." White males who headed households had steady jobs but "the frontiers of [their] career expectations [had] been fixed since [they] reached the age of 35, when [they] found [they] had too many obligations, too much family, and too few skills to match opportunities with aspirations." Inflation would shred their lives.

It was already shredding Johnson's budget. When the administration calculated the cost of the war, it did not adjust for inflation. LBJ might have a deficit of $12 billion for fiscal 1967, a ruinous number likely to swell even higher. The president who loved keeping options open was hearing doors slam shut. To curb inflation and to get deficits under control he would have to work for higher taxes.

THERE WAS RACE Lyndon knew a growing majority of white Americans believed that the administration was going too far and too fast on civil rights. He was troubled by the accusations that his administration, by trying to "understand"—said sarcastically—the roots of disorder, was actually coddling criminals and encouraging more violence. But this did not change his analysis of the problems of the other side of the racial divide. Poverty was the breeding ground of desperation and destruction. Blacks needed more aid and greater opportunities, not less and fewer. Could he allay white concerns while serving black needs? Could he avoid being forced to choose one over the other? The fate of his administration and the future of the nation hinged on his responses.

THERE WAS THE REPUBLICAN PARTY The midterm elections had resulted in significant Republican gains. The GOP's performance had improved its morale and raised its expectations. Elephants were also encouraged by polls registering a decline in the number of voters calling themselves Democrats and an increase in those who were self-identified independents. The cozy alliances Johnson had enjoyed with Everett Dirksen and moderate House Republicans were things of the past. Renewed optimism about 1968 sharpened partisan edges.

That would impact conservative Southern Democrats. They felt their political lives were at stake as they contemplated surging Republican popularity in the South. Given the changing political environment on Capitol Hill and in the nation, raising taxes would be very tough. The price demanded by the Southerners in return would be smaller budgets for existing Great Society programs and a slower pace on enacting new ones. Maneuvering his way around a suddenly potent conservatism would require all of LBJ's skills.

In every one of these areas, Johnson was—in the words of an antiwar song—"waist deep in the big muddy." Would he attempt extrication by pulling back? Would he move forward? The next line was "and the old fool says 'push on' "—which was what he did.

When he looked back on 1967, Johnson recalled the abortive efforts to use such go-betweens as Polish diplomats and a French friend of Harvard professor Henry Kissinger to begin talks with the North Vietnamese. In retrospect, he regretted those failures; at the time, he expected very little from them. LBJ wanted negotiations only on his own terms: no more aggression against South Vietnam. He mirrored his enemy, who wanted America out before talking began. Both sides proclaimed willingness to meet; otherwise, world opinion might turn against them, but for both it was a charade.

Their real focus in 1967 was the military war. For the NVA and the VC this meant avoiding catastrophic defeat, while preserving tactical initiatives in battle and returning afterward to reorganize politically after U.S. withdrawal. For the MACV, the war came down to inflicting heavier and heavier casualties. To do that, said the president in October 1967, "we need to pour the steel on." William Westmoreland had been doing that since January 1.

Throughout 1967, the MACV tried to engage VC and NVA forces in big-unit battles. Operations had two goals: kill as many of the enemy as possible and drive them out of areas that had long sheltered Vietcong cadres. American soldiers were successful at killing; the Pentagon calculated at least 180,000 enemy troops were KIAs. How much of this was based on WEG (wild-eyed guesses) is open to question; more obvious was the fact that the VC and NVA were nowhere near defeat. North Vietnam replaced every KIA and even added reinforcements. Meanwhile, U.S. losses were averaging 200 KIA and 1,400 WIA per week. These totals were not WEG. LBJ felt he had no option but to raise U.S. forces in country toward 500,000 soldiers.

This was because Americans had shouldered the burden of combat against enemy forces. The South Vietnamese were chiefly responsible for protecting efforts at pacification. That, many critics complained, meant nothing was being done to pacify the countryside. Why were we neglecting the political aspects of the struggle? Stung by this criticism, Johnson and his advisers created Civil Operations and Revolutionary Development Support (CORDS), a joint civil–military agency, and placed it under Westmoreland. CORDS would coordinate all the various groups currently struggling with pacification and assess outcomes. As proof of his commitment, Johnson named Robert W. Komer as director.

Washington knew Komer as a no-nonsense, hard-charging bureaucrat. He lived up to his PR, swiftly earning in Saigon the nickname "Blowtorch." Unfortunately, his heat did not light the tunnel's end. Hamlets were most frequently pacified by the removal of the population. Elsewhere, the VC simply returned after American forces swept through, and the ARVN could not dislodge them. Komer did command headlines by trumpeting a "Year of Progress." Journalists in Saigon were skeptical, though few were as blunt as Michael Herr, who labeled CORDS briefings as "psychotic vaudeville" and scorned pacification as "a swollen, computerized tit being forced on an already violated population, a costly, valueless program that worked only in press conferences."

Lyndon himself questioned the CORDS Hamlet Evaluation System. Nor was he pleased by the creation of a South Vietnamese constitution and the resultant elections in September. The Thieu–Ky ticket won an embarrassing 35 percent of the vote, while a political unknown advocating talks with the National Liberation Front took 17 percent. The South Vietnamese government was neither more secure nor more legitimate. No wonder LBJ agonized in October, "How are we ever going to win?"

Could the bombing of North Vietnam hasten victory? McNamara doubted it. After two years of dropping more explosives than had pulverized Japan in World War II, after a year when sorties flown rose to 108,000, he concluded that Rolling Thunder still had no strategic impact. During 1967 Johnson sided with his military advisers against the defense secretary. He permitted attacks on electrical production plants and the only steel mill. He allowed mining of North Vietnam's harbors. He included targets close to the Chinese border. All had been off limits before spring 1967. But after attacking those targets and dropping 350,000 pounds of bombs on NVA units in Laos, there was no decline in the number of soldiers or the amount of supplies infiltrated into the south. Most targets left were those that might bring China into the fighting and spark confrontation with Russia. LBJ could not do this, any more than he could let American regiments pursue the enemy into Cambodia.

In October, McNamara urged the president to suspend the raids in hopes that would encourage North Vietnam to negotiate and would blunt some objections to the war at home and abroad. No military advantage would be lost because Rolling Thunder was strategically irrelevant. LBJ refused. He wanted to "hit them every day and go every place except Hanoi." "I know this bombing must be hurting them," he said. "Despite any reports to the contrary, I can feel it in my bones."

Now there was another factor in planning the war: Lyndon Johnson's "feel." Yet he had no reason to be confident in his instincts. During 1964 and 1965, he had said that were he Ho, he would not quit and would stay confident of victory. Had this feeling changed? Or was he grasping at straws?

He was aware that his patience set him apart from many fellow Americans. However committed people said they were to opposing Communism, their endurance was flagging. As LBJ mused about running in 1968, he told several advisers that the country would not stand for another four years of war. Equally troubling was that upper echelons of the media were getting antsy. *Life* magazine's editorials had been firmly pro-war. In October, Hedley Donovan, the successor to Henry Luce as editor of Time-Life Publications, wrote and published what his reporters said privately. Defending South Vietnam had "proved to be harder, longer, and more complicated than had been foreseen." Given the unending stalemate and increasing dissent, it no longer seemed of great enough significance "to ask young Americans to die for." How much effect would that have on millions of readers? *Life* had complicated Lyndon's life. He had to "hunker down like a jackass in a hailstorm."

There was no hunkering down over Europe, however. LBJ responded to crises there with a vigorous creativity. Francis Bator, a former MIT economist on the White House national security team, understood why. "It is not . . . all that surprising that someone like Lyndon Johnson, who had comparatively little interest in and knowledge of the substance of foreign affairs but was a master of politics and of power and had been enormously successful as Senate Majority Leader, would be both shrewd and wise in coping with the cluster of over-lapping, inter-connected problems we faced in Europe."

As in the Senate, relations with Europe was small-group politics. A finite number of foreign leaders had easily discernible international goals and readily understandable domestic pressures. Their personalities and foibles, their strengths and weaknesses, were well-documented. Lyndon treated foreign leaders as if they and he were members of a club even more exclusive than the Senate.

Each got a mild version of the Johnson treatment. LBJ did not try to bully or browbeat his peers. He spoke with them plainly and powerfully, impressing with his preparation on issues, his grasp of their problems, and his determination to find workable compromises. Key was his recognition that no one could emerge with 100 percent of what he wished; everyone had to take some bad with the good. Also crucial was his willingness to use his position as first among equals to help broker agreements among and between other nations. This he achieved by linking issues and rewarding sacrifices on some matters with gains on others.

Thus LBJ reconciled West Germany to a reduction in U.S. forces and gained assistance for the pound by encouraging *Ostpolitik,* Bonn's effort to seek new understandings with Eastern Europe and the Soviet Union. He gained de Gaulle's acquiescence on monetary reform by having Canada make the U.S. proposal for increasing gold reserves, thereby permitting *le gran* Charles to agree without yielding to "American dictation." Johnson sweetened the pot for France and the European Economic Community by compromising on the level of tariff reductions during the Kennedy Round talks and agreeing on concessions for European agriculture during a successful series of talks on tariffs and trade. He also traded stabilization of

Britain's currency for a continued commitment of some British forces in NATO and in bases in Asia.

Together these deals preserved and even strengthened NATO. Thanks to French politics, in 1966 it had seemed in peril to economic and fiscal uncertainty and to the changing military roles of the United States and Germany. By the end of 1967, these tensions had been alleviated. It was a considerable triumph.

The Middle East posed a different challenge. "The basic problems," mused LBJ in October 1967, "have been there all the time." Issues of ethnicity and religion—inflamed by feelings of humiliation and injustice (the Arabs) and fears about national survival and another Holocaust (Israel)—kept the antagonists from negotiations. In Europe people bargained and compromised; leaders wheeled and dealed. As Johnson ruefully recognized, "We can't solve the Middle East with two men in a room over a highball."

The president settled for trying to keep Israel and the more moderate Muslim countries—Jordan, Iran, and Saudi Arabia—dependent on American goodwill and military supplies. This, he hoped, would stabilize the region. He shipped weapons to all four while assuring the Israelis that the United States would preserve their security. To maintain this balance and head off nuclear proliferation, he actively discouraged Israel's program to manufacture nuclear weapons. The president trusted that reasonable Arab leaders would appreciate his efforts to restrain the Israelis. That, plus half a billion dollars worth of weapons for them, were his carrots. He used his stick as well, by slashing economic aid to Egypt and treating Syria as a pariah in Middle East politics.

Those efforts did not bring peace. The region became increasingly tense during the spring, and both Israelis and Arabs readied for a possible war. By early summer, Israel's leaders saw no alternative to fighting and resolved to strike first. Johnson preached patience and refused to approve an attack. He was not optimistic about his impact. When advisers predicted that Israel would wait, he disagreed: "They're going to hit. There's nothing we can do about it."

Fighting began on June 5 with a preemptive Israeli strike. According to Marvin Watson, LBJ felt that the United States was as obligated to preserve Israel's existence as it was to protect South Vietnam; he also believed that Israel's right to exist was established in the Bible. These were not convictions he expressed publicly. He wanted to be free to broker a ceasefire, and he feared his views might give the Soviets an excuse to intervene for the Arabs. His reticence had one effect: it sparked protests from American Jewish leaders. Their criticism infuriated him. Opposition to the Vietnam War was common among these men; now Vietnam doves had become Middle East hawks. The president seized upon what he saw as hypocrisy to exact a pound of flesh. In a meeting with them, he hinted that the State Department's declaration that the United States would be neutral in word, thought, and act was his real opinion. This left his audience distraught and tearful.

His mean revenge to the contrary, the overwhelming success of Israel's military action pleased Johnson. The U.S. ally would be more secure. He was determined that the Russians would not tip the balance against the Israelis. When a Soviet fleet sailed toward Syrian waters, LBJ sent the U.S. Sixth Fleet to intercept it. Alexei Kosygin contacted him via the hotline installed after the Cuban crisis. "You must turn back your fleet," the Soviet premier bluntly demanded. Johnson's response was terse: "No, you turn your fleet." After some tense hours, the Soviets backed off.

The six-day-long war ended with a ceasefire, but not before Israeli planes and motor torpedo boats attacked the U.S. destroyer *Liberty*, killing and wounding nearly 200 sailors. At first, LBJ and others were convinced this was no accident. They concluded that the Israelis feared the *Liberty* was transmitting information to the Syrians to slow Israeli advances and encourage a truce. Later they realized that there was no convincing proof for their suspicions. Nothing could be gained by rejecting Israel's apology. Johnson readied himself to deal with the aftermath of Israel's victory. Although a sort of peace prevailed, he had no illusions about its permanence.

To LBJ, the Arabs were not the only losers. The USSR "suffered a fiasco worse than the Bay of Pigs." The Russians could not prevent the Arabs' defeat, either by aiding them or by making the United States back down. To recoup reputation, Moscow called a special session of the UN General Assembly; Kosygin flew to New York to demand that Israel withdraw from territory it had seized. He also wanted to meet with Johnson.

The president was unenthusiastic. Kosygin was coming "to try to get some of the polecat smell off of him. . . . He has nothing constructive to offer toward solution" of Middle East problems. Why should he help wash the stink off?

But advisers at State urged LBJ to avoid giving the Soviets the impression that he wanted to embarrass them. His political staff noted that he would be criticized by the Left if he did not talk with

Kosygin. Fulbright's observation that a meeting might lead to talks with Hanoi gave this argument extra heft. And LBJ always had a strong desire to improve relations with Russia and erect defenses against possible nuclear confrontations. He was eager to take the measure of Kosygin. The two men agreed to meet on the campus of Glassboro State College in Glassboro, New Jersey.

Before the meeting, Johnson told Senator George Aiken that his guest had another item on his agenda. Moscow was worried about China—which was testing a hydrogen bomb—and the possibility of a Sino–American deal on Vietnam. This suggested that Kosygin might counter the Chinese with proposals for negotiations of his own. LBJ was not optimistic. Still, he hoped the Russians bringing up China might presage their help with Hanoi in the future.

At first, the president's pessimism about immediate dividends from the meeting appeared justified. Kosygin seemed unmoved by Robert McNamara's passionate concern about the aftermath of nuclear war. Talking about arms control did not interest him. Nor did discussing a ban on anti-ballistic missile (ABM) systems. Johnson was disappointed. He believed if ABMs were not stopped now they would accelerate the arms race and increase the chance of war between the Great Powers. For his part, Kosygin objected to LBJ's uncompromising statement "We will never abandon Israel's cause." Rejoined Kosygin, "Does that include risking possible unlimited nuclear war, which is what you just did?" He left the Soviet premier no doubt: "Yes, even that."

On Vietnam their exchange was predictable. Lyndon insisted all the United States wanted was an independent South Vietnam, and he asked for help starting negotiations with Hanoi. According to Watson, "Kosygin seemed to be receptive." The North Vietnamese "assured him that if the bombing of North Vietnam was stopped they would meet with the Americans." Watson recalled Johnson "responded positively, and Kosygin promised him that he would actively pursue the possibilities of peace."

Later LBJ dismissed this as the old song: "We should stop the bombing and get out of Vietnam." He remained skeptical about how much Moscow was willing to press Hanoi, given that they were competing with the Chinese for leadership of the Communist world. After the meeting the CIA informed him about another reason for Russian caution: the Soviets feared China might send troops into North Vietnam and turn it into a de facto Chinese colony if Hanoi looked like it was willing to compromise with the United

States. Still, Kosygin's comments helped commit him to a diplomatic initiative in late summer.

Johnson left Glassboro encouraged. He felt the Russians were interested in work on a proposed nuclear nonproliferation treaty. Kosygin appeared receptive to his plea that they meet annually. Both men learned—in Watson's words—"that his adversary was a human being, not a demon." They ended two days of "cordial disagreement" with mutual respect. The Cold War could be thawing. Heartened, Lyndon vowed to improve upon Glassboro. He was justified in thinking he had made modest but real progress and in expecting more would follow.

Prospects for the U.S. economy were less promising. Throughout 1967, LBJ kept a close eye on inflation. He understood the need for a tax hike to reduce consumer spending and to bring the budget closer to balancing. He committed himself in principle to an additional surcharge on personal and corporate income taxes, first of 6 percent, later of 10 percent.

Yet he doubted this was possible. The people did not see the need for it; Congress was opposed. If his contemplation of a surcharge leaked out, that would increase resistance. Gossip might even fuel more inflation by spurring consumers to splurge before taxes rose. So he was reserved in his frequent meetings with Gardner Ackley, the Director of the Council of Economic Advisers.

Another reason for his caution was his awareness of what the reaction of Wilbur Mills and other conservatives would be: "no way," unless the tax hike was coupled with reductions in domestic spending. He could not do this, given the worsening state of cities and the unrest and turmoil there. Consequently, he played a dangerous game. New social legislation had to be passed, and current programs spared from deep cuts, before any tax increases could be broached. In the meantime, he gambled that tighter monetary restrictions imposed by the Federal Reserve Board would keep inflation more or less under control. If this discouraged expansion too much, he risked a recession. If tight money did not work, he would have to ask for a tax hike. Whatever he did courted economic crisis and political trouble.

For a time, the Fed's medicine worked. During the first quarter of 1967, the rate of inflation dipped below the 1966 average of 3 percent. Then it began to climb steeply. Delay was no longer a viable option. In August the White House proposed a temporary surcharge of 10 percent on personal and corporate income taxes. LBJ explained that this was the only way to deal with "the hard and inescapable facts" of inflation and deficits. The news of his recommendation had no impact; by fall, consumer prices were rising 0.3 percent a month.

Wilbur Mills did what Lyndon expected: he demanded cuts in domestic spending. And he had what Lyndon feared: a 20–5 vote in October to table the surcharge in committee. The president recognized what inspired Mills's opposition. As historian Robert Collins pointed out, he wanted to "decouple the defining elements of growth liberalism, to separate growth economics from liberal activism." Wilbur did not want the economy's expansion to be the rationale and paymaster for a vast expansion of government programs. His was a sophisticated attempt to remove the cornerstone of the Great Society. It could have long-term consequences for the reception of future policies on Capitol Hill. It profoundly threatened Johnson's dream.

That nightmare worsened when Mills brought up the cost of the war. "I just do not believe," he later said, "that when we are in a war that is costing us $25 to $30 billion a year we can carry on as usual at home." To him, guns *and* butter were not possible. He opted for guns. Unsurprisingly, the war's opponents used the surcharge as proof that the United States should go for butter. Thus those who ordinarily would defend social programs were inclined to respond to the administration's proposal as Mills did, setting it aside until the president and Congress found "a means of implementing more effective expenditure reductions and controls."

Johnson dug in. He had no intention of surrendering to Mills or the doves. Inflation galloped on, immediately raising prices of weapons and supplies for Vietnam. The greater value of goods and services in that country tipped the balance of payments further against the United States; the gap between imports and exports doubled the 1966 trade deficit. The federal budget's deficit more than doubled. This bad news weakened the dollar on international money markets. Foreign bankers converted more of their dollars into gold. And no relief in the form of higher taxes was in sight.

Who would cry uncle first: Lyndon or Wilbur? Charles Schultze, the Director of the Budget, had assured Johnson that Mills was playing "chicken"; once he grasped that the White House would plow ahead, he would swerve away from collision and report the surcharge tax. Wrong! To Mills, this was an ideal chance to end future expansion of Washington's power. He had no intention of flinching.

Nor did LBJ. To him, the present and future of domestic reform depended on white knuckle steering. He did not change course, even when another economic crisis arose.

In November, Harold Wilson informed Johnson that the closing of the Suez Canal after the Six-Day War, a slowdown of the German economy, and a crippling strike by British dockworkers had so weakened the United Kingdom's trade that he had to devalue the pound. Fearful that this would trigger a run on the dollar, LBJ tried to patch together a coalition to save sterling again, but the European nations balked. The United States could not go it alone, and the best he could do was talk Wilson into only a 14.3 percent devaluation, which went into effect on November 18.

Investors immediately lost confidence in currencies and began converting them into gold. The dollar stood to suffer most. Thanks to the negative balance of trade, millions of dollars were in foreign banks. These institutions already doubted the soundness of U.S. currency. If they competed to buy gold with dollars and drove the price above $35 an ounce, confidence in the dollar's buying power would vanish. That reprised the 1930s. Parallels between then and 1967 led LBJ and his economic advisers to believe that the dollar's collapse could bring on another Great Depression.

Confronted by this crisis, the president and his team took swift action. The United States and eight other nations—a "gold pool" formed in 1961—stabilized the gold market at the cost of $641 million between November 20 and 27. (The U.S. share was 59 percent of the total.) The White House reaffirmed the U.S. commitment to $35 per ounce. This convinced other nations to stick with the present exchange rate for their currencies. Finally, LBJ had a message for Secretary of the Treasury Henry Fowler to deliver to Congress: "No single act could more effectively restore and maintain confidence in the dollar, and shore up our balance of payments position— both short and long term—than the passage of an expenditure reduction and tax increase package" in 1967. Speed was essential. "Markets don't wait."

After a good week between December 4 and December 8, during the following five business days the gold pool lost $548 million. The eight partners of the United States agreed to stick it out only after LBJ pledged that he would come up with a new program for reducing the trade deficit. By New Year's Day it was ready.

As his staff devised the plan, Lyndon insisted that unilateral increases in protective tariffs be excluded. He did not want to forfeit his gains during the recent negotiations with Europeans on tariffs. More importantly, he feared other nations would follow suit and repeat the trade wars that helped touch off the Great Depression.

He also ordered his advisers not to ask Congress to approve going below the statutory requirement that U.S. gold reserves be equal to 25 percent of the value of dollars in circulation. He would not give Mills et al. another weapon against the Great Society.

Lyndon and his team finally decided to use presidential authority to restrict direct business investment abroad, to limit the foreign loans U.S. banks could make, and to require businesses to invest foreign earnings at home. Congress was asked to approve programs helping U.S. exporters and encouraging Americans "to see the U.S.A. first."

Congress was also urged to pass the surcharge. The president hoped the gravity of the threat to the dollar would move Congress to raise taxes. Should the buck sink toward the bottom, everything—the Great Society, Vietnam, U.S. international alliances, the U.S. position vis-à-vis the Soviets and Chinese, and U.S. economic prosperity—would be imperiled.

However much LBJ complained about opposition to the war, a majority of Americans, white and black, supported the fight for South Vietnam throughout 1967. Steady increases in the prices of consumer goods did trouble many Americans, but as yet they were not hurting enough to fuel a widespread demand for higher taxes to reduce disposable income available to prospective buyers, depress the number and value of their purchases, and thus compel manufacturers to make the obvious adjustment to reduced market demand and lower prices. In contrast, in 1967 race and poverty had the potential of hurting Lyndon's political future much more, and he handled them cautiously at the beginning of the year.

In his State of the Union address, the president compared the War on Poverty with war in Southeast Asia. In each, "the enemy was difficult to perceive, to isolate, to destroy." Neither fight was "a simple one." This was a crucial shift in Lyndon's thinking. Once he had planned to wipe out poverty. Now he stressed the difficulties of fighting it and was much less sanguine about winning. Martin Luther King thought it ominous that Lyndon was pulling his punches and lowering his sights. King did neither, firing off salvos of criticism.

The gap between the two soon widened further. King determined in early 1967 that he was morally obligated to oppose the war. He announced his decision in a fierce speech on April 4, attacking the U.S. government as "the greatest purveyor of violence in the world." Some of King's closest advisers objected to this language, but he felt softening it would weaken his indictment. Plus, if he was strong, he might win the applause of proponents of Black Power, a step toward reuniting the movement. Finally, King hoped fierce language would end the war more quickly. He was prepared to urge using the billions spent on the war for a "Marshall Plan for the Cities" to reconstruct urban America and ignite its economy, as the original had for Western Europe. He readied himself to call for far more sweeping and radical change than Johnson's War on Poverty.

The president was saddened by MLK's speech at first. Then he went into a rage. It was different from his usual outbursts, noticed his press secretary; this was "cold anger." Lyndon called the speech "an act of disloyalty to the country." He intended to destroy King and the SCLC.

LBJ insisted that the FBI pressure the Ford Foundation to reject an SCLC grant proposal. He was delighted when the foundation reduced a $4 million award to $250,000. Next he told his personal tax attorneys to quietly research if the SCLC's tax-exempt status could be revoked. He and his staff began leaking details of King's alleged Communist connections to sympathetic journalists.

In the midst of this, Johnson nominated Thurgood Marshall, the great African-American lawyer and distinguished solicitor general, to the Supreme Court. The president fervently desired to make this appointment because he believed the elevation of the lead lawyer for the NAACP on the *Brown v. Board of Education* suit would send ringing messages on race to all Americans; one was the distinction between Civil Rights leaders he identified as truly patriotic and those he stigmatized as disloyal.

Soon LBJ could take comfort that MLK had become less popular. On May 22 a Harris poll revealed that 73 percent of Americans disagreed with King's position on the war, while only 9 percent shared his views; 48 percent of African-Americans opposed him, while only 25 percent favored him; and 60 percent were sure this would hurt the Civil Rights Movement, while only 3 percent believed it would not.

Johnson could not gloat for long. Martin's fears about the future of U.S. cities were dramatically borne out. In July, six days of rioting in Newark—26 deaths, 1,500 injuries, massive destruction—were followed by worse days in Detroit—37 dead, 337 injuries, 3,374 arrests, and 1,397 fires. Only after LBJ reluctantly sent army units was order restored. Now he plummeted in the polls. We're "down 15 percent," he lamented, "more than Vietnam [and] inflation." Why? "Every white man says he doesn't want his car turned over . . . [and] his neighbor throwing bricks at him."

Congress was not happy either. During the riots, a common accusation was that some Community Action Programs spurred on rioters. The administration fought off these charges with the testimony of mayors from around the country that CAPS were an important calming influence, but LBJ's budget request for the OEO of $2.6 billion for 1967 (a 25 percent increase over 1966) got mired in committee. Worse, Republicans and some Southern Democrats tried to finish off the OEO.

When the fiscal year ended on June 30, the OEO had no more money. This was not unusual; Congress regularly passed continuing resolutions maintaining disbursements at current levels until next year's budget passed. The OEO got no continuing resolution. After August it could not pay employees. By November 9, there was no spare money. Three Job Corps contracts lapsed, and several CAPS stopped operations. As Scott Stossel observed in his biography of Sargent Shriver, "It looked as though the OEO would die of fiscal starvation before Congress voted on the new bill."

What saved the OEO was the response of local officials, prominent businessmen, and the people. Letters and calls cascaded onto Capitol Hill. Some were spontaneous; some, like Operation Republican Mayor, Shriver organized. The mayors' arguments that "the programs are a positive force in lessening social tensions in our cities," plus their confidence that the CAPS would keep on improving in the future, were persuasive. A continuing resolution passed on November 28.

Lyndon and Sarge Shriver still had to pay a price for the OEO's renewal: greater participation by local officials on CAPs. This compromise was savaged by CAPS' radical supporters as denying the poor a voice and filling patronage troughs. Republicans howled about a Democratic boondoggle. They argued that this was a concession to "bosses and boll weevils" (conservative Southerners) who did nothing to reduce the likelihood for social disorder.

The boll weevil charge had merit. Southerners did play a crucial role in the preservation of the OEO. The agency's opponents sought to kill it by placing Head Start under the Office of Education and the Job Corps within the Department of Labor. They reasoned that once CAPS were isolated from the two most popular programs, they would be terminated and the OEO doomed. Government lobbyists cleverly convinced Southerners to oppose these moves on the grounds that the two departments would use the programs to mount more vigorous attacks on segregation. For the wrong reason

Lyndon got the right result. The amendments to the OEO bill were defeated.

The end of the struggle was a stunning victory for LBJ, Shriver, and the War on Poverty. Congress authorized the OEO for two years, not one. It also allocated $1.78 billion for each of those years. It was, remarked Shriver, the bare minimum for executing all programs. Still, it was an increase over fiscal 1966, and the bill passed by a larger margin than the previous two years.

No one could say the problems of race had been solved, but the best means of attacking them had been preserved. Heartening, too, was the groundswell of support for the War on Poverty. To Lyndon, this vindicated his strategy of creating programs and expecting them to build constituencies. Money might follow later. Not now; not soon. Survival and small steps forward were sufficient victories. Marginalizing Martin Luther King was an additional bonus.

Was Lyndon facing marginalization himself? The GOP had rebounded from total defeat in 1964 to brimming optimism about 1968. Some columnists speculated that the United States was on the cusp of a seismic political shift, away from the New Deal/Cold War/Democratic consensus toward a white middle-class/smaller government/revised foreign policy/Republican majority. Johnson was not so alarmist, but he was aware of uneasiness about civil rights, the War on Poverty, inflation, and Vietnam. Polls showing him vulnerable to a Republican did not shock him.

Of greater concern were the signs of opposition within his own party. His advisers were sure he would have a majority of delegates at the convention no matter what happened in the primaries. But he would have to raise money, give speeches, show up in primary states, cut deals with local Dems, and defend himself from attacks by his party's doves. That news depressed him.

Lyndon had eyed one dove like a hawk for years. His opinion on whether RFK would run shifted often. Gene McCarthy concerned him and his staff less: he was too lazy, too unpredictable, and too tainted by coziness with oil companies to pose a real threat. Still, if he ran he would add to LBJ's woes.

That Johnson viewed 1968 unenthusiastically was not a good sign. That his political staff could not get him to commit much time or attention to the onrushing campaign did not bode well.

He worked up more enthusiasm for addressing the forthcoming campaign's two major issues: race and Vietnam. He combined his political prowess and official powers to deal with both.

Racial issues had become entangled with worries about crime in the minds of the white middle class. George Wallace and many Republicans had long ago figured out that defending "law and order" made opposing more integration respectable. Johnson knew that the political exploitation of crime did not mean that the data were concocted and the concerns of citizens were not justified; what separated him from opponents was his conviction that the roots of crime were economic. Poverty and desperation drove people to crime: if we did nothing but catch and jail criminals, the cycle would repeat itself endlessly. Government needed to grub out the roots. So LBJ linked his crime bill to the War on Poverty. This, he argued, was the right way to get safe streets.

During 1966 this approach had not moved Congress. Gradually the president adapted to its resistance. After the 1967 riots, the administration took the step of proposing federal money for local law enforcement agencies. Other provisions encouraged rehabilitation by emphasizing parole, probation, and participation in community-action job training programs. Opponents of his crime bill made familiar charges. It would intrude on state and local government police powers. It was too soft on criminals. It encouraged moral permissiveness. Lending weight to these objections was a significant swing in public opinion back toward favoring capital punishment. Nevertheless, LBJ remained confident that an effective response to crime as a social problem could be enacted.

Fighting crime helped him against a Republican challenger. Vietnam was the key to dealing with Democratic dissidents. A resolution to that crisis remained as elusive as ever.

None of LBJ's military advisers predicted victory in 1968, but all felt the situation had improved. Their boss dissented. Worn out by work and war, McNamara wanted to leave the Department of Defense at year's end. Gathering his energy, he made another attempt to persuade Johnson to stop the bombing of North Vietnam. He repeated that it served no strategic purpose and energized the antiwar movement. (Though he prudently left this unsaid, failure to try a bombing pause would increase the pressure on RFK to run.) He pointed to the congruency of his proposal with Kosygin's comments at Glassboro. As he made the case, McNamara took hope from August polls showing that 67 percent of Americans disapproved of Johnson's conduct of the war and 71 percent wanted a negotiated settlement as soon as possible.

To Lyndon, these desires overlooked an inconvenient fact: the North Vietnamese did not want to talk; they wanted South Vietnam.

He favored an escalation of Rolling Thunder. He was wary of any policy change that might suggest antiwar protests were getting to him. LBJ believed demonstrations were whipped up by Communists and funded with Red money. Soviet agents, Watson told him, paid stooges in denominations of $20 and less; the Chinese did not balk at large bills. Appearing to give in would lead to stepped-up efforts.

Still, LBJ tested the diplomatic waters. In early September, he secretly approached Hanoi, offering to stop all bombing of North Vietnam in return for negotiations. Conspicuously absent was the usual requirement that the enemy must not use the pause to resupply forces in South Vietnam. Discerning why he took this step is difficult. Did he hope against all expectations that Ho would negotiate? Or did he anticipate that a refusal would prove to McNamara and others how mistaken they were about Hanoi? The suspense was short: North Vietnam did not respond.

Lyndon made his offer public in a speech in San Antonio on September 29. He reinserted his requirement in this version, telling the staff that he did it to stave off criticism from hawks. He clearly hoped to benefit in domestic politics, by keeping hard-liners mollified while appealing to doves. The polls moved slightly in his favor, suggesting that whenever the public perceived him as moving toward getting out of Vietnam, his rating would rise.

Politics may have led him to approve Henry Kissinger's secret contacts with North Vietnamese representatives in Paris during October. When these fizzled out, LBJ reverted to believing that easing off bombing would encourage more resistance from North Vietnam and allow it to strengthen its forces in the south. He also seized upon a consensus among his military advisers that the tide had turned. They predicted one more desperate thrust from the enemy; once that was defeated, light would glimmer.

Johnson wanted to believe them. He did not want more gloomy predictions from a distraught secretary of defense. McNamara had asked for the presidency of the World Bank months earlier; LBJ gave it to him in November.

Robert Kennedy tried mightily to persuade his friend to decline the post and declare opposition to the war. McNamara could not bring himself to do that. Kennedy then planted a story that McNamara had been fired because he argued for negotiations. This false news reinforced the public's correct perception that the president was tilting back toward pouring the steel to North Vietnam. The president's approval rating dropped. A Harris poll at Thanksgiving revealed that Americans favored RFK over LBJ for the presidency by 52 to 32 percent, the widest margin yet.

Looking at a photo of himself during the Six-Day War, Lyndon observed, "There's a picture of a sad man." By the end of 1967, he was a weary man as well. Running for reelection in 1968 would add to his burdens.

That prospect was disquieting. How much so LBJ admitted in the middle of an October 3 discussion of Vietnam. The minutes of that meeting reveal that the president first swore all present to secrecy, then "asked what effect it would have on the war if he announced he was not going to run for another term." "If it were set either way today," he added, "the decision would be that he would not run."

CHAPTER

13

Hell Sucks:
January to March 1968

To run or not to run. Whatever LBJ decided would impact his presidency in ways both obvious and unforeseeable. It would also affect him personally.

Regarding the personal, Lyndon was keenly aware that staying in power until January 20, 1973, would leave him second only to Franklin Roosevelt for longevity. Balanced against this glory was his health. Could he live that long? His male ancestors had died relatively young, and none of them suffered the stresses he had. Having another chief executive die in office would be traumatic for the nation. Most of all, the specter of Woodrow Wilson after his stroke haunted Johnson. He readily conjured up images of himself incapacitated, powerless, and trapped at 1600 Pennsylvania Avenue.

Regarding his presidency, what would happen if he became—to borrow his words—"a crippled water fowl"? When he broached the possibility he might not run on October 3, 1967, he told his advisers, "What I am asking is: 'What would this do to the war?'" Then he mused, "I am afraid it would be interpreted as walking out on our men." The reaction of Dean Rusk—"You must not go down. You are the commander in chief and we are in a war. This would have a very serious effect on the country"—thrust home. Did duty require him to soldier on?

During late 1967, LBJ sought advice from five people. One was his wife. Lady Bird would make the most persuasive case for not running. Two others had been with him since the 1930s: John

Connally and Jake Pickle. Each was a successful politician; Connally as Governor of Texas and Pickle as the congressman from his old district had power bases independent of him. The fourth was Horace Busby, who had worked for him from 1948 to 1965. Like John and Jake, Busby had a successful career apart from LBJ, as a Washington management and political consultant. The final person he consulted was a newcomer: George Christian, the White House press secretary, whom he had hired away from Connally's staff. What impressed Lyndon about Christian was his disinterest in establishing himself in Washington by cozying up to the media. That he avoided the pit Bill Moyers leaped into, and that he planned to return to his Austin public relations firm, confirmed his independence.

No one among these five had personal, policy, or program goals that depended on his serving another term. They would give him advice with the bark off. They would have his best interests at heart. He was confident they would consider what was best for the country as well.

Bird's vote was no. Lyndon had to weigh seriously the possibility that he might die during a second term or be unable to continue in office. Even were he not incapacitated, would he be physically able to keep working the eighteen-hour days the job demanded? Lady Bird judged Lyndon's physical resources dangerously depleted. There was no prospect of rejuvenation: the office would not allow him an R&R leave. Besides, in contrast to August 1964, when she had urged him not to withdraw, many of his tasks were triumphantly finished. He could and would be able to retire and rest easy.

She kept to herself another reason. In 1964 and 1965, the White House had been exciting and fulfilling. She had enjoyed being First Lady. The last two years, however, had been hell. She knew why: "It is unbearably hard to fight a limited war." With no end in sight, she feared neither Lyndon nor she could endure four more years. That was not an argument she could voice. The president's sense of duty and his feelings about being a man were so strong he would never quit if he thought the reason was that events were too tough for him: that would be desertion and cowardice. Bird had to recite his achievements and question his health. That might move him to agree. But he had backed off from retiring too many times for her to be optimistic.

John Connally also advised against running. His reasoning was blunt: LBJ's political problems were too great and his personal unpopularity too widespread. A campaign would end in disgrace and defeat; there was no use pursuing a forlorn hope.

Connally's advice reflected a widening political gap between him and Lyndon. John was much more conservative. Lyndon's approach to race relations and much of the Great Society troubled him, and Connally did not believe he was alone. He concluded that voters were moving decisively to the right. Richard Nixon would take advantage of this and win.

Lyndon Johnson did not need to be told about conservative trends; he had been predicting them for three years. He grasped that he was disliked. Did this equal sure defeat in 1968? His answer was no. As he had pointed out in September 1967 to Max Frankel of the *New York Times,* he had been winning difficult elections since 1937. If Nixon opposed him, he would have an important edge. Privately, Johnson assured his staff that "Tricky Dick" had a fatal weakness: he ran fast and well at the start but inevitably did something toward the end of the race to snatch defeat out of the jaws of victory. Buoyed by these track records, when Frankel asked if he could win in 1968, LBJ did not hesitate. "I sure as hell can. If I decide to run for it, I will win."

Warnings like Connally's would not move LBJ toward retirement. Giving up merely because he feared he would be beaten would be political cowardice. He would also be turning away from a real chance of victory. Living with that would be intolerable.

Christian, Pickle, and Busby also thought Johnson should not run. Each hit independently upon the most persuasive approach. Before LBJ would decide against running, he would have to convince himself—or be convinced—that withdrawing was best for the country because that would make him a more effective president during 1968. All three emphasized that he would accomplish more by removing himself from presidential politics.

The war was an obvious example. Johnson could vigorously pursue negotiations without Hanoi suspecting and doves saying he was doing this for partisan advantage. Foreign and domestic enemies would have to concede that he was making bona fide efforts to achieve peace. The same would be true with domestic programs. Johnson could not be accused of trolling for votes. He plausibly could claim that he was doing what seemed right, with no concern for personal gain. A leader above the political fray, he might get meaningful talks with the North Vietnamese and, for instance, the tax hike from Congress. Certainly he would be undistracted by the troubling dilemmas and wearying pace of partisan politics.

When Connally heard these arguments, he immediately realized how effective they were; they required strength and sacrifice.

Lyndon would not be vulnerable to charges from others and himself of weakness and surrender. Hawks and doves, enemies and allies, could regard him as an eagle, not a chicken. Connally made the same points.

Connally added a note of urgency: the longer LBJ waited, the more questioning of his motives and the weaker his position. Events might even make it impossible to withdraw. No patriot could quit in a crisis. Appearing to race toward retirement when foreign relations were at a critical stage could have catastrophic results. That invited aggression and would leave the president and the country nearly helpless to respond.

Fully impressed and mostly convinced, Lyndon had Busby draft a paragraph announcing his retirement. The president considered reading it during the State of the Union address on January 12, 1968, but the paper stayed behind when he left for Capitol Hill. Later he claimed he had forgotten it to excuse his own vacillation.

That LBJ said nothing did not surprise Lady Bird. The most recent Gallup poll indicated that 48 percent of the American people approved of his performance, a substantial increase over his score in October. Pols in both parties were betting he would beat Gene McCarthy by a margin of 5–1 in the New Hampshire primary. Unmoved by this news, Connally reminded him the clock was ticking. Much more delay, and unpredicted events might choose for him.

Whither Vietnam? As 1968 began, Lyndon drew on the optimism of William Westmoreland, who had informed Congress the preceding November that he could see the light at the tunnel's end. The general also said on television that the United States might be able to start withdrawing troops in two years or less. When asked about the North Vietnamese, he replied, "I hope they try something, because we are looking for a fight." So was his commander-in-chief.

Privately, LBJ forecast that the enemy had one more kamikaze attack left. Fend that off, counterattack in force, and huge NVA losses would cause the scale and intensity of fighting to drop off. He thought that might encourage Hanoi to negotiate, though he remained pessimistic about both the chance for talks or any resultant progress. A more likely outcome would be surging American support for the war and the president.

An indicator of optimism was his choice of analogy. Japanese kamikazes had been suicidal missions. They signaled desperation and presaged defeat. On days that he worried more, he referred to Dien Bien Phu. LBJ did not have to strain to see that parallel.

President Lyndon B. Johnson listens to tape from Vietnam. © Lyndon B. Johnson Library

A marine fire base at Khe Sahn in the remote mountains of northwest South Vietnam was surrounded by NVA regiments. Concerned, Lyndon had the Pentagon construct a model in the White House Situation Room. He brooded over it, finally exploding, "I don't want any damned Dien Bien Phu!" That would destroy support for the war in the United States.

General Westmoreland was positively eager for a fight to the finish at Khe Sahn. Victory there would have a multiplier effect by proving to Hanoi that it could not duplicate the triumph over France. Thus he and his staff paid no heed to a few stray whispers that the enemy was in fact readying attacks against the cities of South Vietnam. Pure disinformation, they concluded.

Whether Lyndon was privy to this intelligence is beside the point: he would not have believed it. Khe Sahn looked, felt, smelled, and sounded like French journalist Bernard Fall's famous description of Dien Bien Phu: "Hell in a very small place." When he studied photographs of marines there, he saw similar messages on their helmets: FAR FROM FEARLESS. BORN TO LOSE. HELL SUCKS.

You would get no argument from LBJ about that last wisdom. On January 25, the North Koreans gave him more brimstone. They attacked the USS *Pueblo,* an intelligence-gathering destroyer cruising in international waters off their coast. One sailor was killed, and the *Pueblo* and its officers and crew were captured. Pyongyang announced its intention to punish them for their "criminal" activities.

Some pundits called for mining the harbor at Wonsan, taking North Korean vessels, blockading, bombing, or even raiding. Johnson had none of these options. The hostages would be at risk. Moreover, both the USSR and the PRC had signed treaties binding them to defend North Korea, and LBJ always tried to avoid escalating tensions between the United States and these giants. He also realized that the U.S. military was already stretched thin in Central Europe and Southeast Asia. Another Korean War would be one war too many.

Off the record LBJ told reporters, "We can't get [the crew] back by military force." Moving some fighters and bombers to South Korea would, he hoped, show enough mailed fist to move the North Koreans toward releasing the prisoners, yet avoid rousing the Russians and Chinese. Most of the work would have to be done with diplomacy's velvet glove. Accordingly, Johnson began seeking help from the UN, Moscow, and a variety of neutral nations.

The *Pueblo* created political problems for Lyndon. Aside from predictable charges of weakness, he could expect accusations that this was more proof of Vietnam leaving the nation powerless to respond to attacks elsewhere. Beefing up U.S. air power in South Korea required the Pentagon to activate some reserve air force pilots, and that made voters apprehensive about more call-ups of reservists. There was trouble ahead.

That was true. But the *Pueblo* would play a minor part in it.

At 1:30 A.M. on January 30, the first day of Tet, the Vietnamese holiday celebrating the lunar new year, VC sappers blasted into the American embassy compound in Saigon. Throughout the country NVA and VC forces launched synchronized attacks on American and South Vietnamese troops. Thirty-six of forty-four provincial capitals were struck; so were five of the six largest cities. Fighting was ferocious.

By 9:00 A.M. the fifteen sappers were dead, along with eight Americans. At 9:20 A.M., Westmoreland proclaimed victory everywhere. All attacks, which he described as efforts to divert reinforcements from Khe Sahn, had been repulsed. Friendly casualties were minimal; enemy losses were staggering.

To reporters who followed soldiers into the compound, this statement was surreal. They saw bodies crumpled, walls pocked with bullet holes, and the U.S. seal askew. The American people saw the same images on television and in newspapers. These scenes became indelible portraits of the war. So did shots of the summary execution of a sapper by the chief of the national police.

Combat raged for weeks. No one has ever settled on how long the Tet offensive lasted or on a final body count. The best guesses agree that as many as 40,000 VC and NVA died out of an attacking force of nearly 67,000. South Vietnamese losses were around 2,300; Americans killed numbered 1,100. An additional 45,000 civilians were dead, wounded, or missing; more than 1,000,000 lost their homes.

Though the military situation troubled Johnson, he was confident U.S. and ARVN troops would prevail on the battlefield. Of greater concern were the psychological and political consequences of Tet. Neither he nor anyone else had trouble recalling Westmoreland's optimistic words. The savageness and scope of the enemy's attacks appeared to give the lie to forecasts that the United States would be out in two years. Worse, the pictures seemed to show that three years of war had left U.S. forces no closer to victory. LBJ had to fight against these perceptions.

On February 2 he insisted to the press that Tet was not a surprise. Technically, this was true. U.S. intelligence had predicted thrusts against Khe Sahn and diversions elsewhere. Left unemphasized was the misreading of where the major blows would fall.

That was damning enough. Then it transpired that claiming the MACV knew something was up raised another question. If foes could achieve success *without* surprise, did that not argue that the war was even further from being won? Johnson hastened to add that Tet was "a complete failure." Then he got down to his real worry. The Communists would claim "a psychological victory." That, he stressed, was not the case: "When the American people know the facts . . . and when the results are laid out for them to examine, I do not believe they will achieve a psychological victory."

Words. Numbers. Served up by a president with a credibility problem. Matched against color photos of marines' bodies stacked on tanks. Here came more trouble, but not right away.

The public rallied to the troops. Polls during February registered a rise in pro-hawk sentiment, with 61 percent favoring stronger military measures, 70 percent wanting the bombing of North Vietnam to continue, and 53 percent desiring either a gradual intensification of military effort or an all-out attempt to end the war before Russia or China could intervene. A gratifying 64 percent hoped that LBJ would not reduce domestic programs, though a majority thought if a choice must be made, guns should rank above butter.

Johnson was not too heartened. Public opinion on Vietnam was complex and volatile. Polls changed rapidly, and they were very sensitive to the nuances of questions asked. Knowing this, doves made points trenchantly and memorably. What would happen, Gene McCarthy asked, if the VC took Saigon? The administration would say they were close to collapse. Senator George Aiken was equally biting: "If this is a failure, I hope the VC never have a major success." Readers of Art Buchwald's columns could draw their conclusions from this communiqué: "The battle of Little Big Horn has just turned the corner, and the Sioux are on the run."

Being the punch line of bitter jokes was a bad sign. Worse was coming. Throughout the decade, Walter Cronkite's even-handed presentation on the *CBS Nightly News* had impressed millions. When Cronkite stared with revulsion at film from Selma, the movement won a major battle. After a trip to Vietnam, the broadcaster told the nation on February 27 that we were "mired in stalemate." He made clear how skeptical he had become of experts who always claimed to see light at the end of the tunnel. Nevertheless, "on the off chance that military and political analysts are right" this time, the United States needed to test whether these attacks were last gasps before talks. Cronkite made it clear he favored negotiations, not as victors but as a country that had done its best. "If I've lost Cronkite," some remembered Johnson saying, "I've lost middle America." Others recalled a different comment: "I've lost the war."

Predictably, some disagreed with this judgment. Was LBJ really on the verge of winning? As usual, he was whipsawed between doves and hawks. Westmoreland and Earle Wheeler, chair of the Joint Chiefs, saw Tet as a great opportunity. They thought they could convince LBJ to widen the war into Laos and Cambodia and to send 206,000 more men to Vietnam. Wheeler urged the president to call up the reserves. He also felt that Tet warranted asking Congress for a declaration of war. Do this, and the United States would crush a reeling enemy.

Soon all the chips would be shoved into the pot. Which hand would he bet table stakes on? Lyndon wanted the advice of Clark Clifford, who was replacing McNamara at the Department of Defense on March 1.

A veteran of political and policy struggles, Clifford counseled considering where the country was and where it was going to be. His reasoning was pure politics: how could LBJ say the enemy had achieved none of his goals and suffered terrible losses, then turn around and say the situation was worse and required more men and possibly calling up the reserves? Absent a compelling explanation, there would be a domestic firestorm. Johnson grasped this immediately. After telling Clifford that the North Vietnamese were "putting all of their stack in now," and thus justifying sending 10,500 reinforcements, LBJ asked him to consider all the options and give him advice "with all the bark off." Clifford took this as a go-ahead to do a wide-ranging review of Vietnam policy.

That review was not fully informed because the enemy's intentions during Tet remained unknown until later. Hanoi did expect to gain a stunning military and political victory, topped off by an uprising by the people and the disintegration of the ARVN. Impacting American opinion was not a consideration; they were not aiming at psychological victory. And they did not get what they aimed at. Tet finished the VC as an effective military force. VC political influence dramatically waned because of battlefield losses and the displacement of peasants into refugee camps and the cities. More completely than was comprehended at the time, the United States won its war with the VC. Even a partially informed review, however, made clear that it had not defeated the North Vietnamese.

Clifford thought about whether the United States could beat them. Considerations other than the purely military and exclusively Southeast Asian shaped his deliberations.

While Clifford pondered, Democrat doves wondered if Lyndon Johnson could be beaten. The occasion of liberals' opposition to him was the war, but that was fertilized by the compost from Senate politics in the 1950s and their growing conviction that the unbending anti-Communism of the Cold War consensus was misguiding American policies. Gene McCarthy spiced these memories and beliefs with a bitter hatred of "that son of a bitch." Still, no one could predict what Tet's impact might be. Robert Kennedy refused to enter the race. The wheel horses of the party could not conceive of a successful challenge to Johnson.

Meanwhile Lyndon showed little interest in the campaign, yet those who urged him to withdraw saw no sign he would retire. John Connally persisted in warning that time was slipping away and events might determine the choice; interestingly, he did not feel Tet would compel the president to run. LBJ kept his own counsel.

Nobody thought anything significant would transpire in New Hampshire. Granite State voters were hawkish; their leaders were for Lyndon. McCarthy did not want to contest the primary, but his staff convinced him to have a go. If he got higher than 10 percent, it would encourage supporters in Wisconsin. His speeches, advertising, and television appearances were calm, quiet, and detached, not like the fire usually burning in insurgent campaigns. As McCarthy's biographer Dominic Sandbrook observed, it was often difficult to tell where he stood on Vietnam. But everyone knew what McCarthy was against: Lyndon Johnson and his stubborn, unbending arrogance of power and failure at leadership.

On March 12, the president received only 49.5 percent of the Democratic vote. "The unforeseen Eugene," as *Time* magazine dubbed him, got a stunning 42.4 percent. Add the write-in votes he got in the Republican primary, and McCarthy came within 230 votes of out-polling LBJ.

Antiwar activists trumpeted the result as a victory for their cause. That version has become part of American political folklore. Yet as Sandbrook has written, it was nothing of the kind. Exit polls revealed that most voters had no idea what McCarthy's position on the war was. His allusive remarks had kept them in the dark. It is impossible to quarrel with his biographer's speculation that "had they known he was a dove, they would have opposed him in greater numbers." Much later, a survey showed that 60 percent of McCarthy's New Hampshire supporters "thought that Johnson was mishandling the war in Vietnam because he was not being aggressive enough." Sandbrook's judgment is well-founded. "In reality, [McCarthy's] vote was an anti-Johnson vote, not an antiwar vote."

The man in the White House understood this. To him, New Hampshire's message was clear: however much his fellow citizens might rally behind the country, they were far less willing to rally behind him. His job ratings confirmed this. Polls in early March showed that voters elsewhere shared New Hampshire's opinion;

63 percent disapproved of his handling of the war, and 52 percent disapproved of his overall performance. These ratings were all-time lows. Lyndon's woes were compounded by the news that 49 percent now believed sending troops to Vietnam was a mistake.

By mid-March, it appeared neither hawks nor doves could stand Lyndon Johnson. They might not know exactly where Gene McCarthy stood, but that counted for less than the fact that he was not LBJ! Most Americans did know where Robert Kennedy stood vis-à-vis Johnson. On March 16, he announced his candidacy. What LBJ had constantly fretted about had come to pass.

Adding to his woes was Tet's contribution to the nation's economic problems. During January and February inflation accelerated. The wholesale price index rose 0.4 percent in January and another 0.6 percent the next month. The Bureau of Labor Statistics concluded that "price increases are becoming more pervasive throughout the economy." Additional spending on the war would speed them up even more.

Less clear was whether Johnson's efforts to reduce the balance of payments deficit were taking hold. This was certain, though: if responding to Tet required massive reinforcements and a national call-up, more dollars would cascade out of the country.

Getting the administration's tax surcharge bill through Congress would alleviate these difficulties. That chance seemed remote. Henry Fowler characterized the House's mood as "almost anarchistic willingness to pull down the temple around their ears on the grounds that our budgetary expenditures are out of control." Wilbur Mills had convinced his colleagues to demand cuts in domestic spending in return for the tax hike. Johnson was not yet willing to give in.

He hoped to pressure the House with this argument: failure to increase taxes would weaken the dollar. Walt Rostow, who had replaced McGeorge Bundy as National Security Adviser, put the case succinctly: the tax hike "has become a symbol in Europe of what the U.S. itself is willing to do." Inaction brought on what Lyndon feared during the first week of March.

Eager to exchange inflated dollars for gold, traders ignited what *Time* magazine called "the largest gold rush in history." To keep the price of $35 per ounce stable, the gold pool countries had to shove nearly $300 million worth of gold into the market. That stimulated more buying. The first four days of the next week, the gold pool lost $769 million. Friday's trading could push the week's losses over

$1 billion, predicted LBJ's financial team, who also urged him to ask the British to close the market immediately and suggested he call an emergency meeting of gold pool countries. Solving the crisis, Rostow summarized, went "to the heart of our nation's capacity to carry its external commitments; maintain the world trade and monetary system; and avoid a serious domestic breakdown in our economy." The situation called to mind the international fiscal crisis of the 1930s. Convinced of the danger, Johnson acted. London shut down the gold market, and gold pool representatives hurried toward Washington.

They were not overreacting. As Robert Collins noted, this was "the most serious economic crisis since the Great Depression." The possibility of a swift and deep slump in financial markets and in the real economy was genuine. That the gold rush got less press than Robert Kennedy's candidacy and has been subsequently neglected by scholars of the 1960s is a tribute to the skill with which the administration handled it.

When the delegates gathered, the U.S. team had a plan to keep the speculative purchases of gold with inflated dollars from forcing the devaluation of the dollar and the pound, and then the rest of the world's currencies. It had been first advanced months before by the governor of Italy's central bank, Guido Carli. His solution was a two-tiered gold market. The United States would supply central banks with gold at the fixed rate of $35 an ounce. Governments could purchase gold for official purposes at that price. This would preserve the worth of their currencies. There would also be a private gold market. There, gold's cost would be set by supply and demand. Speculators could seek the best bargain available. The plan did limit the supply for this market somewhat: governments could not buy gold for official purposes at $35, then sell it on the private exchange, preventing them from undercutting the world's currencies by windfall profit taking. Finally, the plan dealt with the weakest of the Western currencies. The United States and the Western European nations would pledge to support the pound sterling. Since U.S. gold reserves were protected from private speculators, the dollar required no assistance.

Born out of Johnson's patient diplomacy and open-minded consultation with European financiers during 1967, this was acceptable to all except the French. Two weeks later in Stockholm, the United States alleviated their concerns. Johnson agreed to give American allies a powerful voice in the regulation of the official market. The European Economic Community could veto requests to draw upon the official sources for gold. To preserve actual reserves of gold, the United States would treat approved requests, termed Special Drawing Rights, as if they were currency backed by gold. LBJ then pointed to his recent success in persuading the Senate to repeal the requirement that the U.S. Treasury keep 25 percent of U.S. gold in reserve. The United States was then free to use all its gold to stabilize both markets. Lastly, Lyndon told the other nations the United States would control inflation in its own economy. The United States would reduce its deficits and, in Fowler's words, "bring our own financial house in order and, specifically, that we would pass the tax bill." These pledges cemented agreement. The crisis was averted.

That did not mean it might not erupt again. To guard against this, the United States had to raise taxes. Failure to get the surcharge would most likely be followed by renewed loss of confidence in the dollar and U.S. ability to protect it. LBJ used this fear, emphasizing to senators and congressmen that Europe expected a tax increase, which made it the more imperative. Later he claimed, "The international crisis had done what we could not do: arouse the American public and many congressional leaders to the need for decisive action" on taxes. Actually, polls showed a majority still opposed an increase, but he was right about Congress. According to Mills, the "severe run on the dollar in the international market" and the "drastic outflow of gold" moved the Ways and Means Committee toward agreement on a surtax.

As Mills and his colleagues progressed toward a tax hike, Lyndon and his showed their willingness to trim the budget of some domestic programs. He had already warned the cabinet that the devaluation of sterling meant they would have to "slash and stick with reductions in the Budget if we are to save the Great Society and try to get a Tax Bill." Not doing this would let the economy "suffer seriously." He spoke publicly to business leaders about belt tightening, hard choices, austerity, and deferring desirable but less urgent programs. LBJ had conceded cuts must be made. Bargaining could start on how much and where.

When horse trading on domestic cuts began, debate over Westmoreland's recommendations and Vietnam policy was far along. On March 4, Clark Clifford asked Johnson a crucial question: "Do you continue down the same road of more troops, more guns, more planes, more ships?" To Clifford, the outcome of doing this was obvious. The U.S. builds up forces; the opposition builds up forces. Fighting notches up. The present deadlock continues ad infinitum. Clifford himself and his staff at the Department of Defense were not sure "a conventional military victory, as commonly defined, can be achieved." The United States had "gotten caught in a sinkhole." Pushing 206,000 more Americans into the morass would result in "more and more fighting with more and more casualties on the U.S. side, and no end in sight."

The defense secretary did not belabor the political fallout from a huge reinforcement. LBJ learned it soon enough. Westmoreland's request was leaked to the *New York Times*. It was on the front page on March 10, along with news of a serious debate over it at the White House. William Fulbright scheduled hearings before his Foreign Relations Committee; 139 congressmen petitioned LBJ to reevaluate Vietnam policy. Frank McGee of NBC said this would not bring victory, only more destruction. He observed, "We must decide whether it is futile to destroy Vietnam in an effort to save it." And only 25 percent of Americans approved of Johnson's conduct of the war.

Rather than forecasting on March 4 the political reaction, Clifford linked the military's recommendations to the looming fiscal crisis. The president learned that implementing these requests would raise the annual cost of the war by 40 percent in fiscal 1969. This would be *on top of* current Pentagon projections. Budget Director Charles Zwick labeled it "a shock." Equally shocking was this estimate: sending so many troops abroad and pumping those dollars into foreign economies would swell the balance of payments deficit by $500 million during 1968.

Henry Fowler and Dean Rusk immediately pointed out the adverse impact this would have on resolving the fiscal crisis. Other nations had been asking for evidence of U.S. fiscal discipline since early 1967; these projections would make them insist on action. Agreement on a two-tier system of gold markets depended on measures to reduce current and potential deficits. That required us, noted Rusk, to think about what "this troop increase would mean in terms of increased taxes, the balance of payment picture, inflation, gold and the general economic picture." From the World Bank, McNamara chimed in: we had to do everything we could "to prevent the financial requirements from ruining us in foreign exchange [and] in our domestic economic situation." Fowler touched on a point dear to LBJ. The interaction between the financial crisis and Vietnam could jeopardize the dollar, the U.S. economy, and the funding of domestic programs, especially those addressing the problems of poverty and the cities.

Thus by mid-March LBJ had been told authoritatively that a troop increase and a national call-up would not bring victory or peace any closer and would have strongly negative effects on the economy, the dollar, the balance of trade, international financial markets, and Great Society programs. The president could also see what the political impact would be. What was widely called "Lyndon Johnson's war" no longer had the support of the vast majority of Americans. These were compelling reasons to say no to Wheeler and Westmoreland.

LBJ soon uncovered another reason. He asked Rusk what the response of the USSR and the PRC would be to escalating the U.S. military commitment, calling up the reserves, and declaring war on North Vietnam. Rusk was positive that U.S. relations with both would be put under immense strain. This would negate all Johnson had done to fight off North Vietnamese aggression without unduly antagonizing the Russians and the Chinese. It could eventuate in a confrontation threatening U.S. safety and security, just what he had struggled to prevent. It would wipe out his attempts to improve relations with Russia pre- and post-Glassboro and would strangle hopes of arms-reduction talks. In world politics, it would be profoundly destabilizing.

The only thing that might outweigh arguments against escalation was this: did the safety of the American forces in South Vietnam absolutely depend on heavy reinforcements? Convince him of this, Lyndon told Wheeler, and he would agree to the request. No one could do that. For all the talk about "near things" during Tet, American troops won substantial victories. ARVN units had fought well, and, prodded by LBJ, President Thieu announced plans to draft 135,000 more men into that army. Hell still sucked, but there was no reason to fear that the present force could not hold its own. Indeed, successes during Tet gave reason to believe they would have tactical superiority.

By mid-March, the decision had taken on an air of inevitability. Nevertheless, Johnson wanted other eyes to vet the arguments. He convened the "Wise Men," a group of veterans of Cold War policy making, and asked their opinions.

A majority of the Wise Men came down strongly in favor of de-escalation and vigorously pursuing negotiations. This was a complete change of heart since they had met in November 1967, and an angry Lyndon wanted to know how they had been briefed and why they had shifted. As Robert Dallek wrote, this was almost certainly play acting. The Wise Men got the same information he was getting. Their analysis, articulated by McGeorge Bundy, who returned to the White House as a Wise Man, "that the really tough problem you have is the interlock between the bad turn in the war, the critical need for a tax increase and the crisis of public confidence at home," followed obviously from it. So did the blunt advice of Dean Acheson, Truman's Secretary of State, who had been one of the principal architects of policies designed to contain Communist expansion: we were not going to win within a reasonable time. That, "together with our broader interests in [Southeast Asia], Europe, and in connection with the dollar crisis, requires a decision now to disengage within a limited time."

None of the Wise Men's observations on March 26 surprised the president. He had reached the same conclusions. Feigning shock and anger were ploys to let him claim that this advice forced him to de-escalate. If he had to appear hawkish in the future, passing as a man compelled by his advisers' volte-face would be useful.

Johnson played variations on this theme later the same day. When he met with the Joint Chiefs and Clifford, he gave "a painfully sad speech about his own difficulties." The country's fiscal situation "is abominable," he observed. The projected deficit of $30 billion would raise interest rates and threaten the pound and the dollar. Without a tax increase, this situation would be "unthinkable." Getting higher taxes required major budget cuts, not only in domestic programs but in non-Vietnam defense expenditures. This was without 206,000 more troops in Southeast Asia and a national call-up! That would "cost $15 billion [more] . . . [and] hurt the dollar and the gold [reserves]." Then he summed up his political problems: "We need more money in an election year, more taxes in an election year and more cuts in an election year." And there was "no support for the war." By now, everyone knew there would be no reinforcement, no national call-up, no declaration of war, no all-out effort.

What would come LBJ left unexplained, but it seemed clear to Clifford that he "understood the need for a dramatic change in policy." He was right.

Lyndon told the press he would review Southeast Asia policy in a televised speech on March 31, deliberately leaving the impression that the public would hear familiar justifications for escalation and learn about the further buildup of American forces in Vietnam. Behind closed doors, his staff had been working for two weeks on a quite different speech. As Horace Busby discovered on March 30,

"The president intended not only to review American policy but to reverse it."

For starters, the president would announce only 13,500 more soldiers would go to Vietnam. He would stress the need for the South Vietnamese to play a bigger part in their own defense. This role was made more feasible by their improved performance and rendered absolutely necessary by fiscal concerns in this country. He would call again for a tax increase. Most significantly, to encourage Hanoi to negotiate the United States would unilaterally stop all bombing above the twentieth parallel. He would appoint Averell Harriman, a veteran politician and diplomat who had been one of Kennedy's foreign policy advisers, as U.S. ambassador to those talks; Harriman would be ready to go anywhere anytime to negotiate.

That idea had been percolating in LBJ's mind since Rusk suggested a unilateral bombing halt on March 4. The secretary of state noted that the United States had nothing to lose since weather conditions precluded attacks above the twentieth parallel for several weeks. LBJ was enthusiastic, ordering him "to *really* get on your horse on that one—right away!" Even though Hanoi did not respond when informed about this possibility, the president wanted to go forward with it. He would give them what they had always asked for.

Would it work? "It's only a roll of the dice," he philosophized to Busby. Then he revealed that this was not a routine pass for low stakes: "After a moment he added, 'I'm shoving in all my stack on this one.'"

The stakes had changed since January 1. Then Lyndon still hoped for an American victory. Capping U.S. forces signaled a smaller role for them and a growing one for the ARVN. Then he hoped to compel North Vietnam to negotiate; now he tried to entice them to talk. He still desired a free South Vietnam, but he wanted to extricate U.S. forces from that unhappy country, leaving it to defend itself.

Also on New Year's Day, LBJ was ready to press ahead with the Great Society while seeking a tax hike. Now the priority was the surcharge: he had to increase federal revenues.

Three months earlier, his party's nomination had seemed a sure thing. Reelection appeared likely. By mid-March, he had been bloodied in New Hampshire and faced certain defeat in Wisconsin. One of his challengers had momentum; another was the opponent he had always dreaded. A majority of the electorate disapproved of his handling of the war. The next polls could reveal a majority of Democrats did, too.

One decision remained. It was whether he should *not* run. Johnson knew events could force him to soldier on. He also knew if he continued to delay, he would be the only candidate with views compatible to his who could possibly raise the money and win the delegates to defeat Robert Kennedy. Refusing to decide would be a decision to run.

No one can know exactly *when* Lyndon Johnson decided this would be his last year as president. Nor can anyone know exactly *why* he made that choice. He was absolutely alone as he pondered this.

Busby helped him weigh options. In January, he wrote Lyndon that he could not see a clear-cut rationale for withdrawing. "Perhaps," he said, "great power should not be laid down except for great cause." None existed now. If he removed himself for personal reasons, "The nation would be vulnerable abroad—and perhaps at home—to the inherent weaknesses of a lame-duck presidency." LBJ did not reply. His silence, plus his decision against making any declaration during the State of the Union, show he felt the significance of absence of that great cause.

By March 30, Busby had it. "First," he told Lyndon, "under the climate developing in Washington . . . a withdrawal might actually help him in the matter of having his orders obeyed" by civil and military officers. "So many people are convinced that you want power blindly that they are going to be doing all sorts of things to defy you." Each day would bring resignations and talk of more. Not running "would surprise and stun many people, but I think it will permit them to see you in a new light and help to accomplish your objectives."

LBJ agreed. He also knew the same would apply to Capitol Hill. Defending the Great Society, arguing for new programs, and getting the surcharge would be no longer vulnerable to charges that he was doing this to get reelected. They would be seen as the acts of a genuine patriot. That would help a great deal.

Busby made another point, one he felt was most compelling: "Without the withdrawal statement, his order to stop the bombing would be regarded around the world, and certainly at home, as only a self-serving political gesture," an attempt to win votes on April 2 in Wisconsin. After inevitable defeat there, "The bombing halt itself would be discredited and dead as leverage for peace negotiations." Johnson agreed, "even showing some enthusiasm."

Busby's last argument shrewdly solved what had long troubled LBJ: "Everyone in the world thinks you would do anything to hang on to power. That impression has colored the whole public reaction to your presidency." If LBJ would willingly turn loose for unselfish, patriotic reasons, "It will help in the long term for people to see better all that you have accomplished in your administration."

Lyndon immediately brightened. He thought this was right, and that it was a "very compelling" reason not to run. He told Busby to write what he called the "peroration" to his speech on Vietnam.

Those in Johnson's family and on his staff who opposed withdrawal angrily blamed Busby for the decision. That was not fair, though they correctly divined the importance of his intervention.

LBJ was wearied by effort and struggle, disappointed by events in Vietnam and at home, and dismayed by the prospect of a long, bitter campaign for renomination followed by a hotly contested election. He blurted out to Busby, "The biggest reason not to do it is just one thing. I want out of this cage." Yet this "biggest reason" by itself would not have been persuasive. Nor was the news on March 31 that for the first time a majority of Democrats disapproved of his Vietnam policy. What tipped the balance was his conviction that he had to give up to do all he could to preserve the chance for peace and for a more just, better, Great Society. He had to separate himself from candidacy to use his office to accomplish his great goals. It was the right thing; of that he was sure. Right after his speech, he candidly told Jack Valenti, "the reason I made this decision was very simple. I wanted the North Vietnamese to know I had no more political ambitions—that whatever I did from here on would only enhance the prospects of peace. I figured that was the best way to get them to the negotiating table. I had just run out of options." Turning to domestic affairs, he observed, "Now I think I can beat Nixon, but it would be close, so close it would be hard to govern, to get the rest of my agenda passed." These sentiments from LBJ illuminate Busby's contribution. Johnson's longtime friend suggested these reasons and supplied the words describing them.

Busby made one last crucial intervention, when Hubert Humphrey protested that only LBJ had the power to deny Bobby Kennedy the nomination. Noticing the "trapped look" in his eyes, Busby predicted that RFK would prove far more unpopular in the party and nation than he currently appeared, and in two weeks Hubert Humphrey would have the money and delegates needed to thwart him. The president conceded that he might be right. Later he insisted that the speech make clear he was removing himself only from *personal* partisan causes. He wanted to be free to help Humphrey.

At the end of his televised address, Lyndon slowly told the country, "With our hopes and the world's hopes for peace in the balance each day, I do not believe I should devote an hour or a day of my time to any personal partisan causes or to any duties other than the awesome duties of this office. . . . Accordingly, I shall not seek, and I will not accept, the nomination of my party for another term as your president."

Speech finished, Lyndon leaped out of his chair. As he monitored reactions, an assistant noted, "His air was that of a prisoner let free." "We were all fifty pounds lighter," recalled Lady Bird, "and ever so much more looking forward to the future."

The responses from press, public, and politicians were everything hoped for by LBJ. Buoyed, he abruptly decided to go to Chicago the next day and address a conference of television and radio broadcasters. The first intimation people at the conference hotel had that he would be there was when they saw him walking up the stairs. Their applause grew and grew, "thunderous and insistent." Lyndon did not know how to respond. A White House secretary spoke the words Busby thought: "Poor man. He doesn't remember what a friendly crowd sounds like."

One awkward wave, and he hurried on. Moved by the scene, sure the president was "organized" again to achieve more, reflecting on March 31 and the past two decades, Busby was glad he had come along with LBJ.

14

This Hard Time: April 1968 to January 1969

Five days after LBJ announced his withdrawal from the presidential race, Martin Luther King was assassinated in Memphis. Horace Busby was certain that had LBJ not said he was out of the race he would have felt the crisis that gripped the country after King's murder made it his duty to run again.

After scrubbing a trip to Hawaii to meet with William Westmoreland, Johnson spent the next few days and nights talking to big-city mayors and black leaders, counseling restrained police reactions to disorders and personal efforts to calm tensions. He was far from unsympathetic to people in the ghetto. "If I were a kid in Harlem, I know what I'd be thinking right now." He would be telling himself, "'Whites have declared open season on my people, and they're going to pick us off one by one unless I get a gun and pick them off first.'"

Instead of a gun, Lyndon picked up the telephone. He told men and women on Capitol Hill that swift passage of the stalled fair housing bill would be a fitting memorial to King and a clear signal to African-Americans that Congress would address the festering problems of black slums and racial prejudice. Once more, the master of the legislative process had recognized an opportunity. He knew a huge majority in both Houses recognized how desperate the racial situation was; all they had to do was look at Washington burning and troops guarding the Capitol. He believed he could persuade them to do what was best for the nation even though it meant taking a controversial step in an election year. Thanks to his relentless lobbying and their own concern, the bill went through both Houses and became law on April 22.

This success did not delude Johnson into thinking Congress was going to spend more on social programs. The price of the tax surcharge was going to be significant cuts in the federal budget. Encouraged by the swift victory on fair housing, Joe Califano wrote LBJ to ask for an even larger tax hike to raise an additional $3–$5 billion to fund "relatively quick impact programs." Johnson's marginalia on this memo speaks volumes: "No!" "I don't agree." "Ha! Ha!" "Forget it." Fair housing did not require outlays from the U.S. Treasury. More poverty assistance did. Congress was too focused on the bottom line to go along with that. No amount of lobbying by the president was going to change enough minds.

Califano's departure from realism did not cause Lyndon to distrust him. He was not so forgiving of Otto Kerner and the Illinois governor's colleagues on the Civil Disorders Commission. Johnson viewed their description of slum conditions and their conclusion that there were two countries—one white and one black—as indictments of his policies and efforts to embarrass him. Their advice was worthless. How, he asked, could they expect "the same Congress to turn 180 degrees overnight and appropriate an additional $30 billion for the same programs that it was demanding I cut by $6 billion?"

LBJ had an answer. The Civil Disorders Commission was swayed by the many in the poverty programs who were his political enemies, using their positions to further the campaigns of Kennedy and McCarthy. In addition, they were not the only vipers he had nursed at his bosom. The president felt young people and blacks were incredibly ungrateful to him. After all he had done for education, civil rights, and the poor, they were flocking to the standards of "Clean Gene" and RFK.

Though LBJ was not a candidate, this still was a serious problem for him. Liberals and poverty activists were not satisfied merely to agitate against any cuts in Great Society programs; they wanted to fund them more generously with increased tax revenues. Meanwhile, Lyndon was struggling with Wilbur Mills to limit reductions. Liberals would have to trust him to get the best deal he could. Then they must vote to ratify it. If red-hots played campaign politics, dug in their heels, and opposed all cuts, they could torpedo the tax hike. That would bring on an international financial crisis that would deepen into a severe recession. Congress's response to that would be the total dismantling of the Great Society. LBJ's legacy would be lost.

Again he found himself in the middle, between fiscal conservatives fully prepared to bleed domestic reforms dry and liberal supporters blindly committed to transfusing them to bloating. Though he resisted admitting it, Johnson was fighting now to preserve the Great Society. Identifying the tax surcharge as the most important legislation in 1968 prioritized preservation over expansion.

Keeping the Great Society as intact as possible meant flexing political muscle in the presidential campaign. Lyndon could not rely on patronage; others knew his favors were short-term. They would weigh a few months' profit against long-term gains from the next president. He had to show he could intervene decisively in the race. As he mulled over tactics and strategy, he realized he had one powerful weapon and an ideal target.

Most delegates were not chosen in presidential primaries. They were anointed by the powers-that-be in local and state parties. Marvin Watson had long been confident his boss would have a majority of delegates no matter what McCarthy and Kennedy said, did, or won. Lyndon did not release these delegates from commitments to him when he withdrew, and neither McCarthy nor Kennedy dared demand this. Both were regarded with suspicion and dislike by the bosses of large blocs of delegates. Union leaders were especially wary of them, and they could not risk losing the votes and money of organized labor. Thus, a significant proportion of the delegates stayed hitched to Lyndon. This was his weapon.

The target was Hubert Humphrey. Privately Johnson had doubts about his vice president. Hubert talked too much; he was too soft; his position on Vietnam was suspect. Still, if he ran, he would have to defend the administration. Best of all, he did not believe he could win the nomination without Lyndon's support. LBJ played on that insecurity: encouraging him to run, advising him on tactics, making known his appreciation for HHH as his vice president, yet withholding any firm public or private commitment. Left unspoken but painfully obvious was the threat that Johnson could turn on him if he did not toe the line. That he was contemptuous of McCarthy and detested Kennedy was clear, but Humphrey could not be sure he might not in a rage release his delegations to make their own deals. Also possible was Lyndon's manufacturing a draft of himself. Hubert knew how vindictive his leader could be and how quick he had been to exclude his vice president from discussions on Vietnam and race relations. Humphrey was too ambitious and too apprehensive to do other than kowtow. He was dependent on Lyndon.

This gave the president a card to play with those who regarded HHH with affection and respect: congressional liberals, George Meany, Walter Reuther, and other labor leaders. If they did not go along with whatever cuts were required to get the surcharge, he would extinguish Humphrey's candidacy. No one doubted he was ruthless enough to do that.

The power to break Humphrey's campaign did not make the struggle for the tax bill a slam dunk. Mills fought to increase the cuts. In turn, Johnson emphasized "whether he [Mills] realized it or not, the country's economy was about to go down the drain and we had to write a tax bill that we could both live with." After a series of sharp conversations, LBJ agreed to cut $6 billion from social programs to make the surcharge law.

Talks with Meany were sharp, too. The AFL-CIO was committed to zero cuts; it also wanted legislation making the federal government the employer of last resort for the unemployed. Its brain trust did not buy Johnson's doomsday pronouncements. To them, the end of the link between dollars and gold might reduce international commerce temporarily but would have no serious economic impact at home. The president had to resort to arguing congressional practicalities and Humphrey's vulnerability. Meany grudgingly accepted the cuts.

The final ones to be persuaded were Lyndon's staff and cabinet. That they overwhelmingly favored Humphrey helped. Johnson sugarcoated the pill by pretending he was not fully convinced himself. Arthur Okun, the chair of the Council of Economic Advisers, was grilled by the president in meetings. Dubbed "Okun's Chamber of Horrors" by Califano, these staged dialogues featured the diagnosis LBJ had already accepted privately and let others witness his inability to refute predictions of catastrophe. "Take a tax bill with the $6 billion cutback," Okun summed up. "It's hard advice to give but I think it's the best advice. It is the only advice I can give." Following Johnson's lead, his people took it.

The Revenue and Expenditure Control Act of 1968 became law on June 28. It mandated $6 billion in cuts, but Congress managed to slice only $4 billion. The White House preserved major programs and their funding; the only programs pared back were peripheral. Congress's inability to find $2 billion more was a godsend. LBJ refused to do the people's representatives' work for them, and they did not fight him. He had gotten a better break on the most vital programs' budgets than he had expected. That these were still modest funds troubled him less that it did many liberals.

The new law presented another happy result. Lyndon was proud of what he called his practical side: his commitment to balanced budgets and fiscal efficiency. The deficit for fiscal 1968 had been $25 billion. Thanks to reduced expenditures and enhanced revenues, the FY 1969 bottom line was a $2.3 billion surplus. The 10 percent increase for a year in personal and corporate income taxes had also, he believed, staved off an international financial crisis and a domestic recession. The moral he drew from the nation's fiscal difficulties was quite different from his position on the tax cut of 1964. He now believed leaders should resist cutting taxes. That threatened balancing the budget. Moreover, once taxes were lowered, they were devilishly hard to raise. He was proud of accomplishing that as well.

Putting the surcharge first on his agenda and emphasizing the preservation of the Great Society did not mean LBJ lost his enthusiasm for new initiatives. Refusing to let his staff behave like lame ducks, he told Califano that everyone, including himself, would have to work harder and longer.

Listing Johnson's initiatives gives the best sense of his energy. He wanted Congress to improve programs designed to help African-Americans; increase public housing; assist family planning; conserve national resources; improve mass transit; make securities investments more secure; expand food stamps; assist vocational, elementary, and secondary education; increase college loans; approve a constitutional amendment giving eighteen-year-olds the vote; and guarantee access for disabled persons to public buildings. His legislative triumphs included acts improving education; mandating special assistance for educating the disabled; assisting in the suppression of crime and dealing with juvenile delinquency; extending food stamp programs; furthering consumer protection; and offering grants and loans to college students. These laws memorialize LBJ's energy, determination, and skill.

As Robert Dallek has observed, neither attempts nor achievements left liberal Democrats happy. Lyndon did not press with equal vigor for appropriations for programs. He wanted a balanced budget as well as new initiatives. He rationalized this by arguing that these laws would not have passed had he asked for the funding liberals desired. He made his familiar prediction that these programs' constituencies would get them higher funding in the future, and he insisted that the thrust for reform continued to be powerful and its impact would increase apace.

Grandiloquent language had the unfortunate result of raising expectations that could not be met with present funding. Disappointment followed. So did disillusionment, not just with specific programs but with the power of the federal government to affect change or do anything other than interfere and complicate. Lyndon's rhetoric also contributed to doubts about his truthfulness. Historian Robert Collins has aptly pointed past LBJ's glowing words to the real bottom line: "In fiscal year 1969, federal social welfare expenditures (in constant dollars) grew at a rate less than half that of 1965." To Collins, this is far more significant than numbers indicating aggregate spending on social welfare programs continued to rise in 1969 and throughout Richard Nixon's presidency. The dramatic decline in the rate of increase meant "1968 . . . did constitute a sea change, because it shifted the emphasis from an expansion of the Great Society to its preservation." "What was left," he concluded, "was not the powerful reform surge of mid-decade but only its inertia."

Lyndon Johnson would have quarreled with this, but not because he disagreed that his first priority had been to protect the Great Society. He would object because he knew how important momentum was to its preservation. The slowing of a movement once in rapid motion but now without propelling energy behind it meant resistance and defeat. As a superb tactician of legislation, Lyndon knew he had to keep pushing new measures to maintain their appearance of momentum, but he was too keen a student of political conditions not to realize that the window of opportunity for greater change was slamming shut. The glory days were behind him. It was the season to keep winnings safe.

LBJ's fierce determination to do that led to a serious miscalculation. In June, Supreme Court Chief Justice Earl Warren told LBJ that he wanted to retire to keep the choice of his successor out of the hands of Richard Nixon, whom he regarded as dangerously unethical. He wanted Lyndon to name the next chief.

To Johnson this was a heaven-sent chance. He feared more conservative justices would cause "a dissipation of the forward legislative momentum we had achieved during the previous eight years." In particular, he fretted about judicial overturning of federal aid to parochial education; laws protecting consumers and the environment seemed at risk, too. Throughout his career he had regarded the Supreme Court as an intensely political institution and had viewed justices as politicians with unique chances to affect the nation's life for decades. He could not imagine Dick Nixon uninterested in reversing the Great Society. Now he could launch a preemptive strike against constitutional conservatism.

LBJ did not have to think twice about who he wanted. He would nominate Abe Fortas for Chief Justice, promoting him from his place on the Court as an Associate Justice. Nor did he ponder long over who would fill that seat. He would nominate Homer Thornberry, a former Congressman from Texas who now was a federal judge. Thornberry would always be reliably liberal. Fortas was even more valuable. He had actually advised on Great Society legislation, and had the brilliance to dominate internal discussion and set the direction of the court.

So taken was Johnson by this vision that he dismissed his staff's concerns about the difficulty of winning Senate confirmation for these nominees. They cautioned that there would be charges of cronyism. Califano was apprehensive that senatorial cross-examination would expose how often Fortas had advised LBJ. Others warned that some Republicans would resist a blatant effort to deny the appointment of a Chief Justice to a Republican president. Califano also worried that Southern Democrats would be wary of Fortas's liberalism. He urged Johnson to balance the court with a moderate Republican instead of Thornberry. Everyone recognized they would likely have to beat a filibuster. They would need sixty-seven votes.

Against these points were the possible gains. To LBJ, these were worth the plunge. Despite ominous signals from Capitol Hill reacting against rumors of these nominations, he bet he could wheel and deal them through.

Lyndon learned that Robert Kennedy had been shot and killed from Walt Rostow, who called at 3:31 A.M. on June 5. Shocked out of sleep, he blurted, "Too horrible for words."

Words and acts came the next morning. Johnson had asked Congress to legislate Secret Service protection for all candidates, but his request had been the victim of a desire to save money. Now he simply ordered it done and resubmitted the bill. He also ordered his staff to ready gun-control legislation. Once the shock diminished, he contemplated a rearranged political landscape.

One reason LBJ had encouraged Humphrey was that seemed the only way to beat Kennedy. Delegates he controlled were quietly encouraged to back the vice president, an effort so successful that RFK's campaign credited HHH with nearly 1,000 supporters, substantially more than both his opponents. Not satisfied with this, Johnson's White House operatives helped McCarthy in the

California primary. If McCarthy won, Bobby Kennedy would be finished and Humphrey would be the nominee. The staff raised money and funneled it through the HHH campaign to McCarthy, who had no qualms about using it. Their plan failed, but the assassin's bullet tragically produced the same result.

RFK's death still had a profound effect on the race. Veterans of 1968 universally recall that the joy and intensity went out of the contest for the nomination. Neither Humphrey nor McCarthy roused much enthusiasm. LBJ knew why. Here was another martyred Kennedy! No one else could take up the standard. Nixon would win. In this atmosphere, no wonder Humphrey's campaign sagged.

Bitterly, Lyndon wished to Doris Kearns Goodwin that Bobby had become president "so the country could finally see a flesh-and-blood Kennedy grappling with the daily work of the presidency . . . instead of their storybook images of great heroes who, because they were dead, could make anything anyone wanted happen." Meanwhile, the un-storybook Humphrey fell further behind McCarthy and Nixon in the polls.

LBJ publicly committed himself to Fortas and Thornberry in the aftermath of Robert Kennedy's assassination. The changes that were wrought in the dynamics of the presidential campaign steeled his determination to press on. With Nixon's victory more certain with each passing day, all the more reason to push hard for Fortas and Thornberry. That would protect the Johnson legislative legacy from judicial dismantling.

Kennedy's death and Humphrey's decline raised another possibility. Would LBJ reconsider his decision to withdraw? Would he and his staff orchestrate a draft at the convention in Chicago?

Whether Lyndon ever seriously considered reentering the race was not clear at the time and has not been settled since. Marvin Watson, who was in charge of the president's contacts with the Democratic National Committee, was sure he never wavered from the March 31 decision. Doris Kearns Goodwin, often the recipient of Lyndon's thoughts during 1968, believed he thought seriously about doing it. The stunning events of that year, she noted, meant "it was natural to think that anything could happen, or might be made to happen." LBJ believed he was the only Democrat with a chance of winning the South and was confident he could beat Nixon. He told Goodwin that Nixon was "like a Spanish horse who runs faster than anyone for the first nine lengths and then turns around and runs backward." He would "do something wrong in the end. He always does." To her, these analyses were wishful. Sometimes he realized this. Still, "As the convention neared, Johnson began to feel his withdrawal might not be irrevocable, that he might find vindication more real and immediate than the verdict of history—in the vote of the Democratic Party and American people."

Whatever his dreams, Lyndon was determined to hold on to enough delegates to deny Humphrey the nomination. Talk about his reentering the race, observed Marvin Watson, "was used as a threat and a tactical tool to influence the convention's outcome." What LBJ wanted was spelled out by Watson: "(a) the nominee would support his policies, especially regarding Vietnam; (b) the Party platform adopted at the convention [would do] likewise; and (c) the nominee selected [would choose] a running mate compatible with the president's program." Watson put it bluntly when he spoke to Humphrey: "You must stay the course on Vietnam if you expect to be nominated."

The weapons LBJ wielded were nine states committed to favorite sons. Journalists generally called these Humphrey's; in fact, they were under Johnson's control. No one could be nominated without them. Among them were delegate-rich Illinois and Texas, the former under the thumb of Mayor Richard Daley of Chicago, the later ramrodded by John Connally. Neither liked or respected Humphrey; both were ready to nominate LBJ. Lyndon had HHH right where he wanted him.

Lyndon did not do this out of the joy of bullying. He was aiming at ensuring that both parties' candidates supported his position on negotiations. He did not want to give Hanoi any reason to feel his successor would offer a better deal and then hold out until 1969. Moreover, if he could remove discussion of what to do next from presidential politicking, the slide in American public opinion against the war might end. If that happened, the Communists would be less willing to continue suffering military losses and more ready to seek a settlement. He did not believe Nixon, a fervent anti-Communist, would be a problem. It was necessary, however, to keep Humphrey in line.

Another unexpected event of 1968 occurred in April, courtesy of the enemy. Hanoi reacted to the March 31 speech by offering to begin talks. Though he had hoped his withdrawal would demonstrate his sincere desire to make peace and help convince the North Vietnamese to negotiate, LBJ was still surprised. He had expected more of the same: no negotiations without an end to bombing and American withdrawal. This volte-face did not make him optimistic. It was, he reasoned, a ploy to encourage the anti-war movement and drive a wedge between Washington and Saigon. He was sure there would be no slackening of military operations by the North Vietnamese. He had to play along because of his public pledge to negotiate and because he could not cast aside the chance for peace, however remote. He quickly appointed Averell Harriman and Deputy Defense Secretary Cyrus Vance to head the U.S. delegation.

Dialogue bogged down for the next two months over where the talks would convene and whether the National Liberation Front and the South Vietnamese would participate. While diplomats sparred, the Communists launched another series of attacks on Saigon and other cities. To Lyndon, this confirmed his suspicion that the North Vietnamese were not interested in negotiating. Nor was he.

The "mini-Tet" in May was repulsed with substantial NVA losses. These tactical victories encouraged him to hope once more for the military defeat of the enemy. They also buttressed his determination to preserve an independent South Vietnam. Despite many false sightings, Johnson persuaded himself he might really be glimpsing the tunnel's end.

Feeding this vision was the president's conviction that Tet and its aftermath had been major U.S. triumphs. The casualties the enemy suffered, far in excess of the butcher bill for the allies, the performance of the ARVN troops, much better than anyone expected, and the absence of any civilian uprising, confidently anticipated by Hanoi, proved that to his satisfaction. He would have agreed with military historian Victor Davis Hanson: "Tet was a devastating military defeat for the Communist forces in South Vietnam and one of the most lopsided victories in American military history." Continued allied successes during the savage combat in the summer and fall confirmed his belief.

LBJ would have endorsed another of Hanson's points: Tet was perceived then and recalled later "with a strange mixture of humiliation, loss, and regret." To many influential Americans, who juxtaposed the administration's optimism in late 1967 with the massive attacks of early 1968, "that the Communists could lose forty thousand men . . . oddly seemed to reflect power rather than the promised desperation." "Strange" and "oddly" were modifiers Johnson would have chosen.

Lyndon Johnson understood the power of subjective perceptions in politics. That was why in 1965 and 1966 he carefully tended impressions that domestic reform was an irresistible juggernaut. He knew how important it was to prevent feelings of futility about the war and his prosecution of it from flowering further in public opinion.

Knowing this was one thing; doing it was difficult. When Khe Sahn was evacuated in June, there was a predictable uproar, with hawks and doves demanding to know why, if it was not vital, troops were kept in danger there for months. The quarrels over where peace talks would take place was another source of frustration. *Who cared? Let's get down to making peace.* Arguments that place mattered because U.S. negotiators would need secure communications with Washington did not calm emotions. Once the parties agreed on Paris, delaying the start until the shape of the table could be determined seemed crazy and obscene. This dispute was really about the parts the Viet Cong and Thieu's government would have in negotiations. That explanation did not silence the administration's critics. It seemed to Lyndon they simply wanted the United States out, and he could not make them understand that this open desire encouraged the enemy, prolonged the disputes, and jeopardized an acceptable conclusion to the war.

This reaffirmed LBJ's conclusion that nothing would placate those against the war enough to mute their protests. He thought his withdrawal would do. It had not. So he would have to plow ahead. The president took heart from his conviction that a majority of the American people still wanted to preserve South Vietnam's freedom and remained willing to fight for it. He could sense the gathering force of what Nixon called the "silent majority," a broad conservative reaction against peace demonstrations. The problem he had was finding a way to give this a voice, revealing to Hanoi and anti-war politicians that the electorate would stay the course. Controversies over his personality, his prosecution of the war, and his emphasis on civil rights and domestic reform made the problem more daunting.

The place to begin was riding herd on Hubert Humphrey. Convinced in July that he had to reach out to McCarthy and Kennedy Democrats, the vice president drafted a speech hinting that if he was elected he might quit bombing in the hope of speeding talks. When he ran it by the White House, Lyndon quashed the speech and tongue-lashed him. Humphrey gave in.

The vice president's surrender did not keep LBJ from dismissing him as weak and disloyal. Johnson told advisers that the Republicans could be more help in dealing with Hanoi during the next few months than his own party. He arranged a meeting with Nixon on July 26.

After Johnson finished a briefing on the diplomatic situation, Nixon sympathized with him about "this . . . *hard time.* " He would not criticize LBJ so long as there was no softening on negotiations, and he promised not to advocate any unconditional bombing pause himself. This was not disinterested patriotism. Supporting LBJ gave Nixon the excuse not to describe his plans for Vietnam; it also allowed him to conceal that he had none. Halting bombing might speed negotiations on, and the prospect of peace would strengthen Humphrey. Encouraging Johnson to continue insisting on concessions in return for no bombing preserved tensions between him and his vice president and kept the Democrats divided.

Lyndon had no illusions about the motives behind the promises. That did not keep him from welcoming them. If he could continue to control Humphrey, he would achieve consensus among the candidates about the war and the talks.

The next threat to this consensus was the Democratic platform. Insurgents wanted a commitment to negotiations and peace, and they were ready to fight for it. HHH's campaign tried to craft a compromise, one that moved away from Johnson's hard line but not so far as to enrage him. That was futile. LBJ was determined that his party would vindicate him, and he was convinced that if it wavered the enemy would be encouraged. He would force a showdown on the party platform, one he planned to win.

A week before the platform committee met. Lyndon gave a ringing speech to the Veterans of Foreign Wars against "cutting and running" and being "hoodwinked" by the enemy. Humphrey got the message but, desperate to show some independence, pressed on with a plank endorsing a halt while taking "into account, most importantly, the risk to American troops as well as the response from Hanoi." To peace activists, that was weak. It went way too far for LBJ. He was sure Ho would see it as he did: a prelude to caving in. When Humphrey persisted, he ordered John Connally to defeat it.

Connally did everything he could. Back at the ranch, Johnson kept in indirect but constant contact with his old friend, urging him on. Ultimately the Humphrey forces prevailed by a narrow vote in the platform committee on his Vietnam plank.

LBJ did not give up. The official platform of the Democratic Party had greater weight than committee debates. This plank would give Hanoi reason to conclude that as president Humphrey would be less firm than Lyndon. The enemy would never negotiate with Johnson and would continue to fight. Connally was directed to force a floor debate.

Lyndon anticipated he would win. The Soviet Union had just intervened with massive force in Czechoslovakia, abruptly ending the "Prague Spring" of limited reform. Connally argued that this proved Communists were not pacifically inclined. The North Vietnamese helped him. Fighting in South Vietnam became intense and bloody again; during convention week, 308 American soldiers died and 1,134 were wounded. The backlash against anti-war demonstrations in Chicago further heightened resistance to a more flexible stance on negotiations. After a bitter debate, the convention voted to replace the platform committee's recommendation with one acceptable to LBJ by a vote of 1,567–1,041.

Was Johnson tempted by the magnitude of this victory to try for the nomination? In public, he was coy, claiming he had not entered into any politicking on the platform. In private, he never told his aides that this was his desire. Probably he was strongly tempted. Connally asked leaders of Southern delegations if they would support the president; it is hard to believe he would have without LBJ's implicit encouragement. The Southerners' response was emphatic: "No way." That ended any possibility.

Men like Governor Buford Ellington of Tennessee understood that if Lyndon Johnson somehow got the nomination, the Democratic Party would be fatally split. McCarthy delegates would walk out of the convention; liberals would recoil from the campaign. It was entirely possible that they would openly oppose LBJ in November. Ellington, et al. also grasped this fact: any Democratic candidate would have trouble carrying their states in 1968, and Johnson was identified with civil rights and poverty legislation that were anathema to many Southern white voters. They thought Lyndon might be as disastrous for his party in 1968 as Goldwater had been for his in 1964.

Conservative Democrats did agree with his position on Vietnam. They thought it coincided with the majority's opinion in the South and the nation, but they were certain any attempt to get him the nomination would result in a riven, vulnerable party. And they were sure that in the general election Lyndon Johnson carried too much baggage and was far too divisive to win.

Johnson could live with that. Still, he wanted expressions of respect and affection from his party. August 27, 1968, was his sixtieth birthday. He wanted to celebrate in Chicago. For a gift, he wished for a pro forma request he reconsider running. That would give him a chance to decline graciously.

This was denied him. Demonstrators marched through the streets, and the police responded with nearly unrestrained violence. Being in Chicago would be personally dangerous for him and further inflame confrontations. His birthday was, according to Bird, one of the saddest days of their married life; the party at the ranch was somber. No one believed his claim he had never wanted to go to Chicago. Commentators viewed it as another credibility gap. Depending on their politics, they blamed him either for encouraging chaos in the country with his civil rights policy or for causing it with his stubborn insistence on a lost cause. His poll rating sank.

Lyndon took a keen interest in the Humphrey–Nixon race, and in the effect George Wallace's third-party candidacy might have. LBJ believed that his own place in history would be impacted by who won, and how he won. Most importantly, he knew this contest might impinge decisively on what he wanted most from his last months in office: significant progress toward peace in Vietnam. He instructed the FBI to bug the Nixon, Wallace, and Humphrey campaigns. He wanted no surprises, and he wanted to be able to prepare counterstrokes to any changes, particularly from Humphrey.

To Humphrey, the way to peace was obvious: the United States should stop bombing North Vietnam and see if the enemy lived up to the promise to negotiate. Aware of this, Lyndon wished HHH "could grow some balls." Failing that, he pressured the vice president to stick to the administration's conditions.

Then and later, Lyndon's position was often portrayed as sheer stubbornness. Clark Clifford was convinced the North Vietnamese were ready to negotiate in September; the U.S. negotiating team of Harriman and Vance shared his optimism. That LBJ continued to refuse to stop the bombing unless his conditions were met angered and frustrated them.

In defense of Lyndon, however, one should recall that the North Vietnamese continued to launch offensives in August and September. Fighting was bitter; casualties were high. There was reason for him to believe that Hanoi was still aiming at a military victory and hoped to bring that to reality by taking advantage of a bombing halt. Despite horrific losses during and after Tet, the enemy continued to attack. In fact, General Giap's tactics became as predictable as Westmoreland's search and destroy forays. The MACV's new commander, Creighton Abrams, was a much more formidable opponent than Westmoreland; his spoiling attacks on enemy formations before they went on the offensive, plus his uncanny ability to anticipate NVA movements, were very effective. Abrams argued emphatically against a bombing pause. U.S. attacks on enemy staging areas in Laos, Cambodia, and the area around the border between the two Vietnams disrupted and weakened their offensives. For these reasons, Johnson felt he could not dispense with his preconditions and stop the bombing.

That was fine with Nixon. He feared peace might break out before Election Day. Should Johnson relent on bombing and Hanoi respond positively in Paris, light in the tunnel might mark Humphrey's path to victory. To keep abreast of developments, the Republicans managed to talk someone at the White House into slipping them up-to-date information. The Nixon campaign also benefited from Henry Kissinger's reports on his private talks with U.S. negotiators in Paris and his warning that "something big was afoot regarding Vietnam." Armed against surprise, Nixon worked on keeping LBJ from wavering by using evangelist Billy Graham as go-between in September to praise Johnson's performance in tough times. Graham also assured the president that Nixon would continue his policies if elected, give him full credit when peace was made, and refrain from criticizing current actions or the Paris talks.

LBJ suspected this was Tricky Dick fishing for his implicit commitment not to campaign vigorously for HHH. He would not relent on bombing no matter what the Republicans said. Still, he could not help comparing Nixon's stance with Humphrey's. That difference became starker when Humphrey finally broke with the administration in late September, pledging an unconditional halt if he won.

In his memoirs, Johnson claimed that this cost Humphrey the election. Few find this plausible. HHH began to rebound in the polls after the speech, and the possibility this might signal plans for an "October surprise" troubled the Nixon campaign. Was Johnson about to stop bombing and rush to negotiations in an effort to tip the election to his vice president? Losing at the last moment seemed a real possibility to Nixon's men. Soon it seemed even more real.

On October 9, Soviet diplomats passed to the White House news that the USSR was in position to nudge Hanoi into a major concession. Two days later, the North Vietnamese signaled willingness to include South Vietnam's government in the talks in return for a complete bombing halt. The Russians admitted U.S. politics inspired this move. The Soviets were fearful that Nixon's election would heat up the Cold War; the North Vietnamese preferred to deal with Johnson rather than Cold Warrior Nixon. Neither confessed another motive: progress toward peace could boost Humphrey into the Oval Office.

To Lyndon, this was highly promising. He had always believed that if American forces hurt Hanoi enough, the enemy would become eager to talk peace. Now that appeared to be coming true.

Before committing himself further, he checked with the Joint Chiefs and Abrams. They saw no serious military danger from a pause. Clark Clifford, Walt Rostow, Dean Rusk, and the Paris negotiators recommended suspending Rolling Thunder. His impression confirmed, LBJ sent word he accepted. He instructed Harriman and Vance to tell North Vietnamese diplomats in Paris that substantive talks should begin within twenty-four hours.

For reasons still unclear, Hanoi did not want to proceed so rapidly. After a few days, the two sides reached agreement. LBJ would announce the bombing halt on October 31; talks would start on November 2. Election Day was November 5.

Elated with this, Lyndon did not foresee any difficulties with his allies. That is surprising, considering that Clifford had warned him in July that the South Vietnamese government did not want the war to ever end because "they're protected by 540,000 U.S. [troops and a] golden flow of money. . . . Corruption is through all this." But he forgot, ignored, or disregarded this, and was blindsided by the reaction.

The South Vietnamese immediately objected. The presence of the National Liberation Front as a separate party would, the Thieu government claimed, have disastrous consequences for civilian and military morale in South Vietnam. Thieu would not participate until the United States and North Vietnam agreed that there would be one flag on their side of the table and two for the allies, thus symbolizing that only the three sovereign parties were involved.

The president was furious. His wiretaps of the Nixon campaign left him with no doubt that the candidate and his men had told Thieu to stall, assuring him a Republican administration would protect South Vietnam better than Johnson or Humphrey.

When LBJ had informed the three candidates about the prospects for peace, Nixon was publicly supportive, announcing that though some critics might suspect Johnson was playing politics (thereby underlining the suspicion!), he did not. In secret, though, he had foreclosed any hope of a meeting before the election. And he lied smoothly when Lyndon called to quiz him about contacts he might have had with Saigon.

What could be done? Pressuring Thieu resulted only in a half-promise to meet on November 6. Blowing the whistle on Nixon was a tough call. LBJ would have to reveal how he had learned about illegal interference with American diplomacy. Republicans would claim that this was a desperate last-second try to steal victory for HHH. And what if Nixon won anyway? Johnson already had warned friends he would like "to indict us all." This would intensify his vindictiveness. Moreover, if a president-elect were accused of a crime, he might be indicted. What then? Even if a constitutional crisis was averted, Nixon's legitimacy and authority would be fatally weakened. He would not be able to restore peace in the country or the world. Lyndon decided not to decide. He passed the information over to Humphrey, to do with as he chose.

HHH faced the same dilemmas. If anything, he was more vulnerable to charges that this was a dirty partisan trick, pulled out of the hat by a desperate candidate. He stayed silent. Americans went to the polls uninformed about Nixon's intrusion into diplomacy.

Humphrey lost. The margin was paper-thin in the popular vote: the vice pesident wound up with 42.7 percent to Nixon's 43.4 percent and Wallace's 13.5 percent. In the electoral college, Nixon prevailed with 301 votes to Humphrey's 191. That gap was less comfortable than it appears: several states, most notably Illinois, were quite close but went Republican.

Johnson explained Nixon's victory by blaming it on Humphrey's departure from his stance on bombing. Humphrey disagreed. He blamed it on his not distancing himself from LBJ sooner. He had lost "some of my personal identity and forcefulness." "It would have been better," he went on, if "I had stood my ground and remembered that I was fighting for the highest office in the land. I ought not to have let a man who was going to be a former president dictate my future." Equally harmful was the identity of the president who did the dictating. Although Lyndon rarely admitted this, 1968 was essentially a referendum on him as a politician, a policy maker, and a person. He did not fare well.

Polls surveying voter opinions determined that 40 percent of those casting ballots for Richard Nixon supported Lyndon Johnson in 1964. Dissatisfaction with LBJ's handling of the war was widespread, covering—for different reasons—the left, right, and middle of the political spectrum. His inability to get the South Vietnamese to the bargaining table in late October seemed further evidence of bumbling. That charge was unfair, but it was harmful to Humphrey nonetheless.

Disquiet among white voters about the administration's position on civil rights was wide and deep as well. Only 35 percent of white voters were for Humphrey. (In contrast, 97 percent of African Americans supported HHH, despite the fact that a higher proportion of blacks opposed the war than any other group.) Blaming LBJ for this is unjust; he was doing the right thing, but the backlash cost Humphrey.

Inflation had begun to plague the land during Johnson's last years, and it was widely attributed to the cost of his frustrating war and his domestic policies. The cure for that woe—higher taxes—was unpopular. These, too, were Johnson's doing.

The president's argument that crime and disorder had roots in poverty and must be attacked there ran counter to a growing white middle-class conviction that the War on Poverty rewarded certain groups' antisocial behavior and thereby encouraged it. Selling domestic reform had been easier when LBJ could claim it would give individuals the tools necessary to raise themselves. When it appeared these programs were based on a philosophy of group entitlements, they became much more controversial.

Finally, the demographics of the nation—Americans were younger on average in 1968 than now, and senior citizens were less numerous and not as fully mobilized—meant that the blessings of Social Security and Medicare for the middle class were less apparent.

Conservative politicians helped create, then cater to, these beliefs. Nixon and Wallace were merely the most prominent critics. Whenever local Democrats savaged Community Action Programs, they fostered a sense of us versus Washington. Wilbur Mills rejoiced at the "anguished cries of Federal administrators who are feeling the sharp bite of these legislative incisors" tearing at Great Society budgets; how many in the Little Rock Rotary Club helped George Wallace carry Arkansas? Lyndon himself assisted critics by creating agencies that could not deliver the benefits he promised because of shrinking budgets.

Finally, there were LBJ's reputation and personality. Humphrey had to struggle against Johnson's image as the ultimate wheeler-dealer, a man who played dirty pool in politics and feathered his own nest while in office. Every time Box 13 came up, or KTBC's profits were guessed at, this impression was reinforced.

Johnson's plans for the Supreme Court wre effectively portrayed as more of the same from LBJ. Senate Republicans hammered Johnson over Fortas's nomination. More corruption and cronyism, they chorused; another effort by a power-mad man to perpetuate the permissiveness of Earl Warren's court, they growled. Lyndon's persistence when it was clear he could not get cloture made bad worse. He claimed he did it so Fortas could get a majority vote in his favor, and thus appear to retain Senate approval of his position as Associate Justice. Instead, it looked like he was still trying to pay off a pal and pack the court.

Fortas's majority was only 45–43, 22 votes shy of cloture: a dictionary definition of Pyrrhic victory. Republicans realized how inviting a target Lyndon's friend was. Thanks to his greedily charging large fees for teaching and speaking, Fortas would be forced to resign within a year. Before then, he played a part in Humphrey's downfall.

It is hard to believe that LBJ was heartbroken by November 5. True, he had bestirred himself to campaign for his vice president during the last two weeks. True, he was angry at Nixon's meddling with Saigon. Balanced against this was his conviction that the president-elect's position on Vietnam was roughly the same as his, while Humphrey would have gotten out as fast as he could. On the domestic front, Johnson solaced himself with Democratic majorities in Congress. Budget cuts would continue, but his party would preserve most of the programs.

Despite these consolations, LBJ was still haunted by his inability to meet with Soviet leaders, take advantage of the momentum generated by agreements with them on a nuclear nonproliferation treaty, and begin serious arms limitation talks. The Soviet invasion of Prague ended hopes of an early fall summit. That did not discourage him. He had been sympathetic to de Gaulle during the serious unrest in France during May and June; he was equally willing to see Czechoslovakia as an internal matter that should not prejudice building stable, peaceful relationships. Even after Election Day, he hoped to go to Moscow to initiate talks. At first, the Russians and Nixon were agreeable. Then the Soviets concluded nothing enduring could be achieved, and the new president politely signaled his disapproval.

Lyndon was downcast. Convinced that reducing tensions between the superpowers was his foremost duty, he had identified arms limitations as the best way of achieving that. He was sure delay would make momentum for the deployment of multiple-warhead missiles and the development of anti-ballistic missile systems irresistible. He foresaw an immensely dangerous arms race. He lived to see his fears realized. Glenn Seaborg, his chair of the Atomic Energy Commission, later wrote, "Of all the tragedies that befell Lyndon Johnson, this must rank among the most grievous."

As he grieved, did he think if Humphrey had won he would have gone to Moscow? Did he wonder if he should have run for reelection in 1968?

The first answer is "yes." In Great Power and European diplomacy, a Humphrey administration would have been an extension of Johnson's. His launching the process would not have been seen as a last gasp or an effort to usurp policy formulation.

The second answer is "no." Better than many of his friends, Lyndon knew that beating Nixon and Wallace would have required a frenzied effort by him. Nineteen sixty-eight would have been 1937 and 1948 all over again: a race against long odds on a scale much greater than the Tenth District and the Lone Star State. In this one, he could not shrug off his job's responsibilities, which were much greater as well. And he was bone weary and much older.

It was time to go home.

15

The Spent Golden Coin: 1969 to 1973

On her last day in the White House, Lady Bird wrote in her diary, "The golden coin is spent." Her husband's career was over; he was heading back to his ranch. She hoped retirement would be happy and told him she looked forward to twenty years of peaceful life together.

As Air Force One took off, Lyndon hauled out a cigarette and lit up. Aware that his doctors had warned him in 1955 never to smoke again, his daughter Luci objected. Angered, he replied, "For fourteen years I've wanted to smoke when I wanted to smoke and for fourteen years I had a country to serve, children to raise, and a job to do. Now the job is done and the children are raised. It's my turn." Upset, she moved away, the first among friends and family to fear LBJ was committing a slow suicide.

Cigarettes were just one instrument of death. The man who had watched his weight and eaten tapioca demanded huge helpings and sneaked Snickers. The one who commanded Bobby Baker to limit his scotches and water them well drank heavily. The politician who fought through depressed periods and overcame them with sustained bursts of energy and creativity swung between black moods and impotent tantrums. All these self-destroying tendencies Bird struggled against, with mixed success. Her best weapon was this sad fact: Lyndon Johnson, who had gloried in his power and genius and often done what he damn pleased, now depended on his wife completely. As his life neared its end, a friend observed, "She was managing so many of the details of his life—what he ate, what he wore, his general health—that she took her rest when she could get it."

Nothing fully engaged Lyndon. The proposed three volumes of memoirs he contracted to write did not sustain his interest; the one book he completed disappointed him and his readers. He never taught at the public affairs institute named after him. His library lost its fascination soon after its dedication. Almost absentmindedly, he made money from buying ranches and converting them into developments of weekend houses. That consumed relatively little time, but rather than using other hours to direct his media holdings, he sold KTBC and let others run the radio stations. The one exception was the LBJ Ranch. He micromanaged it to comical extremes, going so far as to demand the cowboys write memos each evening. His foreman and hands were miserable.

Bird quickly learned that talking and thinking about politics made Lyndon as miserable as his cowboys. In a courteous tribute to LBJ's interest in space, Richard Nixon invited him to attend the launching of the moon expedition in July 1969. Once there, he discovered he was playing second fiddle to Spiro Agnew. Ranking below a vice president upset him. This proof of his inconsequentiality was followed by clear indications that his successor had no intention of consulting him on policy issues. Nixon stopped informing him very often or thoroughly; he felt no need for Johnson's advice or support, a reaction encouraged by his belief that Lyndon was depressed and distracted. During one of Henry Kissinger's first visits to the ranch, the National Security Adviser realized that LBJ thought he was Kurt Kiesinger, the West German chancellor. Then he noticed that Johnson did not follow his presentation on Vietnam.

To his party, Lyndon became virtually a non-person. In 1972, the organizers of the Democratic National Convention did not ask him to attend. Their rudeness was inspired by George McGovern's promise to extricate the nation from what he called a senseless, immoral war and to extricate the party from the bosses and unrepresentative delegations who had been LBJ's friends and supporters in 1964 and 1968. Probably he wouldn't have gone anyway. Before the convention met, he told General Alexander Haig, who was serving on Nixon's National Security Council, that he thought "a McGovern presidency [would be] a disaster," adding "as a life-long Democrat, he could not vote Republican but he would not vote Democratic either." He would not attend the Democratic Convention, and he would advise prominent Democrats not to support McGovern. He was as good as his word, letting friends know he "despised" his party's nominee on the grounds of ideology and incompetence. Lyndon privately applauded the formation by John Connally and George Christian of Texas Democrats for Nixon. He went to vote in November happy in the knowledge that McGovern did not have a prayer.

LBJ kept quiet about his successor. Familiar with the job's difficulties, he shrank from criticism, even when some Great Society programs appeared in danger. His silence also reflected apprehension. Lyndon thought Nixon was exceptionally vindictive and judged that he would retaliate with the presidency's full might against anybody who crossed him. He feared Tricky Dick would sic the Justice Department on him, dredging up scandals involving Bobby Baker and KTBC in an effort to indict him for fraud. That Bobby had been convicted and imprisoned deepened his worries. When Baker asked for help, Lyndon whined that he did not dare do anything. How far he was from being the master of the Senate or anything else! The one time he stood up against Nixon was in self-defense. In January 1973, the White House tried to bully LBJ into urging Senate Democrats not to investigate Watergate by threatening to disclose he had bugged Nixon's plane during the 1968 campaign. Lyndon turned this blackmail attempt aside with a threat of his own: he replied he would publicize Nixon's interference with peace negotiations right before the election. This episode was quite unique. Customarily, the only critique of the White House he could muster was symbolic. Unlike the well-barbered men there, he let his hair grow. Soon he sported shoulder-length gray curls.

No one claimed Lyndon was a hippie. He remained committed to resisting North Vietnamese aggression, and he doubtless took grim satisfaction that others were having trouble negotiating with Hanoi. His attitude toward the national media in general and the *New York Times* in particular was unchanged as well. When the *Times* began publishing in 1971 a top secret documentary history of the origins of U.S. involvement in Vietnam, an appalled Johnson urged Richard Nixon to seek a federal court injunction forbidding further publication. LBJ was sure, reported Walt Rostow to Nixon, that printing the Pentagon papers was "a serious matter for the fate of the country," because it would discourage candid advice to future presidents and compromise diplomatic relations. Finally, Lyndon stayed bitterly opposed to anti-war Democrats. When the Senate passed an amendment in 1971 setting a deadline for withdrawing all American troops from Vietnam, he snarled to a Nixon aide, "I'm going to do everything

I can to beat the dirty rotten sons of bitches in 1972." Despite these continuities, though, it is not far-fetched to see LBJ as a countercultural figure in American politics during the 1970s and later. The political landscape had been so transformed while he wielded power that the master who had been central to the change became a relic of the past, a man out of step. Much of what he wrought was an enduring legacy to his country, truly golden coins. The change left over was a mixed blessing to the United States and LBJ.

Lyndon regarded civil rights as the crowning glory of his life in politics. Quarreling with that judgment is impossible. De jure segregation was finished by the end of his administration. By 1980, the impact of voting African-Americans in the South and the nation had become exactly what he had predicted in the 1940s and 1950s. The civil rights legislation of 1964 and 1965 and its aftermath were to Johnson vindication of his understanding of the remedy for injustice.

What's more, desegregation and progress toward integration accomplished his other great goal: it brought the South fully into the prospering and expanding national economy and into a potent, decisive role in national politics. Absent LBJ, it is hard to imagine the presidencies of men from Georgia, Arkansas, and Texas, let alone that in 2008 residents of Confederate states will have sat in the Oval Office for twenty-four of the forty years since he went back to the ranch.

Another of his forecasts came true: the South did become Republican. More precisely, it became Goldwater Republican in philosophy. LBJ could see that happening in 1964, when Goldwater carried some Deep South states and got solid minorities elsewhere in Dixie. George Wallace's rise made this clear to him as well. He understood that politicians in the post-civil rights South would find ways to mask opposition to full integration with more respectable talk of states' rights and law and order. He also grasped that race would remain an important consideration for many white voters: they might accept legal integration, but they saw the new situation as a more equal struggle between whites and blacks, and they planned to organize to protect themselves. Lyndon saw this as inevitable. He never pondered whether it equaled a truly integrated society.

Lyndon also glimpsed the power of the backlash against black rights and aspirations outside the South. Polls from early 1965 through 1968 revealed increasing dissatisfaction with his administration's attention to African Americans. Affirmative action, a phrase popularized by Johnson and made executive policy by him, was regarded suspiciously by many whites from the start; it signaled quotas and unmerited favoritism, not correcting historic inequities. Charges that he and his party "coddled" and encouraged criminals and rioters by "understanding" them, then rewarded them with welfare payments and federal grants, pointed to a fundamental problem LBJ had with white middle-class attitudes. In those voters' minds, guaranteeing basic rights to people who were unjustly denied them and providing the education for their eventual success were acceptable actions: conferring federal funds and aid to them as entitlements was not. The more Lyndon and the Democrats became identified with welfare and entitlements, the less popular they became.

The irony in this, of course, was the fact that LBJ lavished benefits on everyone. Federal aid to education, intervention to clean up the environment, consumer protection, Medicare and Medicaid, increased Social Security payments—all these improved the lives of all Americans. Proof of this is how quickly they became untouchables in American politics.

At the same time, federal bureaucracies and government activity in general became objects of popular scorn and inviting political targets. Lyndon earned a generous share of the blame for that. He promised too much, then did not deliver enough funds to come close to fulfilling them. Equally significant, he did not apply his intelligence and energy to overseeing, adjusting, streamlining, and generally increasing the efficiency and responsiveness of federal agencies. Their failures, and his refusal to acknowledge and try to correct them, helped make attacking Washington like shooting fish in a barrel for conservative politicians in both parties. The reason this was so inviting was summarized on February 12, 1969, by David Broder, the judicious and well-respected columnist for the *Washington Post*. According to him, Washington was "a government and a city where most jobs depend on seeing that no problem is ever really solved." A more damning indictment of LBJ's Great Society could hardly be written.

Another easy target for modern politicians was taxation. In part, this resulted from the feeling that dollars were being spent by LBJ's government on wrong-headed projects in a wasteful fashion. More portentous for the future was the simultaneous impression that better results were achieved by cutting taxes. Politicians from both parties in the 1950s were dubious about selling tax reduction as economic wisdom. Sam Rayburn spoke for many. After a cut was justified as an economic stimulus, he warned, it would be very difficult for leaders to reverse their field and get an increase when one was necessary. An enthusiastic advocate for the reductions of 1964,

Lyndon discovered how right Rayburn was when he struggled to get a *temporary* tax hike in 1968. Without the fiscal crisis of those months, he could not have managed it. The next generation of politicians was composed of apt pupils who made opposition to taxes important parts of campaigning and governing. In this case, they followed the example of George Wallace. As early as 1963, Wallace claimed, "Governments do not produce wealth; people produce wealth—free people." His was the wave of the future.

Thus Lyndon Johnson, who believed the federal government could and must address the country's most fundamental domestic problems, helped create an atmosphere in which running against Washington was widely attractive and politically expedient. This development would not have totally surprised him.

Johnson understood the historic commitment to localism throughout the United States and to states' rights in the South. He crafted his legislation on education and poverty to take them into account, and he tried to avoid massive federal intervention in the Deep South because of its traditional emphasis on state governments and the prevailing white folk memories of Reconstruction. We should also recall that he thought the window of opportunity for reform was narrow and closing rapidly. The urgency he felt to get his laws on the books before reaction set in testifies to that awareness, as did his surreptitious escalation of the war to prevent that distraction and excuse for opposition.

Even so, the passion and endurance of anti-Washington rhetoric and reaction would have dismayed him. Lyndon hoped that the benefits the Great Society conferred on Americans would temper, if not reverse, these feelings. Instead, citizens enjoyed their own share of the largesse *and* attacked federal taxes and activity aimed at helping others.

The impact of LBJ's policies in Southeast Asia on American politics was even more pronounced. That the stalemate in Vietnam shattered the Cold War consensus on containment of Communism and divided his own party is obvious. Divisions among Democrats were not, of course, novel in his experience; witness the struggles between isolationists and internationalists during the 1930s. But events had settled these conflicts, and new areas of consensus were created, however grudgingly. Vietnam was different because of the way Johnson characterized his opponents and their effect on the war.

It is not just that LBJ charged them with being fools or tools of Communism. He did more. Privately and publicly he claimed they were abetting the enemy by encouraging them to fight on. That Hanoi was encouraged by dissent in America seems a fair assessment, but how crucial was this to their commitment to keep fighting? Lyndon himself recognized how determined and motivated this enemy was. The North Vietnamese thought they were winning and that they would win, irrespective of American opinion. What made Lyndon's attacks on anti-war Democrats poisonous was how these comments could—and did—morph later into arguments that the United States would have won the war were it not for the peace movement. Did domestic dissent cause losing in Vietnam? That is not self-evident. North Vietnam was a redoubtable enemy ready to fight a long war to the finish no matter what.

Assigning a crucial role to anti-war Democrats for their country's defeat had the effect of raising questions about the ability of their party to deal with issues of national security. These doubts helped sink George McGovern's campaign in 1972. That result did not displease LBJ. Indeed, his private comments reveal the same doubts. As he told Nixon, "He had agreed with most of the positions I [Nixon] had taken during my tenure in office and . . . he found himself in sharp disagreement with the nominee of his party." What he did not foresee was the persistence of this attitude. The charges he made publicly and privately helped the Republicans fashion a weapon they used against Democrats for years after 1972.

Lyndon assisted in the perfection of another tactic politicians employed frequently and effectively after he provided the example. Throughout his presidency, he had been suspicious of the motives of the national media. Always ready to believe that they were out to get him, never satisfied with coverage of his triumphs, forever flinching at real and imagined criticism, he overlooked the fact that he received generally favorable treatment from journalists until well into 1968. Instead, he blamed them for weakening the Great Society and strengthening the North Vietnamese. In 1965, he even told a columnist for the *New York Times*, "I'd have to do it all in six to eight months. The eastern media will have the wells so poisoned by that time that that's all the time I have. They'll have us peeing on the fire."

LBJ also did not hide his opinion that the media were hopelessly prejudiced against Texas and anywhere else beyond the East Coast. In a draft of his memoirs, he scribbled, "The greatest bigots in the world are Democrats in the East Side of New York. [Senator James] Eastland [the segregationist Mississippi senator] is charitable compared to an eastern bigot." This convinced him and his successors that an out-of-touch, unrepresentative, arrogant, and mostly liberal press created and/or worsened most of their problems. For instance, consider LBJ's furious attack on August 1, 1966, on the *New York Times* correspondent in Saigon during 1962 and 1963. "David Halberstam killed Diem. He made us assassinate him. That man is a traitor—so they give him a Pulitzer Prize. They give Pulitzer Prizes to traitors nowadays." Though this tantrum was off the record, Johnson made his feelings known widely as time passed. His rages became a trope of modern popular politics: the press estranging itself from and elevating itself above the concerns of ordinary, patriotic Americans. Johnson contributed to the undercutting of the authority of an institution that had supported his Great Society and his containment of Communism. In the process, he sped the development of a more sharply adversarial relationship between press and politicians.

One consequence of Johnson's accusations was heightening the significance of Vietnam and embedding it in the country's consciousness. To a considerable extent, certainly, that war was important in its own right, but the bitter and corrosive comments by LBJ helped make "Vietnam" as emotional and meaning-packed a word for later generations as "Munich" was for his. Avoiding "another Vietnam" remains a national preoccupation.

The problem was, there was no consensus on the meaning of "Vietnam." Interpreted by Lyndon, it meant the United States had to be unified and resolute in future emergencies to avoid being its own worst enemy and snatching defeat out of victory. The country's major foe was division among its people, as well as their reputation for impatience and softness. Interpreted by his anti-war critics, "Vietnam" signified focusing on foreign matters over domestic ones and being entangled in remote political/military conflicts with the potential for stalemate, defeat, and disaster. That would distract the country from its main national task: a more prosperous and more just United States. Note the contrast with the earlier buzz word. "Munich" meant one thing: not giving in to aggressors because the ultimate reckoning with them would be more hazardous and dangerous. No one disputed that moral.

Clearly, applying "Munich" to Southeast Asia the way Lyndon did was a mistake. By the same token, seeing "Vietnam" everywhere can be equally distorting and misleading. Discerning what is unique in each situation is essential to devising successful policy. That is true no matter how one defines "Vietnam." That moral has been imperfectly understood since Johnson's death. During his lifetime, he contributed to this outcome.

Lyndon Johnson's political career is a textbook illustration of the Law of Unforeseen Consequences. Many of his successes in the Senate and the White House hinged on alliances with Republicans. Yet the end result of many of his decisions was a revved-up partisanship that persists to this day. Confrontation became the way to power for Republicans; it also became the means of staying in power.

It is also true that many of LBJ's triumphs depended on his forging unity among Democrats of disparate views. By 1969, his party was seriously fractured, in part because he chose angry attacks over efforts to conciliate critics and rebuild a common identity. That common identity continues to be elusive for his party.

Lyndon regarded the Right as "the great beast" in American politics in 1965. Ironically, his words and acts helped resurrect American conservatism and set it on the road to power following the crushing defeat he dealt it in 1964. His party was indisputably the majority party when he was president. Now it is struggling to regain that position.

Although he meant for none of this to happen, LBJ was aware that nothing he wanted to achieve would occur unless he was willing to pay a price. As he noted, if civil rights cost his party the South and himself the White House, then so be it. It was a price he would gladly pay because justice had to be done and progress needed to be made. No one today would not honor him for that.

Likewise, LBJ knew that there would be a price to pay for Vietnam. That, too, he was willing to meet, because he thought resisting North Vietnam was crucial for achieving domestic reforms and because failure to stand up would weaken the reputation of the United States, encourage more aggression from Russia and China, and profoundly threaten U.S. security and the peace of the world. Many today would question the wisdom of these conclusions, though much of that questioning is informed by 20/20 hindsight. All would concede he faced tough choices.

Lyndon did compose his own epitaph. It was an honest one, delivered during his State of the Union address in January 1969: "I hope," he told Congress, "it may be said a hundred years from now, that by working together we helped to make our country more just, more just for all its people, as well as to insure and guarantee the blessing of liberty for all our posterity." Then he finished his life in Washington. "That is what I hope. But I believe that at least it will be said we tried."

He may not have believed his own words at the end. Horace Busby worried about this as he watched LBJ leave for Texas on January 20, 1969. "For a while," mused Busby, "Washington had been Lyndon Johnson's, as much as it had ever been any man's." "But," he continued, "it remained that as much as Washington had been his, so Lyndon Johnson would be Washington's. He could never belong wherever else he might be."

Being once more Lyndon Johnson of Johnson City convinced him that he would be forgotten. "All the historians are Harvard people," he railed to Doris Kearns Goodwin. "It just isn't fair." Nobody like him would get a fair shake. He doubted anybody would even remember him. "I would have been better off looking for immortality through my wife and children and their children instead of seeking all that love and affection from the American people. They're just too fickle." His advice to Goodwin: "Get married. Have children. Spend time with them."

Two days later on January 22, 1973, he died, alone.

When Lady Bird heard the news, she was composed: "Well, we expected it, didn't we?" She called her daughters, then some friends and former aides. As she returned to the ranch, she made more calls. When Lynda and Luci arrived, the three Johnson women went into the bedroom where he had passed. They closed the door, and Bird wept for her husband.

Afterward, she asked several old friends to stay with his remains that night. "I do not want him to be alone," she said. "Stand with him."

As they did, lines were forming outside the LBJ Library—some famous people but mostly ordinary folks, waiting to remember, to honor, and to say good-bye to the extraordinary man who changed their lives.

Study and Discussion Questions

Introduction

1. Describe the differences between Lyndon Johnson's treatment of his wife and staff and his relationships with peers in Congress and the Senate. What do you think explains these differences?

2. What institution did Johnson believe was the most powerful in American life? Why?

3. What restrictions did Johnson feel limited his power in foreign relations?

4. Which restrictions did Johnson feel limited his power in domestic affairs?

Chapter 1: A Steam Engine in Pants: 1908–1937

1. What were the prevailing attitudes toward education in Johnson City? How did Lyndon Johnson's ideas differ? Why did they differ?

2. Describe the impact on Johnson of teaching at Cotulla. Why did he react as he did to the situation there?

3. Assess Johnson's performance as a teacher.

4. Several contemporaries remarked on how skilled the young Johnson was as a politician. Why did they feel that way?

5. Why did a staff member claim that Johnson was "a steam engine in pants?"

Chapter 2: The Best Congressman That Ever Was: 1937–1941

1. Explain why Johnson won the special election in the 10th District in 1937. What was the most important factor in his victory?

2. Describe the differences between Johnson and his predecessor as representatives for the 10th District.

3. Why did Herman and George Brown support Johnson? In which ways are the Browns representative of Texas businessmen during the 1930s?

4. What characteristics define a celebrity politician? Explain why W. Lee O'Daniel is regarded as the first celebrity politician in Texas history.

5. Describe the strengths and weaknesses of Johnson's campaign for the Senate in 1941. Why did he lose?

Chapter 3: Trying to Climb a Pole: 1941–1948

1. Why did Johnson feel he could play the martyr in a future campaign against O'Daniel? What does this reveal about his attitude toward voters?

2. Did Johnson's limited combat experience in World War II give him an accurate idea of what Americans in the armed forces endured? Did it influence his position on how returning veterans and their families should be treated after the war?

3. Who were the Texas Regulars? Why did they object to the New Deal and Lyndon Johnson?

4. What lessons did Johnson learn from the Second World War? How did the war influence his attitudes toward foreign relations?

Chapter 4: The Right Place: 1948–1957

1. Why did Johnson defeat Coke Stevenson? What was the most important reason for his victory?

2. Why did Johnson believe the Senate was "the right place" for him?

3. Describe the impact of Richard Russell on Johnson's career in the Senate. Why was Russell so influential?

4. Describe Johnson's attitudes toward race and race relations during the 1940s and 1950s. Why do these define him as a moderate segregationist? What separated him from hard-core Southern segregationists?

5. Describe the role of Dwight Eisenhower in Johnson's career in the Senate. How did Ike help Johnson achieve mastery of the Senate?

6. Why did liberal Democrats in the Senate dislike Johnson so much?

7. Describe the reasons why Johnson concluded in 1957 that he had to manage a civil rights bill through the Senate in order to be a viable candidate for the presidency?

Chapter 5: The Riverboat Gambler: 1957–July 1960

1. Why did the Republican Party press for civil rights legislation in 1957? What sort of opportunities did this create for Johnson?

2. Why did Richard Russell assist Johnson in securing the passage of the civil rights bill?

3. Discuss the strengths and weaknesses of the Civil Rights Act of 1957. Why did Johnson believe it was a significant step forward?

4. Discuss the reasons why Johnson's efforts to win the Democratic nomination for president in 1960 were unsuccessful.

5. Why did John Kennedy offer Johnson the vice presidential nomination? Why did Johnson accept?

Chapter 6: Second Place: 1960–1963

1. What explains Johnson's success in the South during the 1960 campaign?

2. Explain Johnson's conception of what the vice president's role should be and his reaction to what his role was during the Kennedy Administration.

3. Describe Johnson's role in foreign policy during the Kennedy Administration. Why was he excluded from some crucial decisions? What were the effects of that exclusion?

4. Explain the reasons for the fierce dislike between Johnson and Robert Kennedy.

5. Was Johnson in serious danger of being dropped from the Democratic ticket in 1964?

Chapter 7: Free At Last: November 1963–June 1964

1. LBJ felt compelled to keep as many of John Kennedy's appointees in office as he could. Why did he believe this? Was it a wise decision?

2. What were the three goals of the national Democratic Party? How did LBJ plan to meet them? Did he add any goals of his own?

3. What did LBJ feel was his most important task as president? Why did he believe this?

4. Compare and contrast Johnson's approach to Vietnam with his approach to Central and South America.

5. What impact did George Wallace's primary campaigns have on the passage of civil rights legislation in 1964?

6. Richard Russell credited Lyndon Johnson and the clergy with the passage of civil rights in 1964. Was he correct? Should he have added Republican moderates to his list?

7. Why was Johnson concerned about reactions to the new civil rights law in the South? How did he try to reconcile white Southerners to it? Was he successful?

Chapter 8: Walking the Tightrope: July–November 1964

1. According to LBJ, what were the goals of the War on Poverty? Was he concerned about Community Action Programs because they did not fit these goals?

2. Explain why Vietnam posed difficult problems for LBJ. Why did he try to delay a final decision about policy? Did he ever seriously consider an alternative to military intervention?

3. Discuss Johnson's assessment of Ho Chi Minh and the North Vietnamese. How did this assessment influence his desire for a congressional resolution of support?

4. Discuss LBJ's reactions to the Mississippi Freedom Democratic Party challenge. Why did he refuse to make their that cause his

own? Why did this challenge cause him to contemplate not running for president?

5. Was LBJ's campaign against Barry Goldwater an innovative campaign? If so, in what ways?

6. Why did Johnson win the election? Why did he win by a landslide?

Chapter 9: Living in the Middle of It: December 1964–April 1965

1. Why did Hubert Humphrey believe that LBJ had complete freedom of action in January 1965? Why did Johnson disagree? Which one of them was correct?

2. Compare and contrast LBJ's approach to planning for Vietnam with his approach to planning the Great Society. Which are more significant: the similarities or the differences?

3. Compare and contrast Johnson's treatment of powerful interest groups in the debates on federal aid to education and on Medicare. Did these interest groups have an important effect upon the final legislation? How so?

4. When he was majority leader, liberals often claimed that LBJ wasn't concerned about the substance of legislation, but instead focused instead on passing whatever laws he could get. Could that charge be made against him as president on Great Society legislation?

5. Why did Johnson believe voting rights legislation was crucial in 1965? What did he hope it would accomplish? Was he correct?

Chapter 10: Looking for Light: April–September 1965

1. Johnson was not enthusiastic about the prospects for fighting North Vietnam. What explained his pessimism? Why did he go ahead with escalation anyway?

2. LBJ frequently said that the credibility of the United States was at stake in Vietnam. Why was American credibility important to him?

3. Why did Johnson believe anti-war protests were Communist inspired? Why did he feel they were very harmful?

4. Compare and contrast LBJ's handling of Vietnam during these months from April to September 1965 with his reactions to the

Dominican crisis? Which are more significant: the similarities or the differences?

5. Why was it important to LBJ to get Abe Fortas confirmed as a Supreme Court justice?

6. Why did the possible devaluation of the British pound threaten the Great Society? What impact would devaluation have had on Vietnam?

7. Explain why the outbreak of violence in Watts during August 1965 depressed LBJ.

Chapter 11: Impatient People: Fall 1965–December 1966

1. What were the problems with the American strategy of attrition in Vietnam? Why did Johnson fail to raise questions about it?

2. Assess the role of Robert McNamara in the formulation and execution of US U.S. policy toward Vietnam.

3. How did LBJ try to prepare the nation for a long, difficult war? What were the weaknesses in his approach? Why did he have to avoid creating what he called "a war psychosis"? How did this contribute to a credibility gap?

4. How did LBJ try to keep the economy booming during these months? Why did he avoid talk of a tax increase?

5. Johnson was uninterested in increasing the efficiency of federal agencies in the War on Poverty. Why? What were the significances of his decision?

6. Why did the Democrats lose seats in the midterm elections of 1966? Assess Johnson's responsibility for these defeats.

Chapter 12: Waist Deep in the Big Muddy: 1967

1. What major problems confronted LBJ at the beginning of 1967? Rank them in order of importance and significance. Explain your ranking. How were these major problems related to each other?

2. How would LBJ have ranked the major problems of 1968? Why?

3. Explain why LBJ was so successful in dealing with European problems. Why was he unable to transfer this success to Southeast Asia?

4. Discuss the impact of the Six Days War in the Middle East on U.S.–Soviet relations. What encouraged LBJ about the meeting at Glassboro? What discouraged him?

5. Explain Johnson's attitude toward a tax hike in 1967. Why did he regard it as vitally important?

6. In October 1967, LBJ revealed that he was thinking of not running for re-reelection. Why was he contemplating withdrawing from politics? Were his reasons essentially personal in nature, or did they reflect a frustration with Vietnam and the battles over the War on Poverty?

Chapter 13: Hell Sucks: January–March 1968

1. Summarize the arguments LBJ heard in favor of his withdrawing. Which were the most persuasive? Why?

2. What was the impact of the Tet Offensive on Johnson? On the American people?

3. Which of these events had the greatest impact on LBJ's decisions on Vietnam in early 1968?:
   • The Tet Offensive;
   • The international financial crisis;
   • The primary election in New Hampshire.

4. Assess the role of Horace Busby in LBJ's decision not to run for reelection.

Chapter 14: This Hard Time: April 1968–January 1969

1. What were LBJ's misgivings about Hubert Humphrey? Why did he help the Humphrey campaign for the Democratic nomination?

2. What were the significances of the passage of the tax increase? How did it impact the Great Society? What did it reveal about Johnson's strategies in domestic affairs?

3. Was the 1968 election essentially a referendum on Lyndon Johnson? Was Nixon's victory the result of widespread dissatisfaction with LBJ and his foreign and domestic policies? What was the impact of LBS's nominating Abe Fortas to replace

Earl Warren as Chief Justice? Were Humphrey's errors of greater significance than LBJ's reputation?

4. Did Johnson seriously consider re-reentering the race for the presidency? What would have been the results had he done so?

Chapter 15: The Spent Golden Coin: 1969–1973

1. What were the reasons for Johnson's unhappiness in retirement?

2. When he became president, LBJ expressed the hope that he could complete the work of Abraham Lincoln. Did he succeed in this ambition?

3. Johnson struggled throughout his political career against the suspicions many Americans had about the power of the federal government throughout his political career. Did his many accomplishments lessen this suspicion? Or did his failings actually intensify those feelings?

4. Describe the significance on American politics of Johnson's criticism of domestic dissent against the war on American politics.

5. Historians occasionally rank presidents and group them into categories. Recently LBJ's ranking has risen to the category of "near great." Is this a fair assessment of Lyndon Johnson?

A Note on the Sources

The amount of published and archival material on the life and times of Lyndon Johnson long ago reached gargantuan dimensions. It continues to grow; in particular, we can anticipate some new and fascinating work on Vietnam as research in North Vietnamese, Chinese, and Russian sources advances. In this note on sources I have tried to be suggestive rather than exhaustive, focusing upon sources that were very helpful to me as I wrote this book and that will serve to point readers who wish to learn more about specific details of Johnson's life and career in the most fruitful and interesting directions.

Study about LBJ's life should begin with three biographies. Two are multivolumes. The first is Robert Dallek, *Lyndon Johnson and His Times*, 2 vols., *Lone Star Rising, 1908–1960* (New York, 1991), and *Flawed Giant, 1961–1973* (New York, 1998). The second is Robert A. Caro, *The Years of Lyndon Johnson*, 3 vols., *The Path to Power* (New York, 1982), *Means of Ascent* (New York, 1990), and *Master of the Senate* (New York, 2002); Caro is currently working on a fourth volume on the presidential years. The best single-volume biography is Randall B. Woods, *LBJ: Architect of American Ambition* (New York, 2006). Each of these biographies has its own strengths and weaknesses: Dallek's is a balanced, thorough account; Caro's is consistently critical of Johnson's motives; and Woods's work is excellent on LBJ's Texas roots and career in state politics.

In addition to these, Paul Conkin, *Big Daddy from the Pedernales: Lyndon B. Johnson* (Boston, 1986), and Irwin Unger and Debi Unger, *LBJ: A Life* (New York, 1999), are good biographies. Bruce J. Schulman's *Lyndon B. Johnson and American Liberalism: A Brief Biography with Documents* (Boston, 1995), is an insightful survey.

There is also interesting material on LBJ in Jan Jarboe Russell, *Lady Bird: A Biography of Mrs. Johnson* (New York, 1999). Russell's book is especially insightful on the relationship between Lyndon, Bird, and their daughters, and the contributions Mrs. Johnson made to the family's business enterprises.

Several perceptive memoirs deal extensively with Lyndon Johnson. Unfortunately, one of the least intriguing was written by LBJ himself, *The Vantage Point: Perspectives on the Presidency, 1963–1969* (New York, 1971); his desire to present himself as a dignified senior statesman stifled the colorful language in his telephone transcripts and his pungent remarks on events and personalities. Far more illuminating are two recent publications: W. Marvin Watson with Sherwin Markham, *Chief of Staff: Lyndon Johnson and His Presidency* (New York, 2004), and Horace Busby, *The Thirty-First of March: An Intimate Portrait of Lyndon Johnson's Final Days in Office* (New York, 2005). For other interesting perspectives on Johnson, see Bobby Baker with Larry L. King, *Wheeling and Dealing: Confessions of a Capitol Hill Operator* (New York, 1978); John L. Bullion, *In the Boat with LBJ* (Plano, TX, 2001); Joseph A. Califano, Jr., *The Triumph and Tragedy of Lyndon Johnson* (New York, 1991); Clark Clifford, *Counsel to the President* (New York, 1991); John B. Connally with Mickey Herskowitz, *In History's Shadow: An American Odyssey* (New York, 1993); Eric F. Goldman, *The Tragedy of Lyndon Johnson* (New York, 1969); Doris Kearns Goodwin, *Lyndon Johnson and the American Dream*, 2nd ed. (New York, 1991); Katherine Graham, *Personal History* (New York, 1997); Hubert H. Humphrey, *The Education of a Public Man* (New York, 1976); Lady Bird Johnson, *A White House Diary* (New York, 1970); Sam Houston Johnson, *My Brother Lyndon* (New York, 1969); Robert S. McNamara with Brian Van DeMark, *In Retrospect: The Tragedy and Lessons of Vietnam* (New York, 1995); Harry McPherson, *A Political Education: A Washington Memoir* (Austin, TX, 1995); Joe Phipps, *Summer Stock: Behind the Scenes were LBJ in '48, Recollections of a Political Drama* (Fort Worth, TX, 1992); George Reedy, *Lyndon B. Johnson, A Memoir* (New York, 1982); Merle Miller, *Lyndon: An Oral Biography* (New York, 1980); Jack Valenti, *A Very Human President* (New York, 1975), and *This Time, This Place: My Life in War, the White House, and Hollywood* (New York, 2007); and William C. Westmoreland, *A Soldier Reports* (New York, 1976).

For fascinating unpublished recollections of LBJ, readers should consult the extensive collection of oral histories at the Lyndon B. Johnson Library at Austin, Texas. Also available at the LBJ Library are the unpublished sections of Lady Bird Johnson's White House diaries and the secret recordings LBJ made of some telephone conversations and private meetings while he was president. Of the oral history transcripts, 1,150 are readily available at http://www.millercenter.virginia.edu. Extensive selections from the secret recordings may be found in Michael

R. Beschloss, *Taking Charge: The Johnson White House Tapes, 1963–1964* (New York, 1997); *Reaching for Glory: Lyndon Johnson's Secret White House Tapes, 1964–1965* (New York, 2001); and Max Holland, *The Kennedy Assassination Tapes: The White House Conversations of Lyndon B. Johnson Regarding the Assassination, the Warren Commission, and the Aftermath* (New York, 2004).

Further study of LBJ before he became president should begin with Ronnie Dugger, *The Politician: The Life and Times of Lyndon Johnson: The Drive for Power—from the Frontier to Master of the Senate* (New York, 1982). The longtime editor of the liberal magazine *The Texas Observer,* Dugger had a close though somewhat adversarial relationship with Johnson for years and an incredible amount of access to him. As George Christian observed, no one interviewed LBJ more frequently than Dugger. Also invaluable is William Pool, Emmie Craddock, and David E. Conrad, *Lyndon Baines Johnson: The Formative Years* (San Marcos, TX, 1965).

Still useful are three books by Seth S. McKay: *W. Lee O'Daniel and Texas Politics, 1938–1942* (Lubbock, TX, 1944); *Texas Politics, 1906–1944* (Lubbock, TX, 1952); and *Texas and the Fair Deal* (San Antonio, TX, 1954)

Important information relating to Johnson in Texas politics may be found in Julie Leininger Pycior, *LBJ and Mexican-Americans: The Paradox of Power* (Austin, TX, 1997); Joseph A. Pratt and Christopher J. Casteneda, *Builders: Herman and George R. Brown* (College Station, TX, 1999); Chandler Davidson, *Race and Class in Texas Politics* (Princeton, NJ, 1990); and Jane S. Smallwood, *The Great Recovery: The New Deal in Texas* (Boston, 1983).

For Johnson in national politics during the 1940s and 1950s, see D. B. Hardeman and Donald C. Bacon, *Rayburn: A Biography* (Austin, TX, 1987), and James Reston, Jr., *The Lone Star: The Life of John Connally* (New York, 1989). Also informative are Stephen Ambrose, *Eisenhower: The President* (New York, 1984), and *Nixon: The Education of a Politician, 1913–1962* (New York, 1987). A stimulating analysis of LBJ in the Senate may be found in Lewis L. Gould, *The Most Exclusive Club: A History of the Modern United States Senate* (New York, 2005). An interesting account of the impact of events during 1948 on Johnson is Lance Morrow, *The Best Years of Their Lives: Kennedy, Johnson, and Nixon in 1948—Learning the Secrets of Power* (New York, 2005).

Further study of the struggle over the Civil Rights Act of 1957 begins with Gilbert C. Fite, *Richard B. Russell, Jr.: Senator from Georgia* (Chapel Hill, NC, 1991). A fresh perspective on Southern Democrats in the Senate during the 1950s may be found in John Kyle

Day, "The Southern Manifesto: Making Opposition to the Civil Rights Movement," (unpublished doctoral dissertation, University of Missouri-Columbia, 2006). The classic study is Robert Mann, *The Walls of Jericho: Lyndon Johnson, Hubert Humphrey, Richard Russell, and the Struggle for Civil Rights* (New York, 1996). Excellent on the entire era are Richard Kluger, *Simple Justice: The History of Brown v. Board of Education and Black America's Struggle for Equality* (New York, 1976), and Taylor Branch, *Parting the Waters: America in the King Years, 1954–1963* (New York, 1988).

LBJ's relationship with John Kennedy has been discussed in many books. Two thoughtful studies add new insights to this scholarship: Richard Reeves, *President Kennedy: Profile of Power* (New York, 1993); and Robert Dallek, *An Unfinished Life: John F. Kennedy, 1917–1963* (New York, 2003).

On Johnson's presidency and on the tumultuous decade of the 1960s, there are two excellent introductions: James T. Patterson, *Grand Expectations: The United States, 1945–1974* (New York, 1996), and Terry H. Anderson, *The Sixties,* 2nd ed. (New York, 2004).

In my survey on the literature covering LBJ in the White House, I read four works that were extraordinary additions to the scholarship of the period. Each is worthy of being highlighted. They are Robert M. Collins, "The Economic Crisis of 1968 and the Waning of the 'American Century,'" *American Historical Review,* vol. 101 (April 1996), pp. 396–422; Nick Kotz, *Judgment Days: Lyndon Baines Johnson, Martin Luther King, Jr., and the Laws that Changed America* (New York, 2005); Dominic Sandbrook, *Eugene McCarthy and the Rise and Fall of Postwar American Liberalism* (New York, 2004); and Thomas Alan Schwartz, *Lyndon Johnson and Europe: In the Shadow of Vietnam* (Cambridge, MA, 2003).

Irving Bernstein, *Guns or Butter: The Presidency of Lyndon Johnson* (New York, 1996), is a very good overall account, particularly on the economic impact of the war in Vietnam and on the administration's policies on taxation.

Studies of particular Great Society programs abound. Among the best are Hugh Davis Graham, *The Uncertain Trumpet: Federal Education Policy in the Kennedy and Johnson Years* (Chapel Hill, NC, 1984), and *The Civil Rights Era: Origins and Development of National Policy, 1960–1972* (New York, 1990); Lewis L. Gould, *Lady Bird Johnson and the Environment* (Lawrence, KS, 1988); Richard Sorian, *The Bitter Pill: Tough Choices in America's Health Policy* (New York, 1990); James T. Patterson, *America's Struggle Against Poverty, 1900–1980* (New York, 1981); and Gareth Davies, *From Opportunity to Entitlement: The Transformation and Decline of Great Society*

Liberalism (Lawrence, KS, 1996). Scott Stossel, *Sarge: The Life and Times of Sargent Shriver* (Washington, DC, 2004), has an excellent section on the War on Poverty and the relationship between LBJ and Sargent Shriver.

The politics of the 1960s has generated a rich and extensive literature. The following books are particularly helpful in understanding LBJ's dilemmas and decisions. Gary Donaldson, *Liberalism's Last Hurrah: The Presidential Campaign of 1964* (Armonk, NY, 2003), is very good on the Goldwater movement; Robert Mason, *Richard Nixon and the Quest for a New Majority* (Chapel Hill, NC, 2004), is perceptive on Nixon and the GOP's renaissance between 1966 and 1968. On Robert Kennedy, Jeff Shesol, *Mutual Contempt: Lyndon Johnson, Robert Kennedy and the Feud that Defined a Decade* (New York, 1997), is indispensable; Evan Thomas, *Robert Kennedy: His Life* (New York, 2000), is a solid, judicious biography. For very good accounts of George Wallace, see two works by Dan T. Carter, *George Wallace, Richard Nixon, and the Transformation of American Politics* (Waco, TX, 1991), and *Politics of Rage: George Wallace, the Origins of the New Conservatism, and the Transformation of American Politics* (Baton Rouge, LA, 1996). For an excellent account of the role of California in national politics, see Ethan Rarick, *California Rising: The Life and Times of Pat Brown* (Berkeley, CA, 2005).

Politics within the Senate during the 1950s and 1960s are ably discussed in Lee Wilkins, *Wayne Morse: A Bio-Bibliography* (Westport, CT, 1985); Mason Drukman, *Wayne Morse: A Political Biography* (Portland, OR, 1997); Byron C. Hulsey, *Everett Dirksen and His Presidents: How a Senate Giant Shaped American Politics* (Lawrence, KS, 2000); and Randall B. Woods, *Fulbright: A Biography* (Cambridge, England, 1995). The broader contexts of politics during the last years of Johnson's presidency are clearly illuminated in David Maraniss, *They Marched into Sunlight: War and Peace, Vietnam and America, October 1967* (New York, 2004), and Mark Kurlansky, *1968: The Year that Rocked the World* (New York, 2004). For LBJ's relationship with Abe Fortas during the 1960s, see Laura Kalman, *Abe Fortas: A Biography* (New Haven, CT, 1990). A good account of the relationship between Johnson and Nixon between 1969–1973 is in Richard Reeves, *President Nixon: Alone in the White House* (New York, 2001). Interesting material on LBJ and Nixon during 1968 and 1971 may be found in Robert Dallek, *Nixon and Kissinger: Partners in Power* (New York: 2007).

Study of LBJ and Vietnam during the 1960s should begin with analysis of the impact of the Cuban Missile Crisis on his view of international relations. For this, see the relevant chapters in Eric Alterman,

When Presidents Lie: A History of Official Deception and Its Consequences (New York, 2004), and Ernest R. May and Philip D. Zelikow, eds., *The Kennedy Tapes: Inside the White House During the Cuban Missile Crisis* (Cambridge, MA, 1997).

The classic overview of United States involvement in Vietnam is George C. Herring, *America's Longest War: The United States and Vietnam, 1950–1975*, 4th rev. ed. (Boston, 2002). A very good summary is Patrick Hearden, *The Tragedy of Vietnam*, 2nd ed. (New York, 2005). Events during the crucial year 1968 are thoughtfully discussed in Ronald H. Spector, *After Tet: The Bloodiest Year in Vietnam* (New York, 1993). For a suggestive interpretation othe lingering impact off battles during the Second World War and the Tet Offensive, see Victor Davis Hanson, *Ripples of Battle: How the Wars of the Past Still Determine How We Fight, How We Live, and How We Think* (New York, 2003). For a discussion of developing historical controversies about the origins and prosecution of the war, see Marc Jason Gilbert, ed., *Why the North Won the Vietnamese War* (New York, 2002).

Historians of the war tend to fall into one of two broadly defined camps. Orthodox historians generally view U.S. involvement as mistaken and bordering on immoral. Revisionists believe that American had legitimate interests to defend in South Vietnam but improperly executed the preservation of that nation. To my knowledge, no effort at synthesizing the two interpretations has as yet been published.

Important orthodox interpretations of the Vietnam War include Lloyd C. Gardner, *Pay Any Price: Lyndon Johnson and the Wars for Vietnam* (Chicago, 1995); Michael H. Hunt, *Lyndon Johnson's War: America's Cold War Crusade in Vietnam, 1945–1968*; Fredrik Logevall, *Choosing War: The Last Chance for Peace and the Escalation of the War in Vietnam* (Berkeley, CA, 1999); and David E. Kaiser, *American Tragedy: Kennedy, Johnson, and the Origins of the Vietnam War* (Cambridge, MA, 2000). Important recent revisionist interpretations are H. R. McMaster, *Dereliction of Duty: Lyndon Johnson, Robert McNamara, the Joint Chiefs of Staff and the Lies that Led to Vietnam* (New York, 1997); Michael Lind, *Vietnam, The Necessary War: A Reinterpretation of America's Most Disastrous Military* Conflict (New York, 1999); Arthur J. Donnen, *The Indochinese Experience of the French and the Americans: Nationalism and Communism in Cambodia, Laos, and Vietnam* (Bloomington, IN, 2001); C. Dale Walton, *The Myth of Inevitable U.S. Defeat in Vietnam* (London, 2002); and Mark Moyar, *Triumph Forsaken: The Vietnam War, 1954–1965* (Cambridge, England, 2006).

Index